LIFE GUIDE:

Keys to Emotional Strength

Human Services Institute
Bradenton, Florida

TAB BOOKS
Blue Ridge Summit, PA

Human Services Institute publishes books on human problems, especially those affecting families and relationships: addiction, stress, alienation, violence, parenting, gender, and health. Experts in psychology, medicine, and the social sciences have gained invaluable new knowledge about prevention and treatment, but there is a need to make this information available to the public. Human Services Institute books help bridge the information gap between experts and people with problems.

FIRST EDITION
FIRST PRINTING

© 1992 by **Sid Cormier**.
Published by HSI and TAB Books.
TAB Books is a division of McGraw-Hill, Inc.

Clinical examples appearing in *Life Guide* are based on actual case histories. Names and details have been altered to protect the identities of the patients.

Library of Congress Cataloging-in-Publication Data

Cormier, Sid.
    Life guide : keys to emotional strength / Sid Cormier.
        p.   cm.
    Includes bibliographical references and index.
    ISBN 0-8306-4054-1   ISBN 0-8306-4053-3 (pbk.)
    1. Conduct of life.   2. Emotions.   I. Title.
BF637.C5C67   1992
158—dc20   92-8260
                                                    CIP

TAB Books offers software for sale. For information and a catalog, please contact TAB Software Department, Blue Ridge Summit, PA 17294-0850.

Acquisitions Editor: Kimberly Tabor
Development Editor: Lee Marvin Joiner, Ph.D.
Copy Editors: Pat Holliday and Pat Hammond
Cover by Holberg Design, York, PA

Questions regarding the content of this book should be addressed to:

Human Services Institute, Inc.
P.O. Box 14610
Bradenton, FL 34280

Contents

Acknowledgments . . . iv
Introduction . . . v

1. SITUATIONAL ENGINEERING
   Your problems are not all in your head! . . . 1
2. YOUR FEELINGS
   How to recognize and handle your emotions . . . 31
3. YOUR PERSONAL RIGHTS
   How to stand up for yourself . . . 51
4. LETTING GO
   of the past . . . 73
5. WHAT YOU NEED
   And how to get it . . . 99
6. YOUR EMOTIONAL INVESTMENTS
   What hooks do you hang your life on? . . . 117
7. BEHAVIOR DYNAMICS
   How your actions can lift your moods . . . 135
8. GETTING BACK IN CONTROL
   The power of relaxation and imagery . . . 157
9. YOUR SPHERE OF INFLUENCE
   What you can and cannot control . . . 181
10. NEUTRALIZING DISTRESS
    *Finding the emotional strength to survive
    and overcome . . . 203*
11. YOUR INNER VOICE
    *The power of beliefs, expectations
    and self-talk . . . 221*
12. POSITIVE RELATIONSHIPS
    The healing power of love . . . 239
13. TIME TO START LIVING . . . 255*

Notes on Sources . . . 267
Index . . . 275

This book is dedicated, with unending love and respect, to my parents, Frances and Sidney Cormier.

Acknowledgments

I wish to gratefully acknowledge the giants in the field who laid the foundation for *Life Guide*. While pioneering researchers, clinicians, and scholars have all contributed to the foundation of this book, several masters from the past and present deserve special acknowledgment: Sigmund Freud and Carl Jung for their brilliant clinical acumen, and structural and dynamic insights into the human psyche; William James, considered by many to be the founding father of psychology; B.F. Skinner, whose pioneering work in the field of behaviorism led to dramatic changes in the practice of psychology; Abraham Maslow and Carl Rogers, founders of the field of humanistic psychology; Fritz Perls, creator of the open-chair and other powerful emotional ventilation techniques; Wayne Dyer, who taught a generation to be assertive; John Bradshaw, whose insights allowed individuals to let go of shame and other problems from their past; Albert Ellis, considered by many to be the father of modern cognitive psychology; Peter Lewinsohn, whose focus on the primacy of behaviors led to breakthroughs in the areas of behavioral medicine and depression; Joseph Wolpe, discoverer of the power of desensitization procedures; William Kroger and William Fezler, for their pioneering work in the field of clinical hypnosis and imagery; Martin Seligman, for his research into the areas of perceived control and how it affects helplessness and resourcefulness; Norman Vincent Peale, inspirational leader of the twentieth century; and, Leo Buscaglia, who reminds us all of the incredible healing power of love.

On a more personal and practical level, I would like to thank my wife, Julie, and our three children, Reneé, Christopher and Cheri, who tolerated numerous hours of abandonment while I was locked up in my study working on *Life Guide*. My thanks are extended to Dawn Kofford, whose tireless typing brought *Life Guide* into book form. And finally, to Dr. Lee Marvin Joiner, whose encouragement, insights, and valuable editorial comments brought *Life Guide* into its final form.

Introduction || Beyond Existing

To live is the rarest thing in the world, most people exist, that is all.
-Oscar Wilde

Wouldn't it be nice if, the day you were born, life came with a complete set of instructions telling you:

- Which of your problems are really all inside your head;
- What your feelings are and how to use them to help you;
- How to stand up for yourself and be assertive;
- How to let go of unnecessary baggage from your past;
- What your needs are and how to go about meeting them;
- How to discover and live your values;
- How to use your behaviors to lift your moods and improve your self-esteem;
- How to return your mind and body to their natural state of calm relaxation;
- How to handle seemingly impossible problems;
- What you should and should not worry about;
- What kinds of things you should be thinking, believing, and saying to yourself; and
- How to develop and maintain warm, loving, trusting relationships?

Or in short, not only how to cope with life's most difficult challenges, but how to get happy and stay that way . . . at least most of the time.

Unfortunately, many of us live from one crisis or problem to the next without gaining control over our destinies. I see these people day after day in my practice: the negligent husband, the nagging wife, the recently divorced man, the continually depressed woman, the senior citizen who feels discarded, the mature adult in a mid-life identity crisis, the compulsive workaholic, the employee trying to deal with an impossible boss, the person who can't kick the drug or alcohol habit, the lost souls who have fallen into the criminal justice system, and more.

These people have much in common. They remain in miserable situations that offer them little if any chance to fulfill their dreams. They block out or hide from distressing emotional experiences. They either let people walk all over them or lash out with inappropriate anger and alienate others. They are often prisoners of past resentment, guilt, fear, and loss. They spend months or years worrying needlessly over things they have little if any control over. They have completely forgotten how to allow their mind and body to return to a natural state of calm relaxation. They have become victimized by their responsibilities and either ignore them completely or assume responsibilities for things they have no business taking on. They continually talk negatively to themselves and set up meager expectations for their future. They have forgotten how to play and have fun, real fun. They have lost touch with the tremendous power of their unconscious mind and write off intuition and imagery as "mystical." Or worse, they've completely lost faith.

They develop anxiety, depression, ulcers, high blood pressure, and other stress-related diseases. They often turn and fight with those they truly love. In frustration they seek escape through drugs, alcohol, workaholism, or other addictions. At best, they just exist. They desperately look for an excuse for their misery. Dysfunctional family? Codependency? Addiction? Abuse? Molestation? Neglect? Mental illness? But what they really want are answers that make sense and that work.

Fortunately these answers exist. With the publication of the *Principles of Psychology* in 1890, William James began what many people feel is the art and science of psychology. In the over one hundred years of its existence, the diverse practitioners of psychology have developed the tools necessary to eliminate most human emotional suffering and distress. The problem has been that, while the tools are available, they have never been organized into an understandable, practical strategy that anyone can apply not only to solve problems, but also to live life to the fullest.

Unlike many psychologists, I have never been interested in figuring people out. I have been dedicated to helping people live their lives to the fullest every moment. I have kept a keen eye out for what really works for my patients, my loved ones, and myself. I have searched not only within psychology, but also in philosophy, religion, and, most importantly, plain old common sense.

In my search, I have discovered some real answers. Answers that represent pieces to the puzzle of the human condition. Answers that represent a mixture of clinical secrets and common sense. Dynamic answers that, when put together and used, unlock the true power of human potential.

To find answers, an open and receptive mind is required. Some answers become obvious as soon as you ask your questions correctly. Some you already know, but haven't realized their significance. Some may seem hard to understand now. Others may seem even counterintuitive.

To get back on course for living and not just existing, imagine that the following twelve principles represent a set of directions for guiding you through the course of life.

1. Your problems are really not all inside your head. It's virtually impossible to be happy when you are in a chronically unhappy situation. You've got to either engineer your situation into something that's acceptable to you or leave it.

2. Your feelings, both pleasant and unpleasant, are your friends. They are there to help you, and the sooner you learn to recognize, experience, and fully express them, the sooner you'll be on your way to living life to the fullest.

3. To keep from being victimized by others, it is necessary to learn to stand up for yourself and be assertive.

4. Before you can let go of the problems from the past, you must learn from them.

5. You must know what your basic needs are and how to go about meeting them.

6. Your emotions, like your money, are investable. It is not enough merely to *know* what is important. You must *show* it in your everyday behavior.

7. There are behaviors and experiences that are good for your physical health, mental health, spiritual health, and self-esteem. Whether you feel like it or not, you can dramatically improve your mood just by doing the right behaviors.

8. Your mind and body were designed to be calm and relaxed, so quit fighting it and learn how to let go. When you do, you will perform better in all areas of your life.

9. For those problems that seem to have no answer, realize that when your body is profoundly relaxed and remains relaxed, you cannot be emotionally upset, no matter what you think about or experience.

10. You will save yourself much wear and tear by discovering your personal sphere of influence, that is, learning to control the things you need to control, accepting the things you cannot, and developing the wisdom to recognize your boundaries.

11. The power of your beliefs, expectations, and self-talk is crucial in shaping your feelings, behavior and the course of your life. You must get the little voice inside your head—your self-talk—on your side.

12. Perhaps the most powerful key of all is a loving, trusting, warm, honest relationship with another person.

My purpose in writing *Life Guide* is to show you how to use these keys developed by dedicated men and women in the fields of psychology, philosophy, and religion to help you experience the most meaning, excitement, joy and love in your life as possible.

1 Situational Engineering

Your problems are not all in your head!

Your problems are not all in your head! They really aren't. As B. F. Skinner put it, ". . . don't try to change yourself, change your environment." No matter how emotionally stable and well adjusted you are, it is virtually impossible not to go nuts if you stay in a chronically stressful or crazy situation. Some situations can destroy you. There are examples of the overwhelming power of the situation on a person's behavior.

On November 18, 1978, in the dense jungles of northwest Guyana, a healthy young woman takes a last long look at her dead husband and dying friends as she puts a cup of poison to her small daughter's lips and then her own. They cuddle up together, and join over nine hundred others in a convulsive and finally peaceful end to their lives. They have committed their final act of religious commitment to their prophet, the Reverend Jim Jones.

The most powerful instinct in human beings is the need to survive. Yet at Jonestown, people chose to go against the very core of their being. What force can be so powerful to make people take their children's lives and their own?

A situation can be a force of light or darkness, liberating or imprisoning you. Even the most difficult situations can bring out the best in the human spirit. Consider the gallant response of the King of Denmark during the Nazi occupation in World War II. Thousands of Jews were trapped in Denmark and, in order to persecute them, the German high command issued an edict demanding that all Jews wear a yellow star. Upon learning of this, the King of Denmark, a Protestant, placed a yellow star on his lapel. The rest of his countrymen followed in kind, thereby confounding the German authorities. What force is so powerful to cause people to personally challenge the edicts of a mighty and despotic state?

In the comfort of your living room, reading this book, it is easy to speculate and weigh what you would or would not do under certain conditions. But when you are in the actual situation, there are determinants that impel you in a direction, often without your conscious consent. Psychologists have studied, in controlled scientific experiments, how far people can be pushed.

HOW FAR CAN YOU BE PUSHED?

In the late 1960s, psychologist Stanley Milgram conducted a fascinating series of experiments on obedience to authority. Results showed that the demands of a situation are usually more powerful in determining human behavior than an individual's conscience or force of will. In these experiments, people in a psychological laboratory were told to carry out some behaviors that increasingly came into conflict with their conscience. The main question Milgram asked was how far the participants would go in complying with the experimenter's instructions.

In one experiment: Two people come to a psychology laboratory to take part in a study of memory and learning. One of them is designated a teacher and the other, a learner. The experimenter explains that the study is concerned with the effects of punishment and learning. The learner is led into a room, seated in a chair, his arms strapped to prevent excessive movement, and an electrode attached to his wrist. He is told that he is to learn a list of word pairs; whenever he makes an error, he will receive electric shocks of increasing intensity.

The real object of the experiment is the teacher. After watching the learner being strapped in, he is taken into a main experimental room and seated before an impressive shock generator. Its chief feature is a horizontal row of thirty switches, ranging from 15 volts to 450 volts, in 15-volt increments. There are also labels that range from *slight shock* to *danger* to *severe shock.* The teacher is told that he is to administer the learning test to the person in the other room. When the learner responds correctly, the teacher moves on to the next test item; when the learner gives an incorrect answer, the teacher is to administer an electric shock. The teacher is to start at the lowest shock level (15 volts) and increase the level each time the learner makes an error, going through 30 volts, 45 volts, and so on up to 450 volts.

In Milgram's experiment, the teacher is an unsuspecting person who comes to the laboratory to participate in a learning study. The learner, on the other hand, is an actor, who receives no shock at all. The main point of the experiment is to see how far the teacher will go when ordered to inflict increasing pain on a protesting victim.

Although no shocks are actually administered, the teacher's conflict is intense and obvious, increasing along with the discomfort of the learner as shock levels are raised. At 150 volts the learner demands to be released from the experiment, by 285 volts he screams in agony. On one hand, the suffering of the learner presses the teacher to quit, while on the other hand, the teacher feels compelled to continue by what is perceived as legitimate authority.

Milgram discovered that, while many subjects experience stress and may protest to the experimenter about what they're doing, approximately two-thirds of the subjects will continue to shock the learner up to the final level of 450 volts on the shock generator.

One explanation for this behavior might be that the subjects are hostile, aggressive, or even evil. On the contrary, Milgram's interviews with these people showed that they are ordinary people, just like you and me. They come from all walks of life and may be managers, secretaries, factory workers, or students. Most of the people who delivered shocks at the ultimate level had no history of violent or aggressive behavior and felt genuine guilt over continuing the shocks they delivered. But they responded to situational pressure with behavior contrary to their conscience.

The equation, *Behavior = (f) Organism x Environment*, is a psychologist's way of saying that your behavior is due to factors within you interacting with your environment. Factors within you (the organism) include such things as your temperament, physical abilities, height, weight, intelligence, personality organization, values, and attitudes.

The environment, or situation, includes such things as where you are, who you're with, the air temperature, the noise level, what people expect of you, and what people are telling you to do.

Most self-help books focus on helping you change conditions within yourself. You may be taught to talk better to yourself, to do things that are good for you, to make self-affirmations, and so on. But your situation can be much more powerful in determining your behavior than anything within you.

FORCEFUL OTHERS

A forceful aspect of your situation or environment is the people who are important to you. Most people want desperately to be loved and accepted by those important in their lives. In the late 1950s, psychologist Irving Goffman wrote an authoritative book entitled *The Presentation of Self in Everyday Life*, expanding on this point. Not only did Goffman believe that our behavior is strongly influenced by what we feel other people think of us, he went so far as to say that all of our behavior and personality is strictly a reflection of what we think other people want of us. In short, Goffman's idea was that we are all actors, giving a show for others.

Although I personally believe there's a lot more to people than "how they look to others," Goffman's point is well taken. If you think about it you will realize that much of what you do is measured to fit what you believe others require or expect of you.

Not all forceful others are authority figures; many are our peers. Perhaps the best example of peer pressure influencing behavior comes from the drug culture. For the past several years I have been director of psychology at a drug and alcohol rehabilitation center. Part of my job is to assess individuals who come in for treatment. Routinely, I try to find out how they got started using drugs. Almost invariably, I hear the response, "Well it started out just partying in high school with my friends and boyfriend/girl-friend. We liked to party on the weekends, and I had to drink or do drugs to fit in."

Tina is a twenty-six-year-old woman who entered therapy for anxiety attacks following an auto accident. During my history taking with Tina, she told me that she had a long history of smoking pot and taking barbiturates. Tina had never been through an alcohol or drug rehabilitation program but had been off drugs and alcohol for approximately five years. Here is Tina's story:

Well, I started smoking pot when I was about twelve. All my friends were doing it, and I had a crush on a boy who was fourteen and he was a stoner. We would basically get loaded every day during recess, and after school. On the weekends we would go over to a friend's house and all get high.

I guess I was under some pressure at the time from school and my family, but I really wasn't aware of it. To be honest with you, I don't think I really had that many problems, but just fell into a group of people who liked to use drugs. When all of my friends and my boyfriend were using drugs, it seemed only natural for me to use them too. When I was about fourteen, the most important people in my life were my friends. I still loved my mom and dad, but I felt that they really didn't understand me. So when my friends and my boyfriend used drugs, they expected me to use them too. Nobody thought anything was wrong with it. The people who thought drugs were bad we considered nerds. In my school, the people who weren't using drugs or partying were not cool.

By the time I was twenty, I was living with a heroin addict who was going nowhere but down the tubes. When I started to date other guys, I found that all of them were equally going nowhere. Finally I figured out that everybody I hung out with had a drug problem. So I decided to apply for a job in another city. Luckily, I got the job.

When I moved, I found myself surrounded by new people. I was lucky enough to find a boyfriend who was a really nice guy and not into drugs. My new friends at work were also straight and they seemed pretty happy. I've been married now for three years, and overall get along really well with my husband. I haven't used drugs for over five years, and feel no real desire to do so. I really feel the most important thing in getting off drugs is to be around people who support you in not using drugs and make you feel like you don't fit in if you do use drugs.

Tina's self-rehabilitation from a drug problem is a common but little-noticed phenomenon. Often, it does not require extensive rehabilitation, counseling, or structured support groups to overcome a drug addiction, if there is a situational change. A situational change is distinctly different from the "geographical cure" condemned by AA. While a geographical move may help, usually the most powerful effect of the situation is the qualitative aspect, that is, what kind of people you are around and what they expect of you. In fact, AA uses this principle (peer pressure) to help members maintain sobriety.

Another example of peer pressure is gang violence. Psychologists call people who belong to a gang "sociopaths." Nevertheless, it is important to realize that gang members do have a conscience——a strong allegiance to members of their own gang. They are very devoted, protective, and sincere toward each other. The gang members I've worked with think of their gang as a family that gives them the love, attention, and protection they never received from their family of origin. When one of their gang members is shot or killed, it is as though a member of their family has been attacked.

Kenny was an eighteen-year-old former street gang member who had recently moved to Northern California from Los Angeles. Here is Kenny's story showing, his escape from a powerful malevolent situation:

I just moved up here because it got too hot in L.A. I knew I was going to be next in line to get shot.

I remember we was sitting on the steps last year and a car drove by and some guys started shooting. Mike and Trevor (gang members) and some lady I didn't know all got shot and there was blood all over and they were killed. I was scrambling just to stay alive. So three of our guys got together, drove by their spot, and paid them back.

It's like you always have to watch your back. You know somebody's gonna be comin' for you. If you don't get them, they gonna get you.

Kenny's story is an example of adaptive paranoia. He had been in a street gang where the situation dictated kill or be killed. Kenny had a history of neglect by his original family and had taken the gang as his family. Kenny's gang provided him with a sense of love, belonging, attention, and protection that he never received from his parents.

While research, headlines, and stories like Kenny's demonstrate the power of situations in bringing out the best or the worst in people, situations also exert a pervasive effect over the course of your life.

GATEWAY SITUATIONS

Certain situations mark and guide the developmental progression of your life. These are what I call *gateway situations*. They are likely not only to affect your behavior and your feelings, but also to alter your life's course.

Education

Ever since the age of five or six, you have been involved in the most powerful and pervasive series of gateway situations in our culture: the educational system. As a child you learned to sit when told, raised your hand to ask questions, asked permission to go to the bathroom, did homework assignments, tried to please your teachers and impress your fellow classmates, and, hopefully, learned as much as you could. You were given a diet of facts about getting along in life that older, wiser people felt were important to know. You were graded or evaluated on a scale from superior to absolute failure. Vacations, family get-togethers, athletics, and leisure pursuits were all scheduled at times when you were not in school.

What happened when you graduated and entered the real world? If you stopped your education with a high school diploma, you may have found that landing a preferred job was difficult. You may have found yourself having to take a job you disliked, getting paid not enough, or working the hours you did not prefer. In short, with your high school diploma came opportunities, but they were limited.

A college degree opens up different situational opportunities. During college you probably developed a clear idea of what you liked to do and spent extra hours in the educational system becoming qualified to do this. Your level of pay, hours of work, and leisure activities became more consistent with what you wanted than was true for the high school graduate.

At a graduate level, you achieved a Ph.D., M.D., J.D., or M.B.A., the highest levels of education possible in the formal education system. With an advanced degree, you had a higher earned-income potential, a more flexible schedule, and training that put you on a par with the state in your particular field.

The question to ask yourself regarding your education is this: "Have I received the education I need to do what I want to do in life?" If the answer to this question is "No," it is best to try to stay in, or return to, school. An extended education can lead to superior situational opportunities down the road, despite the short-term costs.

Occupation

Your chosen occupation is what you will spend most of the rest of your life doing. The average working person will spend eight hours a day, five days a week, fifty weeks a year, for forty to fifty years, doing his or her job. While your marriage may be more important to you in one way, the odds are you are going to spend a lot more time doing your particular job than you are going to spend with your husband or wife.

> Wayne is a forty-year-old journeyman carpenter. The youthful zeal with which he used to pound nails and frame houses in order to make an easy paycheck to pay for his bachelor pad and sports car has long since faded. His skin is chaffed and prematurely aged. His lower back and elbows are beginning to show signs of arthritis. His wife begins to complain because the money is never enough. And Wayne's dreams are knocked down as he bumps his head on the ceiling of his chosen profession. What seemed like a good career choice at twenty has turned into a disaster at forty.

So when considering your occupational situation keep the following points in mind:

- Most importantly, try to do something that you would enjoy doing even if you were not paid for it.
- Don't underestimate the value of money. Although most of us would agree that money is not the most important thing in our lives, the amount of money we make determines, to a large degree, the freedom you have, and the opportunities which we can pursue doing the things we like.
- If possible, choose an occupation that gives you some flexibility. If are doing the same thing over and over, you are likely to become burned out. If your job involves diversification with many different tasks within a big job, you are likely to have enough flexibility and diversification to continue to enjoy doing it for a number of years.
- Never quit a job until you have another job. If at all possible, never give up a source of income until you have secured another source of income. Yes, your health and happiness is more important than money, but how happy can you feel when

your mortgage forecloses and you are standing in line for food stamps?

- Assess the supply and demand nature of your career. Whatever you chose, try to see the probable market for your skills on the horizon.

Marriage

To most of us, marriage is the most important personal commitment we will make in our lifetime. You have spent years looking for a person you can love and with whom you can be happy. Nearly all of us have had disappointments in relationships, but eventually most of us say "I do."

Now a dramatic situational change occurs. Instead of being an individual, and just caring for yourself, you become a couple and have to deal with the realities of your commitment and obligations to your partner.

While we all are responsible for our own behaviors and feelings, a totally negligent husband, a wife-beater, or an unfaithful wife can have dramatic consequences for your feelings. How mentally healthy can you be when you are frightened that your drunken husband is going to come home and beat you senseless; or when you go to work not knowing whether your wife is sleeping with someone else?

Despite what some self-help psychologists tell you, it is not all in your head. People strongly influence other people. If you are in a relationship where you are being emotionally or physically victimized, it's time to try to either correct the situation or, if you cannot, get out.

Becoming a Parent

Another gateway situation, a major life transition, is having your first child. That little bald-headed, blanketed, bundle of joy represents a shift from being a couple to being a family. Now there is a new, helpless, totally dependent human being on the scene, looking to you to meet his or her survival needs. For most women this means taking care of the baby for at least the first year or two of life. For men, it means seeking financial security so the family's needs can be met. For both, there is considerable pressure.

When you add other children to your family system, things become complicated quickly. More than anything else, children need attention when growing up, and if you fail to give it, they often do very undesirable things to get "negative attention." Your spouse and children all need attention, but with each new child, some of the time that you had been giving to your other children, your spouse, and other areas of your life has a way of vanishing. Parents find themselves pulled in five or six different directions between children, spouse, job, and personal wants. So think about the level of time and commitment required before you take on the job of becoming a parent.

Divorce

Unfortunately, more than fifty percent of today's marriages will end in divorce. With divorce, you are thrust from a couple or family situation into some form of loneliness, at least temporarily.

David, a thirty-six-year-old state middle management worker, just couldn't understand why his wife was considering leaving him. In a last desperate attempt to get her to stay, David had agreed to come in for marital counseling.

His wife, Maureen, seemed agreeable to counseling during the first session. She told me she wanted the marriage to work and what she needed from her husband that she wasn't getting. In the middle of Maureen's fourth session, she admitted that she had been unfaithful to her husband for the past ten years. She had been involved in relationships with at least five different men and was now in love with another man. In short, no matter what David did, Maureen was going to leave him.

David took stock of his situation. He had many friends, several attractive female acquaintances, a reasonably good job, and hobbies and activities he enjoyed. He accepted the reality that his wife was going to leave him. Learning that his wife had been unfaithful for years, David found it even easier to accept the divorce.

Two months after the shock of the separation, David reported that he was beginning to feel like a new man. He bought some new clothes, started to work out more frequently, and before too long was landing a few dates.

David reported that an ulcer problem he had been developing for several years disappeared and that he no longer had trouble sleeping. He told me "I always kind of knew something was wrong. Maureen would always make different excuses for coming home late, and they seemed to get weaker and weaker as the months and years went by. There always seemed to be a thin layer of ice between me and Maureen, and I knew something was really wrong. It's really hard to learn to live on my own, and it's really scary sometimes but I think I'll get through it."

Once David removed himself from the disastrous marital situation, his life began slowly to improve.

While David's case represents a successful adjustment to divorce, consider for a moment some negatives commonly experienced in divorce: (1) you do not receive the attention you were receiving from your spouse; (2) your sexual needs usually go unmet, at least temporarily; (3) you lose a former friend (your spouse); (4) the duties and obligations you and your spouse once shared are thrust upon you alone; (5) your friends are likely to become divided over the divorce and to take sides; (6) your children, no matter how friendly the divorce, will feel conflicting allegiances; (7) the stability of the family system will be shaken, and your children cannot help but feel insecure; (8) you are likely to be plagued by thoughts of anger or guilt; (9) you are likely to feel you were a failure; and (10) at the very best, you'll admit you made an error in judgment when you chose the person you married.

So, before leaving your husband or wife, try to find one ember of the love that once burned so brightly for your beloved and try to rekindle it. Yes, sometimes divorce is the only answer. But if you exert your best effort to save the marriage, you'll not only give your partner a chance to come around, but if you do leave, you will leave with a much clearer conscience.

Retirement

Robert, a sixty-year-old middle management executive, had spent thirty-five years working his way up the corporate ladder, working forty to sixty hours a week for the company. A large part of Robert's self-esteem and personality revolved around what he thought his supervisors thought of him. He had been a dedicated employee. He had made significant contributions to the company, and was loved and respected by all.

Robert had accumulated enough money and was ready to retire. Suddenly, he had a gap of forty-to-sixty hours a week——a void without his job situation. Robert confessed:

> I really didn't think it would be like this. When I started out with my job, I was doing it for the money and really didn't like it. But as I made more money and got better at what I did, I guess I somehow came to like middle management work. I really liked the people I was working with. The company's really been very good to me. I'm set up well with stock in the firm, and really don't have any financial problems.
>
> I guess in the back of my mind, I had some idea of a pot of gold at the end of the rainbow. Now that I'm no longer working, I feel a huge gap in my life. I really don't know what to do with myself. I guess my job just got to be kind of automatic, and now that I'm not doing it, I feel worthless. It's bad enough to turn sixty, but when you also lose your job, and all of the people you've worked with, it really does set you back. I feel as if I've been put out to pasture. I guess I'm just not handling retirement very well.

Robert was a man who learned to love his occupation. Probably the worst thing that could happen to him was to have his job taken away. Like many, he had equated money with success.

Robert is dramatic proof that success is actually a process. There really is no magical state of existence we can achieve, like that "pot of gold at the end of the rainbow."

In dealing with retirement, there are five unpleasant situational truths: (1) you are suffering a major loss (your job); (2) you may have a lowering of self-esteem due to being removed from your job role; (3) usually your income will be reduced; (4) you will be removed from friends and coworkers you saw daily; and (5) you'll have a huge chunk of empty time . . . at first. On the positive side, with retirement comes a tremendous opportunity. You may, in retirement, have an opportunity, for the first time, to pursue your dreams. In Robert's case, his dreams had faded away while his ideal became corporate life. But with a little support and encouragement, within two years, Robert and his wife had rekindled an earlier dream of building and sailing their own twenty-foot sailboat. Again we see the give-and-take of situational power.

The Empty Nest

Frances had spent the last twenty-five years raising four children. She had cooked, washed dishes, washed and ironed clothes, attended PTA meetings, carpooled, been a scout leader, organized school candy sales, been a den mother, shopped for clothes, administered time-outs and spankings, and worried a lot. She was a professional, full-time mother.

When her last son left for college, Frances was devastated. She went into the children's rooms, gathered up their toys and clothes, and cried over the loss. Unfortunately, childhood and active motherhood, just like life, are always terminal.

Like Robert, Frances had a block of time, she used to spend doing things for her children, now vacant. Fortunately, Frances was able to redirect her emotional energy into new activities. She and her husband bought a farm and started raising vegetables. They began to spend more time fishing and made plans to travel.

The years passed quickly. One day a station wagon rolled up in front of her house and out sprang three lively grandchildren. And thus the cycle continues.

Here is some advice on how to cope with the empty nest syndrome:

- Recognize that you will always be a mother, but the most active years of your motherhood are likely to be during your children's first eighteen to twenty years.
- Enjoy your children while they are still children. Yes, there are going to be times when you want to pull your hair out and scream, but it won't go on forever.
- Support your children's desire for independence as they approach adulthood. The more you cling to them, the more likely they will rebel.
- Develop a friendship with your children as they approach adulthood. Make them want to come to see you not because they should, but because you are a friend and they enjoy being with you.
- Share interests and activities with your children as they develop into adults. If you and your children both like to ski or play tennis, this shared interest will give you common ground later.
- Provide an emotional safety net for your children. That is, always try to be there for them when they need you. This does not mean giving your children money whenever they ask for it, but being emotionally supportive and willing to listen.
- Having established a foundation for keeping your children emotionally close and friendly, channel some of your emotional energy into things you may always have wanted to do but have never done. (See Chapter 6 on emotional investments.)
- Consider developing a new career or returning to work. This will occupy you and keep you from focusing on who is not there for dinner.

RATING YOUR SITUATION

Now that you know how powerful situations can be in determining your behaviors, feelings, and even the course of your life, let's take a good, clear look at your present situation from several different perspectives and see how it measures up.

Situations may be thought of as personal environments offering either opportunities to pursue your needs, values and goals, or constraints that block these pursuits. I have found it very useful, with many of my patients, to use a measuring technique I have created called a situational rating scale.

The situational rating scale was designed to measure your perceptions of the constraints or opportunities different parts of your living situation offer. Specifically, you will be asked to list important areas of your life, and to judge the extent to which your present situation offers you opportunities to pursue your goals and values, or constraints that block these pursuits.

Here is how it works. First, take each important area of your life and write it at the top of a sheet of paper. For instance: job, marriage, recreations and hobbies. Then, subdivide each area into specific parts that are important to you. For instance, important aspects of your job may include: (1) income potential, (2) enjoyment of duties, (3) relationships with coworkers, (4) upward mobility, (5) job security, and (6) working hours and conditions. Then, rate each of these areas separately on the following scale:

constraints				opportunities
-2	-1	0	+1	+2

Rating:

-2   Your situation offers almost no opportunity for fulfilling your goals, and many constraints.

-1   Your situation offers many constraints, and very few opportunities.

 0   Your situation offers an equal number of constraints and opportunities to pursue your goals and values.

+1   Your situation offers a moderate amount of opportunities for the fulfillment of your goals and few barriers.

+2   Your situation offers many opportunities for the fulfillment of your goals, and few if any barriers to pursuing them.

After you have rated each of these areas, add up the number for each important area of your life. If the sum is a negative number, you have a problem. The more negative the number, the greater the situational constraints or problems. On the other hand, a positive number represents more situational opportunities, and the higher the positive number the more situational opportunities exist for you.

For instance, Bill, a state government middle-management worker, with a part-time real estate practice, rated important aspects of his job as follows:

- income potential +1
- enjoyment of duties +2
- relationship with coworkers +2
- upward mobility -1
- job security +2
- working hours and conditions +2

When adding up the scores, Bill's job situation rating came to +8. In fact, Bill was quite happy with his job although he knew there was no tremendous upward mobility in state government. He rated his income potential as positive because of the supplemental work he had been doing in real estate.

But remember, some aspects of a domain or particular area of your life may be much more important than others and need to be given special consideration.

Zak, a worker at a local mill takes pride and pleasure in being a lumber grader. To Zak, his income potential is fine. He enjoys his duties, gets along great with his coworkers, and is gradually working his way up within the mill. His working hours and conditions are excellent. Unfortunately, Zak learned that the mill may be closing, and over fifty percent of the workers face a layoff. While Zak rated the other dimensions of his job as +2, the -2 rating on job security tended to overshadow an overall rating +8. Recognizing this gave Zak the presence of mind to join with other workers in his union doing what they could to salvage their jobs. At the same time he began to look for alternative employment.

To understand how powerful this rating technique is, let's apply the situational rating scale to important areas of your life.

Your Job

Your chosen occupation is what you will spend most of the rest of your life doing. The average worker will spend eight hours a day, five days week, fifty weeks a year, for forty-plus years doing their job. In terms of importance, your occupation or job cannot be overestimated. While your marriage may seem more important to you, the odds are that you will spend a lot more time doing your job than you will spend with your husband or wife.

Rate the important aspects of your job, considering the extent each offers you opportunities for fulfillment, or constraints and barriers: (1) supervisor, (2) coworkers, (3) income, (4) job security, and (5) upward mobility. Select the number that best describes your judgment about each.

How did your ratings turn out? Do you have a coworker or supervisor that you just can't stomach, but love the money? Or is it vice versa? Do you feel stale and stuck with no upward mobility? Too much pressure? Do you have to take your work home and does it interfere with your family life? Do you feel as if your life is on the chopping block when you get word that your company has become a takeover target? Or, can you just not tolerate another day sitting in front of that same computer terminal?

When you add your ratings of job components (supervisor, coworkers, income, job security, and upward mobility), if your sum is a negative number, you should carefully consider the long-term personal cost and whether or not you are willing to pay it.

If you decide to take action, first try to change your job situation in the problem area. For instance, if you have constant conflicts with coworkers, talk with them or your supervisor about it and see if you can resolve the problem cooperatively. Need more money? If so, ask for it. Talk to the people who can change your situation and see what can be done. Only if this fails to correct it, should you start looking for another job.

Your Living Situation

Where you live has a strong impact on how you feel. You may be bringing home a nice paycheck and be perfectly happy with your marriage, but how secure can you feel about yourself and your family if you are living in a neighborhood that is riddled with crime and violence? A little later we will look at special aspects of your living situation, such as recreational and educational opportunities but, for now, consider some of the basic situational realities of where you live.

Rate the following components of your present living situation: (1) housing, (2) neighborhood safety and security, (3) air and noise pollution, and (4) overcrowding. By rating each area of your present living situation, you may become more aware of exactly which aspects of your situation are good and which are less than ideal. You may, for instance, have trouble adjusting to the excessive noise and pollution in your city. You may feel terrified to go out of your house at night for fear of being mugged. Or, you may be squeezing your spouse, four children, and yourself into a tiny, two- or three-bedroom apartment.

Your Relationships

From our earlier discussion on peer pressure, you know that your personal relationships with others has one of the strongest influences on your behaviors and feelings. Think of how powerfully your parents' behavior affected you as a child. The expectations and behaviors of your teachers also had a strong impact on how you responded. Think about the people who were your role models and how their behavior influenced you. What about the school bully who picked on you and teased you mercilessly? How much of what you did in high school revolved around the opinions of your friends or boyfriend/girlfriend? And what about today? How much time do you spend trying to impress your boss or spouse? How do you get along with your own children?

Your relationships with others is one of the most important influences on how you feel. So, rate each important or significant person in your life. Specifically, what you will be rating is the extent to which each important person in your life offers you the kind of relationship you want with respect to: (1) communication, (2) mutual respect, (3) similar values, (4) shared interests and activities, and (5) mutual need fulfillment. The following example illustrates this rating process.

> Bart rated his marriage to Judy very positively. There was good communication and shared values, and they enjoyed playing tennis and golf together. Bart and Judy respected each other and each was capable and willing to meet the other's needs. Judy's parents, on the other hand, presented a problem for Bart. No matter how much he tried to win their favor, they constantly put him down. Bart's need for their acceptance was being blocked, not by what he himself did, but by their hypercritical attitude. This, in turn, led to poor communication and other problems.
>
> Bart had met a situational barrier in the attitude of his in-laws. His desire for a warm, communicative, friendly relationship with them had been completely frustrated. After repeated efforts to fix this problem, Bart realized it was in his own best interest simply to avoid contact with them.

In short, use the situational rating scale to assess your relationships with the important people in your life. After looking at the ratings, do everything you can to make things right within the particular problem areas. Create time and space for the people who make you feel warm and secure, and who meet your needs. But avoid people who seem to enjoy frustrating you or driving your crazy.

Leisure Activities

Recreation and leisure activity is becoming increasingly recognized as essential to your emotional health. I have, in fact, devoted an entire chapter (Behavior Dynamics) to this topic. The fact that recreations and leisure pursuits are so important justifies their being rated as a special part of your living situation. What you will be rating is the extent to which your present living situation offers you opportunities, to pursue your recreational and leisure activities, or constraints which block these pursuits.

Consider how your situation stacks up in providing opportunities to pursue your preferred leisure activities, recreations, hobbies, pastimes, and play. Rate not only the things you know you would like to do, but the things you feel you might enjoy doing someday. Be sure to include not only physical recreations and hobbies, but also intellectual activities (e.g. reading), artistic activities (e.g. calligraphy), and culture pursuits (e.g. attending concerts). Apply the situational rating scale to each recreational or leisure activity that you find, or think you might find, enjoyable. Rate the extent to which your present situation offers the opportunity to engage in these activities.

People get stuck in particular sets of hobbies and activities that eventually become boring. A way to break the boredom is to shift to something completely different, even something that you think you might dislike. I have often noticed how professional athletes with extremely physically demanding careers find relaxation and enjoyment in low-key physical activities such as golf, reading, and artistic pursuits. A scholar, on the other hand, often finds a sense of joy and excitement by taking up more physical hobbies, such as white-water rafting or downhill skiing. Diversity in your recreations and leisure activities is the key.

After rating your present situation for opportunities and constraints, you may become aware of several things you would love to do that your present situation simply does not permit. Conversely, your present living situation may offer bountiful opportunities to pursue leisure activities that you would find very enjoyable.

For instance, on a recent vacation to Louisiana there were no opportunities in that state for two of my standard recreations, snow skiing and mountain biking. But when my friend introduced me to bass fishing, I had one of the best times of my life. Similarly, when I first moved to northern California from Manhattan, I was disappointed to discover that there was no Metropolitan Museum, no Greenwich Village, no Broadway, no major university library. On the other hand, I soon became aware of the situational opportunities and took up snow skiing, wind surfing, mountain biking and rock climbing.

It does not matter what you find enjoyable or fulfilling. The point is to determine the extent to which your present living situation offers you either opportunities or constraints. Find out what your situation has to offer for recreation and leisure activities and take advantage of it.

Education

Another area to rate is the extent to which your present living situation offers constraints or opportunities to pursue the education you want. We have already established that your education is a crucial gateway in determining the course of your life.

If you are eager to achieve a master's degree or Ph.D. after working for years as a teacher's aid, you will be disappointed if you discover that the area you live in has only junior colleges and no major university. A recent patient became extremely frustrated when she learned, after receiving her master's degree, that the school which specialized in the doctoral training she desired was 400 miles north of where she and her family lived. She was then faced with the dilemma of deciding what was more important to her, her doctoral education or all the conveniences and securities of her present living situation?

Educational opportunity can be rated along the following dimensions: (1) availability of a college or university, (2) kinds of degrees offered, (3) courses offered, (4) quality of instruction, (5) educational costs, and (6) course scheduling.

SO HOW DOES YOUR SITUATION STACK UP?

When you have finished rating the situational constraints and opportunities of your living situation, job, relationships, leisure activities, and education, add your ratings to learn if the sum is positive or negative. If the sum is negative, it says that you have a significant problem in one or more areas of your present situation. If the number is positive, it is a signal that you have more situational opportunities than constraints, and probably should be taking advantage of them. If you are like most of us, your situation probably has many excellent opportunities that you may either ignore or take for granted.

Remember, the rating scale does not take into consideration that certain parts of your living situation are likely to be much more important than others. You may, for instance, be extremely happy in your marriage, have several recreations and hobbies, a very good job, and live in a great neighborhood, but have only a few friends. You may find that changing your situation simply to pursue more friendships is not worth threatening other positive features.

If one or more areas of your life is frustrating, that is, not offering you opportunities you truly want, the first thing to do is try to fix it. Usually, assertive problem-solving behavior is the necessary first step. If, for instance, you are having problems with your boss, the first thing to do is assertively and appropriately tell him/her the problem. If you are having major problems with your husband or wife, leaving home is not the first step. First, do the best you can to express your feelings and solve the problem with your partner. Then, turn to professional help if needed. Having the help of someone with an objective point of view can go a long way toward finding solutions to seemingly insurmountable problems. Only as a last resort should you leave the problematic situation. If you leave without addressing you problems, you may be running from them for the rest of your life.

APPLICATIONS OF SITUATIONAL ENGINEERING

Trauma

Pat was a healthy twenty-six-year-old policeman, husband, and father who was forced to take a medical leave of absence from duty. Pat described the sequence of events that led up to his problems.

It was about 12:30 a.m. and me and my partner were driving around the back of a grocery store. I thought I saw somebody duck into the alley, and I told my partner to slow down and then go back. We began to pursue the suspect on foot, and I really couldn't tell very much about what he looked like. He jumped over a fence, and knocked over one of the trash cans and we followed.

We ended up in a blind alley, and he seemed to have disappeared into thin air. Then, suddenly, he sprang from behind a fifty-gallon drum, and pointed a forty-four about five feet from my chest. Time stood still. Then I heard the loud crack of two shots.

I remember a tremendous pressure in my chest as the first bullet hit, and I remember being thrown backwards. I don't remember feeling the second bullet hit, but I went down in a kind of a haze. On pure instinct alone, I came up with my 357 firing. I know the first two shots hit the suspect, but I don't know whether the third did or not. He dropped his gun and went down.

My partner and I went over to him, and we saw that he was pale and shivering. He was breathing shallow, and the look of panic in his eyes soon turned to glass.

At first, Pat seemed to have gotten over the traumatic experience fairly well. He was back on duty within a few days and seemed able to perform his job. The relaxation training I had taught Pat seemed to work well, and he appeared to ventilate his fear and distress thoroughly.

Unfortunately, after about three weeks, Pat began to get nervous and shaky every time he had to question a suspect or approach a parked vehicle. His hands and feet would get cold and clammy, his heart would begin to race, and he would notice a fine film of perspiration all over his body. Each time he approached a suspect, Pat experienced a brief flashback of what had occurred. He wondered if he might be shot and killed. He began to imagine what life would be like for his wife and children if they were left without a husband and father.

Certain people or situations reminded him strongly of the justifiable homicide. The criminal's brother and friends would walk by Pat, hold up a finger, and point an imaginary gun at him. Dreams about the event began to recur. Pat was suffering from what psychologists call a posttraumatic stress disorder.

Pat decided at a very deep level that to continue with his job as a policeman posed a threat to his life. When this realization finally dawned on Pat, he made the decision to go into vocational rehabilitation. He successfully landed a job as a manager in a grocery store, and pursued a college degree through night classes.

Two years after Pat changed jobs, he reported that things were going well. He admitted that he missed his job as a policeman but told me that he could at least sleep at night. He was no longer plagued by intrusive recollections of his near-death experience. Pat told me, "I don't feel like every morning when I kiss my wife and baby daughter goodbye that there's a good chance I may never see them again."

Financial Insecurity

Laurie, a twenty-eight-year-old mother of four, wondered what to do. Her husband had recently divorced her, leaving her and the children in a medium-sized northern California city. Once the shock of the divorce wore off, Laurie faced financial difficulties. She was forced to sell the family home, take a part-time job and pursue her education with night classes.

Laurie was uneasy talking with her husband's former friends because she felt they were too sympathetic. She sensed pressure from her children and felt that she had to take care of all their needs.

After using the situational rating scale and examining her responses carefully, Laurie realized that she had extensive personal and financial support systems in the Los Angeles area. It took some doing to get Laurie to overcome the embarrassment of calling her parents and sister, but once she did, things rapidly started to turn around.

I received a letter from Laurie about two months after her move to Los Angeles.

Hello Doctor,

Things are going great! My sister's friend got me a job with the city two weeks ago and the kids and I will be moving out of mom's into a rental home for a while. I've got a boyfriend who was recently divorced himself, and we have a lot in common. I really thought my problems were all inside my head and that everything was my fault. Thanks for making me aware of how my living situation influenced how I feel, what I do, and the course of my life. I'm already using your situational rating scale to help me engineer situations in my life in Los Angels which will offer me opportunities to be the person I really want to be.

Thanks,
Laurie

A Violent Partner

Sharon was a twenty-two-year-old young woman whom I began treating in a chemical dependency unit. She had a serious problem with amphetamines, and her boyfriend was an abusive alcoholic. Sharon was not the victim of an abusive father or mother but had fallen into a situation with a man who "loved her" but had trouble controlling his temper.

On three separate occasions, Sharon was seen in the emergency room of the local hospital for severe cuts, abrasions, and bruises. Once, she suffered an incomplete fracture of her collarbone. Despite the many physical assaults, Sharon felt crippled by her relationship with her boyfriend and unable to leave him. She was an insecure young lady who feared that she would be unable to keep her boyfriend or find another one if he left.

Sharon had an adverse reaction to some amphetamines and had entered the hospital for treatment. Once there, she developed a support network of other recovering amphetamine abusers and alcoholics, which gave her the strength and social support to leave her abusive relationship. Through counseling, Sharon became aware that her fear of loneliness had been stronger than her fear of being beaten or even killed by her boyfriend.

I ran into Sharon at an aftercare meeting about two months ago. She let me know that she had developed a comfortable and secure relationship with a recovering alcoholic who was participating in treatment.

Vacation: A Situational Relief

A situational change does not have to be permanent. Probably the best example of a temporary situational change is the vacation.

Fred was a forty-five-year-old contractor who had made a commitment to build a neighborhood of over 200 homes in just two years. In response to grueling sixteen-hour days and seven-day weeks, Fred developed high blood pressure and ulcers. His sleep was disturbed, he began to lose weight, and he began to suffer from tension and cluster headaches. He responded favorably to relaxation training and was able to cut down on some of his hours. By delegating responsibility to his subcontractors, Fred allowed himself to take a three-week vacation in Mexico. Shortly before leaving, Fred told me that he felt better already, and was looking forward to doing some swimming, sailing, and sunbathing.

Fred had a delightful and carefree vacation in Mexico and came back refreshed, recharged, and eager to complete his project. He reported that he was no longer taking his ulcer medication and that his high blood pressure was under control.

He did not have one headache during the entire three-week vacation.

Most of us would have difficulty leaving a situation that is in critical need of our time and attention. Through counseling, Fred agreed to spend a large amount of his time before his vacation working on his contracting project. When he had accomplished what he felt was enough for the time being, he turned over responsibility to others and decided to take a break. During his vacation he avoided thinking about his contracting project.

Fred's vacation not only gave him a physical relief from the demands of his job, but also an essential *emotional vacation* from its demands and pressures.

Remember the following points when using a vacation as a situational change:

- Make your vacation enjoyable and restorative. A vacation is a situation in which you recharge your emotional, physical, intellectual, and spiritual batteries. Do not make your vacation into a job or a task.
- Learn to relax on your vacation. How important is it if you have only six, versus eight, hours at Disneyland, or ski three, versus four, days?
- Use every hour of vacation time your employer allows. This will help you avoid emotional and physical burnout.
- Compartmentalize when you're on your vacation. That is, don't allow pressing problems, job requirements, or other issues to interfere with and clutter up your vacation.
- Take frequent minivacations. Take two- or three-day weekends to escape from the everyday grind. Don't underestimate the power of these minivacations. They can sometimes be more restorative than extended vacations.
- Give yourself at least one day to do something primarily for yourself. You can include your spouse or children in this, but it must be something that *you* thoroughly enjoy doing.

IN SUMMARY . . .

As I was driving back from vacation across the remote deserts of the Southwest, I came upon a little town. I wondered if a potential Shakespeare, Mozart, Van Gogh, or Einstein might be there, endlessly pumping gas or working in an oil field for the lack of situational opportunity.

No, your problems are not all inside your head. It is a big mistake to think that you should be happy and successful regardless of your situation. You may be stuck in a miserable situation that offers you little or no opportunity to pursue and fulfill your dreams.

Take a good, long, clearheaded look at your marriage, your family, your job, your friends, your living situation, and other parts of your life. Ask what is really for you or against you. Then, *fix it or leave it*. You don't deserve to be miserable.

2 || Your Feelings

How to recognize and handle your emotions

Are you a feeling stuffer? Do you try to block out distressing emotions with the hope that someday they will evaporate? Or do you intellectualize away your feelings as unnecessary symptoms of a weak and undisciplined mind? Do you often find yourself saying or thinking, "I feel strange," "I don't know what to make of that," or "I don't know how I feel"? If so, odds are you're having trouble recognizing and expressing your emotions. This is important because, as Fritz Perls creator of the open-chair and other powerful emotional ventilation techniques discovered, "Once a feeling is fully expressed it disappears."

WHAT ARE EMOTIONS?

Psychologists define emotions as: "Feelings or affective responses that result from physiological arousal, cognitive processes, subjective evaluation, and bodily expressions." But what the heck does that mean? To understand this, let's look closely at the components of an emotion.

First, there are your body's physiological reactions. These are your heart rate, blood pressure, the dilation of the pupils of your eyes, the rate at which you breathe, and your level of muscular tension. Second, there is the behavioral component. This means what you do on both obvious and subtle levels. It may involve everything from frowning, to speaking in a sarcastic tone, to throwing a book across the room in a fit of anger. The third component, the cognitive, emphasizes the importance of what you believe——your thoughts, your expectations, and the things you say to yourself in determining the type and intensity of your emotional response. Finally, your evaluations decide if your feelings are good or bad.

When you combine these components, the outcome is the personal experience of an emotion. A good way to understand the ingredients of emotions and how they work is to look at an experiment done by psychologists Stanley Schacter and Jerome Singer in the early 1960s.

Thinking, Doing and Feeling

Schacter and Singer divided their experimental subjects into three groups and gave each one a shot of a drug called norepinephrine. This drug produces a high state of arousal (increased heart rate, blood pressure, respiration, and perspiration, pupil dilation, a high level of motor activity, and some constriction in the blood vessels of the hands and feet). These bodily responses mimic what your body does when you face a life-threatening situation——the *physiological* part of an emotion.

Each group was told something different. Group one was told that the shot they received was a powerful vitamin, and they were led to expect all the bodily responses that would arise. The other two groups were either uninformed or misinformed about the shot they were getting. Members of all groups were then placed in a room with a confederate (a man who collaborated in the experiment). At one time the confederate acted angry, and at another, happy.

Schacter and Singer found that the people who were correctly informed about what to expect showed no significant emotional responses. They recognized their bodily reactions simply as a response to the powerful vitamin they received.

On the other hand, the people who were misinformed or uninformed tended to mimic the emotions of the experimental confederate. That is, people who were around the angry confederate reported feeling angry, while subjects around the happy confederate reported feeling happy.

Schacter and Singer's experiment reveals how powerfully your expectations and thoughts can influence your emotions. The same bodily responses resulted in three different emotions, depending on people's situations and expectations.

This research suggests that while your body's responses and behaviors are key components of your emotional response, the labels you put on your feelings and what evokes them are the primary determinants of your real emotional experience. The practical applications of how your thoughts determine your emotional experiences will be covered in detail in Chapter 11.

Other psychologists, such as Peter Lewinsohn, believe that your behaviors are just as important in determining your emotional experiences. Lewinsohn had depressed patients engage in activities that are inconsistent with depression, such as dancing, jogging, laughing at comedy routines, and doing vigorous physical exercises. Lewinsohn, and other researchers, showed that when depressed patients engage in vigorous activities, there is a dramatic improvement in their depression. In one study, depressed patients forced to do daily aerobic activities showed a seventy-five percent decrease in depression compared to people who received no treatment.

Types of Emotions

Now that you know some fundamental facts about your emotions, let's examine basic types of emotions, the purposes they serve, and some examples of each. The following material is organized around Dr. Robert Plutchik's color wheel of emotions. Plutchik postulated that there are eight basic emotions which, combined in different ways, create all other emotions.

TABLE 1. Basic Emotions

EMOTION	PURPOSE	EXAMPLE
Anger - A feeling of strong displeasure turned against anyone or anything that has hurt or wronged you or someone else.	To prevent you or someone else from being hurt in the future.	Honking your horn at someone who cut you off in traffic, or shouting at your son for hitting your daughter.
Disgust - A strong or sickening dislike characterized by such feelings as loathing and repugnance.	To remove you from a situation which is sickening, distasteful, or harmful.	Refusing to eat a sandwich made of rancid meat, or refusing to associate with a criminal.
Sadness - A feeling of sorrow, grief, or distress associated with some type of real or potential loss.	To demonstrate your feelings to others and give them an opportunity to offer you comfort and solace.	Divorce, loss of a job, death of a loved one, loss of activity level due to a physical injury.
Surprise - A feeling caused by something happening suddenly or unexpectedly.	To give you a sudden recognition that something has happened, so you can learn to anticipate such occurrences in the future.	Receiving a bouquet of roses from your negligent husband, receiving an unexpected bonus or promotion, or bumping into an old friend.
Fear - A feeling of distress composed of a sense of personal vulnerability, a real or potential danger, and a sense of inability to overcome that danger.	To prevent you from being hurt, injured, or even killed. Without fear, many of us would have already been killed.	Nearly being hit by a tractor trailer truck on the freeway, or concern over your children going to a dangerous school.

Acceptance - The act or feeling of taking what is offered or given to you. A favorable reception, involving approval by others.	To allow you to acknowledge in yourself the feeling of approval from others.	Being congratulated by your superior on doing an outstanding job, being told you're loved by your spouse, or being complimented on how beautiful your garden is.
Joy - A strong feeling of pleasure, happiness, and excitement characterized by such adjectives as bliss, delight, rapture, and gladness.	Your body's way of telling you that you are doing something that makes you feel very good.	The birth of a child, getting married, your first job, or overcoming a serious physical injury or illness.
Anticipation - Involves looking forward to some future event.	To prepare you for an actual sequence of events that are about to happen.	Looking forward to receiving a promotion or a good grade in a class you studied for.

The following are secondary or combined emotions. Secondary emotions are a blend of two primary emotions. Let's look at some of the more common of these secondary emotions.

TABLE 2. Secondary or Combined Emotions.

EMOTION	PURPOSE	EXAMPLE
Love - A mixture of joy and acceptance.	To signal that your behavior is acceptable not only to you but also to others.	Protective love toward your children, and romantic love toward your spouse.
Remorse - A deep painful regret for a past wrong.	To prevent you from making the same mistake again.	Feeling bad about cheating on an exam, or feeling overwhelmed by despair over battering your spouse.

Optimism - The tendency to look on the bright side of things with the belief that everything will turn out for the best.

To give you hope during times of despair and to keep you going.

Holding out with hope when you have a serious physical disease, and hanging in through the difficult times during your marriage.

Disappointment - Failing to have your expectations met.

To prevent you from getting your hopes too high in the future.

Being denied your request for a raise, making a lower grade than you expected.

Aggression - An act or attitude of hostility, usually arising from feelings of inferiority or frustration.

To keep you from being exploited or to serve as potential protection.

Fighting off a mugger or standing up for yourself and arguing with your boss.

Awe - Fear and respect inspired by power. It also has a positive definition involving a feeling of wonder and reverence inspired by something of great beauty, majesty, or power.

To put human beings in their place, and make us aware that there are forces much more powerful than us in the universe.

Witnessing an earthquake, observing a total eclipse of the sun, or simply gazing at the heavens.

Contempt - The feeling that a person or act is mean and low. The object of contempt is scorned, despised, or disgraced.

To show severe disapproval, and to try to modify or change the behavior of others.

In 1990, Iraqi president Saddam Hussein earned the contempt of the United Nations when he invaded Kuwait.

Submission - The act of yielding to power, control, or authority of another. It includes as compliance, acquiescence, or surrender.

To accept an unpleasant situation to protect you from further conflict, danger, or damage.

Withdrawing a request for a promotion when you hear a rumor that you may be fired, or handing over your money to an armed robber.

Besides the primary and secondary emotions noted by Robert Plutchick, there are many others and two common ones need to be mentioned here.

Envy is a feeling of distress when you feel your personal qualities, possessions, abilities, or achievements don't measure up to those of people important to you. Although envy has received negative publicity and bad press in the psychological community, beneath the surface of envy is a useful purpose. It could motivate you to measure up to your standards and achieve your potential. Negative examples of envy include sitting around complaining about not making as much money as your neighbor. A positive approach to a feeling of envy is to spur yourself to excellence at your job, to work longer and harder.

Jealousy is related to, and often confused with, the emotion of envy. Jealousy is the feeling that arises when an actual or desired relationship with another person is threatened. It may involve wanting to have a relationship with someone who is already committed, or feeling threatened by your spouse's admiration of a friend. A positive purpose of jealousy is to motivate you to protect and improve your relationships. A negative example of jealousy is following your spouse and spying on her business luncheon with an attractive coworker of the opposite sex. Positive uses of jealousy are losing that extra twenty pounds, or paying more attention to your mate. The latter two behaviors will make you more attractive and desirable to your spouse and reduce the threat of losing him or her to someone else.

Intellectually recognizing your emotions is not enough. To be content with them and to let them serve their purpose, you must also experience them at an emotional or gut level. This means being genuine.

Expressing Your Feelings Genuinely

One way to tell if you are being genuine with your emotions is to listen to the tone of your voice and notice your facial expression and general behavior. In 1972 psychologist Paul Ekman traveled to remote areas of New Guinea to study nonverbal communication. There he found that members of nonwestern tribes were easily able to recognize the emotional expressions on American students' faces, and vice versa. Not a single word was said, yet emotions were easily recognized simply by looking at pictures of faces, even though the faces were of people from a remote culture.

An example of an inconsistency between your emotions and what you say is the furious individual who forces a smile and says that nothing is wrong. Another is the person who has just lost home, job, and family but smiles when describing the disastrous sequence of events leading to the loss.

When experiencing emotions, notice not only the content of what you say, but also how you say it——how you look, and what you do. If these are consistent, you are being genuine in expressing your feelings.

Never be afraid to label and experience your feelings in your everyday behavior. Look for opportunities to experience and express not only positive emotions like joy, but also unpleasant emotions like disappointment. Emotions themselves are neither good nor bad, but serve a constructive purpose in your life. Above all, when you are in touch with experiencing and expressing your emotions, not only do you know where you stand in life, but other people know as well.

Emotions are telling you and others that something has touched an important need or value in you. It is unpleasant to experience emotions like anger, fear, sadness, disappointment, or disgust, but recognizing, accepting and ventilating these feelings is necessary for mental health. Do not make the mistake of trying to block or ignore distressing or unpleasant emotions, or otherwise incorrectly handle them.

IN DEFENSE OF YOUR EGO

Powerful emotions that were once distressing often become blocked and shut off for years. The longer they stay blocked, the scarier they are to experience. These emotions are often incorrectly handled by what psychologists call psychological *defense mechanisms.* There are ten common psychological defense mechanisms that may be blocking you from your feelings and hanging you up emotionally.

Suppression means being aware of an unpleasant feeling and trying to block it out or not think about it. It is important to realize that suppression involves something you are aware of, at some level, yet consciously try to avoid thinking about. An example of suppression might be withholding an angry comment when your spouse forgets a luncheon date.

Denial is a severe form of suppression. In denial, the emotions are so painful or distressing that the individual refuses to accept facts. An example of denial is often seen in the early stages of grief, in which someone refuses to believe that a loved one is gone. Sometimes denial can be healthy and adaptive, as when people "deny" their own mortality and this keeps them from fretting over the inevitable. The main problem with denial is that it prevents you from seeing and handling problems that you could solve.

Acting out is the externalization of emotional conflict through inappropriate behavior. Acting out is a behavioral representation of a blocked-off feeling. An example of acting out is suddenly punching an obnoxious clerk who refuses to accept your perfectly valid credit card.

Displacement is a shift of emotion from the person or object toward which it was originally directed to another, often unrelated person or object. Usually it means taking out your frustration on someone who doesn't deserve it. An example would be yelling at your child when you are angry with your spouse.

The defense mechanism of *rationalization* involves attributing the wrong reasons to a feeling or event. A classic example of rationalization is the parable of the fox who wanted some grapes. Unfortunately, the grapes were too high on the vine and could not be reached. After repeated failure to get the grapes, the fox rationalizes away his frustration and disappointment by saying, "Oh, the grapes were probably sour anyway." Rationalization usually involves some type of after-the-fact excuse or explanation for why things happened as they did.

Intellectualizing is a defense mechanism that employs your intellect in trying to understand or explain a distressing problem so you can avoid the emotion it evokes. Or, the feeling is bombarded with intellectual baffle-gab. An example of intellectualizing is the man who goes into great detail about the anatomy and what happened when his beloved wife had a heart attack while acknowledging no feelings of fear or sorrow.

The defense mechanism of *projection* involves attributing to other people your own distressing emotions or faults. If you have found yourself reacting strongly to someone's arrogant or condescending attitude, there is a good chance that you sense these traits in yourself.

Reaction formation is a defense that consists of counteracting an unpleasant feeling, emotion, or impulse with its opposite. An example of reaction formation is the person with strong homosexual impulses, and underlying guilt, who crusades vigorously against homosexuality.

Identification is a defense mechanism consisting of the imitation of another person when trying to master unpleasant feelings or impulses. You may act as you feel others would if they suffered the same distressing emotion. Identification is not necessarily bad if the person you're identifying with is appropriately handling his or her emotions.

Minimization involves trying to play down or minimize unpleasant reactions or feelings. When your proposal to your loved one is rejected, you write off the crushing disappointment by saying, "I'm a little disappointed, but life goes on."

If you continually use psychological defense mechanisms, you may have walled off your feelings so completely that you have become what some psychologists call "emotionally constipated." To learn if you are emotionally constipated ask yourself the following questions:

- When was the last time I cried?
- When was the last time I lost my temper and shouted at someone?
- When was the last time I told someone "I love you" and really meant it?
- When was the last time I allowed myself to feel fear?
- Have I ever let myself experience a "rebel yell," that is, a verbal expression of joy or jubilation?
- When was the last time I experienced a full-blown belly laugh? (Chuckles or giggles don't count.)
- Do I often find myself using psychological defense mechanisms?
- Do I sometimes feel as if I'm an "emotional zombie," that is, not reacting strongly to emotional events that I know should evoke a strong response?
- Do I ever experience the "leaky onion" phenomenon——that is, finding that my feelings tend to seep out gradually but persistently over a long period of time?
- Do I often find that I put off expressing unpleasant feelings, only to find that I never get around to experiencing them?

RELEASING BURIED FEELINGS

If you have trouble remembering the last time you fully experienced an emotion, or recognize that you rely on any of the psychological defense mechanisms, you are probably emotionally blocked or constipated. So how do you break the blockage?

Catharsis, a term defined by Sigmund Freud, refers to the expression and discharge of blocked or pent-up emotions and ideas——like steam pouring out of a hot radiator. The most important thing to know about catharsis is that if you continue to block and suppress your feelings, they tend to build. The more you block feelings, the stronger they become. And the stronger these blocked emotions are, the more they will adversely affect your behavior. You will finally build up so much emotional pressure that you can no longer tolerate it. Then, a minor event will provoke a huge release of feelings. This surprising cathartic release of feelings can be frightening.

A humorous example of catharsis was reported to me by a woman who had been married to a very condescending, arrogant man. He had continuously put her down over the thirty-three-year course of their marriage. But she had endured the criticism.

Finally, one evening, her husband commented about how the roast "wasn't cooked quite right." The woman walked over to the counter, picked up a pot of hot noodles, and placed the pot upside down on her husband's bald head. She smiled gleefully as he frantically slapped hot noodles about the kitchen.

The Open-Chair Technique

The key to handling your feelings is knowing that when they are fully ventilated and expressed, they disappear . . . unless rewarded by someone. It's similar to hearing one of your favorite jokes repeatedly, and laughing so hard you just can't laugh anymore.

Therapist Fritz Perls developed a powerful and effective technique for expressing and ventilating pent-up emotions, which became known as the *open-chair technique*. The open-chair technique is a psychological tactic for ventilating and expressing blocked feelings. In an open-chair exercise, you will get in touch with some powerful feelings, such as anger, grief, or remorse. Often the open-chair technique will produce a cathartic ventilation of emotions, and if you are not prepared, it can be frightening.

The typical procedure for an open-chair technique is as follows:

1. Arrange to spend an uninterrupted thirty minutes to an hour working on what is bothering you. Make sure you are in a quiet room where you will not be disturbed. Give yourself permission to express your feelings, including those of rage, hurt, resentment, and frustration.

2. Allow yourself to experience whatever you are going to feel, for as long as you need to feel it. It is important to make sure

that you will not injure yourself or anyone else while doing this exercise.

3. Close your eyes and imagine the person you need to talk to about your feeling is sitting in a chair, across from you in the room. Go into vivid detail about what the person is wearing, how he or she is sitting, and how the person is looking at you.

4. Then tell the person exactly what you need to say. Speak to the person directly, as though he or she is in the room with you.

5. It is essential to go into specific details. Use examples of real events, times, and places. Express the feelings. Do not just go through the motions of saying the words.

6. When you have said all you need to say, imagine that you are the other person. Now, look back at yourself. Say aloud what you think that person would tell you.

7. When you are finished expressing what you think the other person would say, then imagine becoming yourself again, and reply.

In the open-chair technique you should feel free to ask any questions you need to ask and to answer them as you think the other person would. For the technique to work, you must be able to move back and forth freely between yourself and the other person, ventilating your feelings until a resolution is achieved.

Here is a sample of an open-chair session with a young woman who had just lost her father in an accident. Cindy was instructed to sit in a comfortable chair, close her eyes, and imagine vividly her father sitting across from her. She was then instructed to tell her father whatever she needed to say. Here is what happened:

CINDY: Dad, I just wanted to let you know how much I love you and miss you. (Patient begins to cry.) I feel so awful that the last thing that happened between us was an argument. I was so proud of you for overcoming your alcohol problem, but I guess I wasn't really ready to tackle my own problem with drugs. I think back on all the good times we had and it just overwhelms me.

You're such a good dad and were always so kind to me. I remember the time you bought me a horse for my sixth birthday. I remember all of the attention you used to give me, and I remember how I was your first and only little girl.

But I have to admit it wasn't all that good all of the time. I remember when you and mom divorced, I was really angry with you. I blamed the divorce on you, and got really upset with you when you married Debra. I felt like Debra slowly drove a wedge between you and me, and lots of times I found myself really hating you for not paying attention to me like you used to. Although I'm still angry with you for not paying as much attention to me, and giving a lot of your time to Debra, I'll try to understand it.

DAD (Cindy now responds to herself as she thinks her father would): Cindy, honey, you know I love you. (Patient begins to cry again.) You've always been my number one girl. Your mother and I had some really serious problems, but it had nothing to do with you. Ever since you were a little girl, I guess you really didn't understand what it was like for a man who had always been married to suddenly be lonely. Loneliness is really scary, and I thanked God that Debra came into my life when she did. I'm sorry I didn't give you any more attention, but I realized that you were growing up, and soon would find your own special person.

CINDY: Dad, life really isn't fair. I will always love you.

DAD: I love you too, honey, take care of yourself.

In this open-chair session, Cindy became aware not only of her devastating feelings of loss and grief over the death of her father, but also of some buried childhood resentment and anger over his remarriage. Through expression and ventilation of these feelings, Cindy was soon freed not only of her grief, but also of her guilt over her suppressed anger.

Although the open-chair technique is an extremely effective and powerful tool in the arsenal of a clinical psychologist, it is difficult to use unassisted. Fortunately, there is another effective technique you can try.

When In Doubt, Write It Out

While therapeutic journal writing has helped people express their feelings, another effective way to express your feelings is through letter writing. Therapeutic letter writing should be done just like the open-chair technique; that is, use the first person present tense, hold nothing back, and go into the details.

Letter writing has several advantages over the open-chair technique: (1) it prevents the occurrence of what psychologists call *secondary gain*; that is, receiving attention and approval for dramatically expressing your feelings; (2) it gives you something concrete and explicit that you can keep with you long after the experience is over; and (3) it minimizes the potential embarrassment of talking to someone who is not really there.

Therapeutic letter writing can be extremely helpful in ventilating and expressing your feelings. But to be effective, some basic rules of the open-chair technique must be followed. The letters must not be written half-heartedly. You need to go into precise and exact detail about what occurred, when it occurred, how you felt about it, and what you want to do about it.

The therapeutic letters may actually be sent to people with whom you have some unfinished business. On the other hand, patients often write letters to people who are no longer available, or even alive.

There may be situations in which writing a letter to someone could prove very damaging to that person or to yourself. What if you have major unresolved anger toward your mother, who has a serious heart condition? Confronting her with a therapeutic letter may prove too much for her to handle.

The main purpose of the therapeutic letter is to put you in touch with your feelings. The therapeutic letter allows you to express your feelings fully and to learn from them. Just like the open-chair technique, allow yourself to imagine the person to whom you wrote writing a letter back to you. You don't have to go into too much detail about what you think this person might say. Simply get in touch with all you can remember about this person and write what you think he or she would say. If you become stuck, use your best guess—your intuition. You will often find that things that come out spontaneously are accurate.

Connie was a mother, wife, and owner of a small business. She was an intelligent woman and was often complimented on how effectively she handled her business. Connie had learned to cope with problems by holding her feelings in, being strong, and not expressing anything unpleasant. Over the years, she had suffered significant emotional hurts due to her husband's actions and omissions, yet had blocked any expression of these feelings of resentment. In short, Connie had become severely emotionally constipated.

To further complicate the problem, Connie's husband had no idea how he affected her. Connie simply endured, while her husband wondered why she didn't like him.

When I first asked Connie to express her feelings of hurt or resentment, she felt extremely uncomfortable. She said, "No one's really hurt or disappointed me. My life's been pretty good."

After a little pushing, she admitted that her husband had often let her down. Connie was uncomfortable about expressing these feelings in front of me, so I encouraged her to write one or more letters to her husband, fully ventilating and expressing whatever she needed to tell him. She was encouraged to go into detail, including exactly what happened, where it happened, when it happened, and how she felt. The following is a portion of one of Connie's letters:

Dear Brad,

I can't begin to express how much rage I feel toward you. When I think of what you did, I start to shake all over and I can't control myself.

I've often wondered why I've had thoughts about wishing you were hurt or dead, but now I know why. I remember fifteen years ago when you went to that conference in Canada. You told me everything was fine, and there were no problems. I remember a week after you returned your telling me that I would have to go the doctor because you had just found out you had caught gonorrhea while sleeping with a prostitute. Then we never talked about it.

What a double whammy. I thought you had been faithful to me all of those years, but now, who knows how many whores you've slept with? Furthermore, the idea that you would sleep with a prostitute is something I can't believe. To make matters worse, I caught a disease I only thought sleazy or disgusting people would ever have. I'm not that kind of person, and I find it hard to live not only with you, but with myself since this happened.

I really feel like you deserve anything bad that happens to you for what you did. I've had to put away these feelings for the sake of our three children, but now that they are almost grown, I'm feeling more and more urges to leave you. So when you see me acting strange or distant, I want you to know exactly why. It is because I don't trust you, and I don't know if I ever will again.

Besides expressing her rage over her husband's faithlessness, Connie wrote other letters revealing tremendous anger toward her husband for his neglect. The following is a reply Connie wrote to herself as she felt her husband would have:

Connie,

I'm very sorry I hurt you by being with someone else all those years ago. If I could go back in the past and undo it I would, but that's impossible. I've learned from my mistake, and I can promise you I won't do anything like that again. I can promise you that is the only time something like that has happened, and there have been many opportunities I've ignored. With respect to not paying enough attention to you, that's going to be a tougher one to work on, but I'll try.

Connie's anger was protecting her from further emotional hurt. She had emotionally distanced herself from her husband so that she would not be so disappointed if he was unfaithful again. In therapy, Connie learned to substitute realistic caution and emotional withdrawal for her overwhelming anger. After expressing these feelings, she was able to live with her husband in reasonable comfort.

Letter Writing and the Leaky Onion

A "leaky onion" is a metaphor for a person who has suppressed or blocked feelings that nonetheless gradually leak out over a long period. This was true for Tara.

Tara had an overwhelming amount of tragedy in a single year. She lost her husband in an airplane crash and her teenage son in an automobile accident. As a result, she had a tremendous amount of underlying grief that could be expressed intensely over a short period or gradually over an extended period. When Tara was encouraged to express her feelings, through the open-chair and letter-writing techniques, she expressed some feelings, but when she started to cry she quickly shut them off and stopped the exercise.

The turning point in Tara's therapy came when she asked me how to cope with her deceased son's birthday. Surprisingly, the day before the birthday, Tara went home and wrote a lengthy letter and allowed herself to sob deeply for over two hours. When she saw me two days after her son's birthday, she reported that his birthday went by with no real problems, and she felt a huge relief. The blocked grief had been released and Tara was able to start rebuilding her life.

IN SUMMARY . . .

Yes, your feelings, even the most unpleasant ones, are your friends. They are there to help guide and direct you through life. Just knowing the wide range of emotions you are entitled to as a human being is not enough. You have to fully experience and express them at a gut level.

When you try to block out or hide from distressing or unpleasant experiences using psychological defense mechanisms, they don't go away, but build in strength and intensity. Often, they lead to such clinical syndromes as chronic anxiety, depression, or substance abuse.

Clinical techniques such as the open-chair procedure and therapeutic letter writing are excellent ways to get in touch with your feelings and to release them. In terms of individually helping yourself, therapeutic letter writing is extremely effective because it gives you something concrete to look back on and precludes receiving support or secondary gain from someone to whom you express your feelings. Don't be surprised if you become extremely angry or cry when writing a therapeutic letter. Remember your goal: once any emotion has been fully expressed and ventilated it will disappear.

3 | Your

Personal Rights

How to stand up for yourself

How often do you: (1) feel powerless to refuse an unreasonable request? (2) feel guilty or uncomfortable when saying no to someone? (3) feel uncomfortable or uneasy asking someone for a favor? (4) feel spiteful and unable to express how you truly feel? If you answered "often" to any of these questions, you probably have a problem being assertive. Fortunately, you can do something about it.

Assertiveness training is based on the idea that nonassertive behavior is learned and therefore can be unlearned—replaced with new, rewarding, assertive behavior. Once you begin to notice positive results from being assertive you are likely to continue standing up for yourself. The new assertive behavior can become a permanent part of your personality.

ARE YOU AGGRESSIVE, SUBMISSIVE OR ASSERTIVE?

Assertiveness involves expressing your feelings clearly and appropriately when communicating your message. Submissiveness, on the other hand, allows other people to have their way with you. When you are submissive, you often feel victimized and rarely get what you want. Assertiveness does not have to involve being aggressive. Aggressive behavior is characterized by anger and intimidation. It reflects the philosophy of "winning through intimidation." Although you often achieve the results you seek through aggressive behavior, you do so at others' expense. To better understand the difference between assertive, submissive, and aggressive responses, consider these illustrations.

1. After years of drinking and taking pills, you have sobered up. Now your wife is asking you to fix some things around the house. You are busy doing something else and respond, "Is this what I got sober for, to be your slave?"

This is an aggressive response to a request. Although you may feel put upon by being asked to do something you prefer not to do, you are dragging up unnecessary material from the past and using it to intimidate someone.

2. Your husband remains silent instead of saying what's on his mind. You say, "I guess you're uncomfortable talking about what's bothering you. I believe you and I can work it out . . . if you'll tell me what's irritating you."

In this situation, you are being assertive and appropriate. You are telling your husband what you think is wrong, respecting his feelings, and offering a possible way to help him.

3. For the fourth month in a row, your wife has cashed her check and spent most of it before coming home. You are upset, but say, "That's okay honey. After a difficult day at work, you deserve to spend a little extra money on yourself."

This response is submissive. You are upset that your wife has spent money, but you bury or suppress these feelings for fear of creating an argument. As you know from Chapter 2, suppressed anger does not go away, but builds up like pressure in a volcano. The odds are that later you will do something later to get back at your wife.

4. Your boyfriend comes home drunk and late for dinner. You feel angry and upset and say, "You're drunk again. Can't you ever come home on time?"

This is again an aggressive response. Although you probably have a right to be angry with your boyfriend, and to know why he does not come home on time, you are expressing your feelings angrily, not assertively. The odds are that if you respond aggressively, you will put your boyfriend on the defensive.

An assertive response would be: "Honey, I'm really disappointed you're late. I notice you're drinking again, and I'm getting concerned that you might have a problem with this. I wonder if there is anything I can do to help you."

5. A coworker asks you for a ride home after work; it's inconvenient because you're already late. The drive will take you at least thirty minutes out of your way. You say, "I'm pressed for time today and can take you to a nearby bus stop, but I won't be able to take you all the way to your house. I'm late for another appointment."

This is an assertive response. You stated precisely why you could not do what was requested. There is no indication that you felt guilty, and you offered help that is close to what your coworker requested.

6. Your husband promised that he would have a talk with your son about his incessant talking during class. The promise has not been kept. You say, "I thought we agreed last week that you would have a talk with Steve about his talking during class time. So far you haven't done this. I still think you should talk to him soon. I wish you would do it sometime tonight."

This is an example of assertive behavior. Your husband promised that he would have a talk with your son and has not followed through on his promise. This was disappointing. You expressed your disappointment and asked that he honor his promise.

7. A very dominating acquaintance has asked to borrow your car for the evening. You do not want him to have it, but say, "I don't know. . . . Well, I really don't want to get into a fuss about it. You can borrow it, but I should warn you that I've been having trouble with the brakes."

This is an example of submissive behavior. You allowed yourself to be dominated by a more assertive individual, and you did not express exactly and precisely what you felt. Instead, you half-heartedly agreed with his request, made a lame excuse about why you would rather not, and hoped that he would take the bait.

8. Your roommate is about to leave for work and tells you that her friend needs a ride to the airport later in the day. She has volunteered your services. You say, "You've got your nerve committing me without asking first. There's no way I'm going to the airport today. Let her take a cab like everybody else."

This response, although close to being assertive, is more aggressive. You are expressing your indignation. However, you could express these feelings more diplomatically by saying, "Usually I wouldn't mind giving your friend a ride, but today I have something else to do. I'll be happy to do favors for you, but you need to give me advance warning."

9. A loud stereo upstairs is disturbing you. You telephone and say, "Hello, I'm your neighbor downstairs. Your stereo is loud and it's bothering me. Would you please turn it down?"

This is an assertive response. You are stating what is occurring and how you feel about it, making a request for a change.

10. Your wife continues badgering you about going shopping with her in the mall. You have other things to do on the weekend,

and don't want to go. You say, "Honey, although I love to spend time with you, going to the mall is not something I'm interested in. My weekends are very valuable to me, and I like to spend them doing things that I enjoy or that we can enjoy together. Let's go to your favorite movie instead."

This is an assertive response: stating how you feel, refusing a request, yet offering a reasonable alternative. Assertiveness involves expressing your feelings, your needs, and your ideas, and standing up for your legitimate rights without violating the rights of others. Assertive behavior is usually direct, honest, expressive, and self-esteem building. When you are assertive, you make your own choices and feel good about your behavior.

Submissive behavior is evasive. It is characterized by not directly expressing your feelings, needs, and ideas—ignoring your own rights—and allowing other people to victimize or take advantage of you. Submissive behavior is usually emotionally dishonest, indirect and inhibited, and lowers your self-esteem. Submissive people allow other people to choose for them and to take advantage of them. They often end up feeling anxious and disappointed over having caved in, and angry and resentful toward the people who have victimized them.

When you are aggressive, you stand up for your own rights, but ignore and even violate the rights of others. Aggressive behavior expresses your feelings, needs, and ideas at the expense of the rights of others. Aggressive behavior is expressive, but it is often defensive, hostile, and self-defeating. Aggressive people try to make choices both for themselves and others. When others fail to comply or follow through, the aggressive person feels angry and self-righteous.

Self-Defeating Beliefs of the Nonassertive

Submissive people often are surprised to hear that their unwillingness to stand up for themselves is learned. Somewhere in the past, submissive people have come to accept as true certain beliefs or rules that encourage their passivity. These mistaken beliefs are sometimes taught indirectly in school, but more often they are part of a family tradition. Consider the following nonassertive beliefs, and see if you agree with them.

- Other people have the right to judge my thoughts, feelings, and actions.
- I must always have a reason or justification for my thoughts, feelings, and actions. Everything I do must make perfect sense.
- I must always be consistent and never change my mind.
- I must never make a mistake. If I do, I must admit it.
- I don't deserve to be treated with respect, especially when I've made an error. When I make a mistake I should continue to feel guilty about it.
- I must know everything and answer every question. I must never appear uninformed or stupid.
- I am responsible for finding solutions to other people's problems whenever they request.
- I must always be grateful for and dependent upon the good will of other people. When other people are kind to me, I must do exactly as they wish.
- Everyone I meet must like me and approve of what I do.
- I am responsible for and have control over the consequences of other people's behavior.
- I am not entitled to my own feelings, and must reflect to other people what I think they want me to feel.
- I must always conform to the expectations and wishes of others.
- The people who love me will always approve of what I do, no matter what it is.
- If people don't approve of my actions, it means that they don't love me.
- I cannot feel love and anger toward the same person.
- Anger and hatred are the same thing.

The above beliefs form a core of assumptions that guide nonassertive behavior. They are based on unrealistic desires and expectations and have little foundation in factual reality. At the foundation of these faulty beliefs and assumptions are two principles: (1) you have to be perfect and you're not, and (2) because you are imperfect, other people have the right to judge you.

The truth is, all of us know we are imperfect and feel guilty about our shortcomings. All of us also want very badly to be loved and accepted by others. But if you take these two basic beliefs and run in the wrong direction, soon you will find yourself feeling and acting like a second-class citizen.

Your Assertive Bill of Rights

Once you have challenged and dismissed the previously discussed nonassertive beliefs, you must find something to replace them. Fortunately, psychologists over the years have developed an assertive bill of rights. This bill of rights is based on the assumptions that you are a unique individual and entitled to self-worth, and if you don't take care of yourself, no one else will.

1. Every human being is entitled to respect, dignity, and courtesy.

The most important word in this right is the word "respect." Respect means being able to acknowledge and understand a belief, behavior, or feeling that is different from your own. An example of respect would be acknowledging that someone is very good at playing the violin, although you cannot stand violin music.

2. Human adjustment requires that you stand up for your own rights.

This assertive right means that if you do not take care of yourself, it's unlikely that anyone else will. Adjustment means being flexible in interacting with other people and your environment.

3. By not standing up for your rights, you encourage others to victimize and take advantage of you.

Think for a minute about what it means to people when you let them take advantage of you. In my practice I have often encountered nonassertive patients. I know that if I am late for an appointment, they will say nothing. If I make a lame excuse, they respond, "Oh, well, that's okay." Through the message of their behavior, these nonassertive patients are teaching me that I can be late because they will not mind.

4. If you don't exercise your right to take care of yourself, you should not resent it when people take advantage of you.

Resenting people who are assertive and take care of themselves is a form of envy. At some level you probably admire this behavior in others and wish you could do it yourself. If you feel resentful or envious of people who are assertive, allow it to motivate you to become equally assertive.

5. By not expressing yourself, you allow things to build up inside that may later lead to inappropriate anger and an aggressive or hurtful response toward someone.

This assertive right expresses the philosophy that resentment and suppressed anger are cumulative and build up over time. They illustrate the phrase, "the straw that broke the camel's back." It is ironic that the nicer you try to be to people by not expressing your angry feelings towards them, the more your own anger builds up, and the more likely you are to explode later. The psychological defense mechanisms of acting out and displacement can also come into play here, and you can find yourself lashing out with inappropriate anger and hostility towards someone who clearly does not deserve it.

6. It is unnecessary and undesirable to live your life without ever hurting someone's feelings. Sometimes taking care of yourself involves putting others in their place.

To take care of yourself, sometimes you may have to step on people's toes. To be yourself and feel good about yourself, sometimes you must let other people down or disappoint them. When this occurs, ask yourself a simple question: "Whom do I care more about, the other person or me?" Although it might sound selfish, the answer to this question should be, "me."

7. Being submissive for fear of being rejected is a sure way either to destroy a relationship or prevent it from developing.

If you are polite to someone out of fear, you are being submissive. If you are afraid of or intimidated by someone, you should speak up. By trying to cover up your fear and intimidation with politeness, you mask your true feelings, not letting others know where you stand. This encourages insincere or dishonest relationships.

8. It is selfish to not let other people know how you feel and what you think. Without this information they cannot learn who you are and what you stand for.

If you want to relate to other people and develop relationships, you must let them know how you feel. Then they can decide if they want to have a relationship with you. Not letting other people know what you are all about is a serious form of selfishness. You are not allowing others to decide if you are worthy of a relationship.

9. If you don't tell people what you think and feel, you don't give them an opportunity to change.

Think about what happens when you disagree but remain silent. You say to yourself something like, "I feel this way but I'm not going to let them know. They wouldn't understand. Or, if I really let them know how I felt, they probably wouldn't agree with me." When you hold back feelings or ideas like this, you prevent others from seeing things as you see them. You may have a novel way of looking at things. Others may sincerely respect and appreciate your disagreement, and learn from it.

10. Emotionally healthy people stand up for their rights and do not suffer under a tyranny of "I should do for others."

Your shoulds are of two types: what you feel you should do for other people, and what your conscience demands. Although it is necessary to follow your conscience, it is not always necessary or even desirable to behave as others think you should. Emotionally healthy people behave in keeping with their own beliefs, not according to how they think other people feel they should behave.

STANDING UP FOR YOURSELF

How To Say No

Being assertive involves being able to say how you truly feel, even if it means refusing to comply with a reasonable request. Saying no is not necessarily rude, it's just expressing how you feel. This is the problem of "just say no." As a slogan, it sounds simple. In practice, nonassertive people cannot seem to resist going along with requests for their time, assistance, cooperation, or involvement and the result too often is overcommitment. Only after they run out of time, resources, and strength do these unfortunates stop complying. Having never said no, they must feel guilty because they failed to carry the burden placed on them by others, with their own consent.

Failure to say no when, or as often as, you should does not necessarily mean you have a major psychological problem or are abnormal. If there are too many times when you should have said no but said nothing, you may simply need tutoring in the art of saying no gracefully. Saying no is simple, if not easy, once you learn and begin to follow three rules.

1. *Be brief*. If you begin a long-winded excuse about why you're refusing a request, your answer loses much of its power. Keeping your answer brief also makes your answer simple and avoids confusing the other person.

2. *Be clear*. If you cloud your answer with excuses and confusing reasons, the simple no is likely to get lost. People who get involved in a long list of confusing justifications often change their own minds. So be explicit in what you are saying. Begin your answer with the word "no," so your answer is not confusing or ambiguous.

3. *Be firm*. Firmness communicates that you are sincere. Remember, what you communicate is not only composed of what you say, but also how you say it and how you look. If you say no in a wavering fashion, you are asking to be manipulated out of your answer. Firmness implies commitment. Once you've decided to refuse a request, stick to your guns.

Never begin your reply with, "I'm sorry, but . . ." This introduction implies that you have something to feel guilty about. It suggests that you can be moved from your position because you feel uncomfortable even before you have gotten a reaction from anyone else. A better way to overcome any insecurity you may feel about saying no is to postpone the decision long enough to think through your options. Tell the person making the request that you would like some time to think about it.

Try reading the following examples aloud as a practice exercise for learning to say no.

- No, I won't do that. I have something else scheduled that day.
- No, I don't feel like going shopping today. I had planned on doing some gardening around the house.

- No, I don't feel like I know you well enough to go over to your house.
- No, I find it very uncomfortable spying on someone for you.
- No, I'm not going to buy you coffee this time; you owe me too many coffees already.
- No, I'm not going to lend you twenty dollars. You still owe me sixty dollars from two previous loans.
- No, I can't play golf today. How about next Sunday?
- No, I'd like to go with you to the art exhibit, but not today.
- No, you should give that job to Bill, since he hasn't done his share of work.
- No, that's not in my job description.
- No, I respect your feelings but choose not to do that for you.

BENEATH YOUR WORDS

Beneath your words is what psychologists call your *nonverbal behavior*, meaning such things as your tone of voice, eye contact, posture, hand gestures, facial expressions, and the distance you maintain from others. When you compare submissive, aggressive and assertive styles you will find noticeable differences between them in nonverbal behaviors. The following are extreme portraits of submissive, aggressive and assertive people, drawn with their nonverbal behavior. They are only meant to be illustrations, because no one individual would show the complete pattern of nonverbal behaviors outlined below.

Submissive Nonverbal Behavior

Submissive people often speak in a soft, low, weak voice, avoiding eye contact, and keeping their eyes downcast or looking off to the side. Their speech is slow and hesitant—not fluent. They close their messages with questions, searching for approval.

The submissive person's posture is a dead giveaway—stooped—often with the head tilted downward. They use hand gestures that are inhibited or fidgety. They smile or giggle excessively.

Submissive people tend to feel unsure of themselves and try to cover up their insecurity with excessive smiling.

Submissive individuals often avoid physical proximity to others, but engage in a behavior called "head nodding." Their head nodding lets others know that they are paying attention.

Aggressive Nonverbal Behavior

An aggressive person's voice quality is loud, hard, and authoritative with a fluent, fast, and pressured speech pattern. Angry people maintain eye contact in a staring, cold, glaring, and intimidating fashion.

Aggressive persons often appear extremely tense, and try to look tall and intimidating. Males will push out their chests and flail their arms, often making threatening gestures like clenched fists. They adopt a hard, cold, and angry expression, usually with a furrowed brow and a firmly set jaw. Aggressive people invade other's space, often moving in, leaning in or standing erect to look down on them.

Assertive Nonverbal Behavior

An assertive person generally speaks in a conversational, moderate tone. Their speech is fluent, moderately paced, firm, and confident. They maintain frequent direct eye contact, but do not stare or glare at the other person. Assertive posture is relaxed, with the head straight and the body correctly aligned. Assertive people tend to use firm, definite hand gestures for emphasis and have facial expressions that are relaxed——either pleasant or neutral.

An assertive person doesn't invade another person's space, yet does try to maintain a comfortable distance and an eye-to-eye level for communication. If the other stands, an assertive person stands; and if the other sits, an assertive person sits to talk.

CREATING OPPORTUNITIES TO BE ASSERTIVE

By now you may be asking yourself what are all of these things? Why are they here? And, what am I supposed to do with this stuff? So, let's now go from the abstract to the concrete and look at some ways to create opportunities to be assertive.

Greeting Talk

It is good to be outgoing and friendly with people whom you would like to get to know better. A good way of meeting people is to smile brightly and maintain direct eye contact while saying, "Hi, how's it going?" or "Wow, I haven't seen you in months," and "I've been looking forward to seeing you."

Feeling Talk

Express your likes and dislikes spontaneously. Be open and direct about what you are feeling. Above all, don't bottle up your emotions. On the other hand, don't let your emotions take over and control you either. Some examples of feelings talk: "That dress is beautiful on you," "You look terrific," "I hate feeling this bad," "I'm totally exhausted and have to take a nap," and "This show is hilarious."

Assertive Talk

Don't allow other people to take advantage of you. Expect to be treated with justice and equality. Characteristic examples of assertive talk include: "I was in line first," "Please turn down your television," and "You're late again."

You have a right to disagree with people, and when you do, it does not mean that people will dislike you. Avoid acting like you agree with people for the sake of keeping the peace or winning approval. A way of indirectly disagreeing with people is to change the topic or to look away and not pay attention. This is not a good way to disagree. When you disagree with people, do so actively; let them know exactly where you stand. Other people will respect you for it.

Ask for reasonable explanations from authority figures such as teachers, older relatives, doctors, and lawyers. You deserve respect, and you have the right to know why people want certain things from you. Make other people understand that you will live up to your commitments, but you will not cave in to unreasonable demands.

Talk About You

If something good or exciting happens to you, it's a good idea to let other people know about it. Let people know how you feel about things. Relate personal experiences and details of how you felt. Don't monopolize the conversation, yet don't be afraid to bring the conversation around to you when it's appropriate.

Agree With Compliments

Learn to accept compliments. If you have trouble acknowledging compliments, it is a sign that you have low self-esteem. Never devalue yourself or become unnerved when someone compliments you. Offer a sincere "Thank you." Or, reward the person's compliment by saying something like: "That's a supportive thing to say. I really do appreciate it."

ASSERTIVENESS TECHNIQUES

Once you have mastered the above strategies and created opportunities for yourself to be assertive, you are ready to learn some tried and true assertiveness techniques that are little known to the general public yet commonly practiced by the pros.

The Broken Record

The broken record technique is a communication skill wherein you repeat the same request several times during a conversation without becoming irritated or upset. This technique gets its name because you will sound like a broken record, saying the same thing repeatedly without allowing yourself to be manipulated. The broken record technique is particularly effective in helping you ignore all manipulative and irrelevant issues brought up by the other person.

Consider my recent encounter with a clerk:

Me: I bought this racquet here, it is materially defective, and I would like my money back.
Clerk: Hold on, I'll have to get the manager.
Me: I bought this racquet here, it is materially defective, and I would like my money back.
Manager: Did you buy the racquet here?
Me: I bought this racquet here, it is materially defective, and I would like my money back.
Manager: I don't see any more on the shelf, are you sure you bought it here?
Me: I bought this racquet here, it is materially defective, and I would like my money back.
Manager: Hold on I'll have to make some phone calls.

Ten minutes pass.

Manager: Yes, it's one of ours. Would you be willing to accept a store credit?
Me: I bought this racquet here, it is materially defective, and I would like my money back.

The manager then instructs the clerk to give me my $53.00 back.

Workable Compromise

Invariably, when two assertive people are around each other for long there will be some conflict. The workable compromise technique and is designed to work out an agreement. In a workable compromise, your self-respect is not in question, and you do not bully or intimidate the other person. For instance, recently my wife and I went out with a married couple who are very good friends. The topic came up of where we were going for dinner and what movie we were going to see. Given the fact that we were four very assertive people, eight possible answers emerged. The four of us then agreed that the two women would agree upon where we would go for dinner, and the two men would select the movie we would see.

Free Information

The free information technique is a listening skill whereby you listen closely to other people, evaluate what they say, and follow up on the information they give you about themselves. This technique often makes other people feel very comfortable talking to you. It also takes the burden off you for continuing the conversation. An extreme form of free information is a psychological technique called "reflective listening." Reflective listening means reflecting back to the other person almost exactly what they're saying. Not only does this give you information about people, it also is designed to help other people feel better about themselves.

Consider the recent interaction I had with a patient named David:

David: I don't feel like I'm ready to go back to work yet.
Me: The idea of going back to work makes you feel uncomfortable?
David: Yeah, I think if I go back to that place right now I'd totally go nuts.
Me: You know good and well, right now, if you returned to work you'd have a nervous breakdown?
David: Yeah. There's just something about that place that makes me crazy. As long as I stay away from it I'm okay.
Me: You're a perfectly normal and sane guy, but being in that work place drives you nuts?

David: Yeah doc, you really understand.

Self-Disclosure

In some situations it is essential to reveal information about yourself to others, letting them know what you think, how you feel, and what you want. In self-disclosure, you give away free information about yourself, thereby encouraging others to feel free to self-disclose what they feel and think.

Self-disclosure is a common technique used by practicing psychotherapists and often makes patients feel comfortable and connected in the therapeutic process. Consider the following, brief vignette:

Patient: Ken finally left me and I feel like my life is ruined.
Therapist: I remember the shock and disappointment I felt when my ex-wife left me.
Patient: Every time the phone rings or I hear the doorbell, I think it's Ken calling to tell me he's on his way home or showing up.
Therapist: I remember, for about a year after my wife left me, every time the phone rang, I thought it was her calling to say she wanted to come back.
Patient: Yeah, I can see you really know what it's like.

Fogging

Fogging is a technique designed to cope with manipulative criticism. When using this assertive technique in response to criticism, you avoid denying any of the criticism. Simply keep the other person talking until you get to the core of the message. Common statements used in fogging include such sentences as: "Tell me more," or "What do you want?" Fogging allows you to avoid appearing defensive and permits you to offset criticism by offering very little resistance.

Negative Assertion

Negative assertion involves coping with criticism by openly acknowledging your faults and errors. It will promote respect for you in many situations involving social conflicts. It is not likely to be useful for you in situations involving physical or legal conflict.

Negative Inquiry

A negative inquiry is an assertive communication skill in which you encourage others to examine the basis for their feelings. It involves questioning people in an open and neutral fashion. It may include statements like, "I don't understand why you're saying all men are jerks," "What makes you say all doctors are rude?" and, "Why do you feel all lawyers are sleazy?"

GIVING AND TAKING CRITICISM

Do you feel defensive, rejected, or angry when you are criticized? What do you do when you're criticized? Do you counterattack, withdraw from people, try to laugh it off, change the subject, or feel guilty? When receiving criticism, keep the following points in mind.

First, realize the simple fact that you are not perfect. Although you may receive criticism about a particular behavior, you may choose not to change that behavior. An example of this would be saying, "I really feel okay about myself, although I recognize I have a bad temper sometimes."

Second, remember that if you are being criticized fairly you are being criticized for an act or behavior, not being rejected as a person. If you are being rejected as a person, this is probably coming from someone with many more problems than you have.

Third, remember to behave in a way that makes you feel good about yourself. Trying to change the way you are, or what you do, to meet what somebody else wants you to be will be "bending yourself out of shape."

Finally, people will often criticize you about something that is not the main problem. When this occurs, you have to continue asking questions to get to the root of the real problem.

Some basic responses to valid criticisms about yourself might include statements like these.

* *I understand you don't like my behavior, but I feel okay about it.*
* *I'm working on being less selfish, but I'm not where I want to be yet.*
* *Although I recognize I'm bossy, I'm choosing not to try to change that right now.*

What about situations when you encounter unjustified criticism? In those situations it is extremely important to stick up for yourself. For example, if your boss unfairly tells you that she's tired of your loafing on the job, you might say, "You know and I know that's not true. I'm one of the hardest working employees in this company."

If your child inaccurately complains that you are never there for him, you might say, "How can you say I'm ignoring you when I spent two whole afternoons with you this weekend?"

Often people will feel uncomfortable giving you negative feedback, and they will have trouble getting their point across. Still, you must know exactly and precisely what you are doing that bothers others before you can change. To find out what this is, you must help other people to be specific about what they think you should change. For instance: "Please give me some examples of how I come across as arrogant."

Sometimes you will encounter a "put down" form of feedback. This is feedback given to you in a way that is unacceptable and makes you feel depreciated. When this happens, it is important to let the other person know precisely how you feel. For instance, "Just because I got fired doesn't mean I'm a lazy, good-for-nothing bum. I really feel put down when you call me that."

When offering criticism it is best to follow some simple rules. First, refer to how you feel, not how other people are making you feel. For instance, instead of saying, "You're a slob or a drunk," say "I get tired of picking up after you" or "I really feel disappointed when you come home drunk every night."

When giving criticism be specific. Give precise details of what occurred, when, where, and how. For instance: "Last week when you went to lunch with Ed, I felt very anxious." Finally, when you are giving criticism don't "beat around the bush." The more you show a lack of direction and firmness in what you say, the more likely the person you are criticizing is to become confused. So be specific, firm, and to the point.

Sandwich Technique

In my practice I have found that an effective way of giving criticism is to qualify it, using the "sandwich technique." The sandwich technique begins with telling people something good about themselves. This is followed by your criticism. Close your remarks by mentioning yet another thing you like about them. For instance: "I really appreciate you being my friend for all of these years. I was disappointed when you missed my wedding because of a fishing trip. I hope we can get together soon." The sandwich technique is extremely useful in important relationships, like those with your spouse, your supervisors, or your employees. An example of a work-related sandwich to your boss might be: "I really respect the way you're running this company but I was very disappointed you didn't give me last Tuesday off to visit with my parents. I know you're a fair person, and hope you'll consider my feelings more seriously in the future."

Role Playing

Now that you know the principles of assertiveness, practice being assertive before you get into situations where you need to use this skill. An effective technique for practicing assertiveness is "role playing." Role playing involves rehearsing what you will say to someone before saying it. It is often a good idea to try out role playing with your friends or your spouse. Role playing gives you the opportunity to say what you need to say and a chance to receive feedback from someone who is not as important as the person you will be talking to in real life. If you can find no one to rehearse with, express your assertive statements aloud and see how it sounds to you. Writing out your assertive responses can be effective, too, even more so when followed by writing out what you think the other person will say.

Worst Case Scenario

A technique that I often use with my patients is what we call the "worst case scenario." This involves assertively stating what you need to say and imagining the other person comes back with the most awful put-down imaginable. Once you become aware of the worst response possible, it becomes easy to prepare for it and accept it if it happens. The worst case rarely happens in reality.

IN SUMMARY . . .

Being assertive prevents distressing feelings from building up. By being assertive you refuse to be victimized, and you teach others how you wish to be treated. You stand up for yourself and become your own best friend. In short, you develop self-respect and self-esteem, while commanding and receiving the respect of others.

4 Letting Go

of the Past

$\mathbf{A}$re you a prisoner of your emotional past? I believe that all the emotions and distressing experiences that you have left unresolved go into a special place called your Personal Emotional Septic Tank (PEST). Not just anything gets thrown into your PEST. The emotional material must be (1) something that is distressing, (2) something you can no longer do anything about, and (3) something that keeps you from meeting your present needs and achieving your optimal potential in life. Usually the emotions have been there for a long time, and have become powerful.

Any distressing feeling may fall into your PEST, but there are four big categories of emotions that always seem to end there. Those are: (1) guilt, (2) fear, (3) grief, and (4) anger. By neutralizing or eliminating the cause of these distressing emotions, you will obtain optimal enjoyment from living.

GUILT - "And Forgive Us Our Trespasses"

Guilt, according to my psychological dictionary, is "The realization that one has transgressed a moral, social, or ethical principle, associated with the lowering of self-esteem and a need to make retribution for the transgression." This may seem complicated and confusing. A simpler definition of guilt is: "Guilt is the emotional jail time you give yourself for doing something that you felt was wrong, without doing anything to correct it." The purpose of guilt is to prevent you from repeating a mistake. If you do something wrong, receive no punishment and feel no guilt, you have no motivation to avoid repeating that wrong.

The first step in handling guilt is to find out if it is handicapping you. In my practice I have noted several things to observe that suggest an underlying problem of guilt.

- You may find it difficult looking for positive things in life and seem preoccupied or obsessed with problems or difficulties, no matter how trivial.
- When things are going well, you become uneasy and feel as if things are probably going to fall apart because you "don't deserve it so good."
- If your life does not fall apart spontaneously, you do something to upset the balance and return yourself to the sorry state of affairs you feel you deserve.
- Your mind may be plagued by many "I should" or "I should not have" self-talk statements.
- You are likely to be on guard and suspicious of others.

Sound familiar? If so, there is a good chance that you are doing emotional jail time for something you feel guilty about.

There are two types of guilt: guilt caused by mistakes of commission, and guilt caused by mistakes of omission. Mistakes of commission occur when you harm or injure someone by your actions. An example would be the spreading of rumors behind someone's back. Mistakes of omission occur when you fail to do something you could or should, and as a result someone is harmed.

Techniques for Exposing Suppressed Guilt

Your psychological defenses can block out guilt, and often you may be completely unaware that guilt is a problem in your life. You experience the crippling effects of guilt, without knowing what is wrong. The most common guilt blocker is *suppression*. It is your mind's way of blocking out things that are unpleasant to deal with. But, if you block out or suppress things that you're guilty about, you can never know what you did wrong and never profit from your mistakes. So how do you overcome suppression and find out what's really bothering you?

Clustering. A technique used by creative writers, clustering is an extremely effective tool for uncovering what you feel guilty about. Clustering also may reveal other distressing emotions hiding in your PEST. To practice clustering, first write the word "guilt" on the top of a piece of paper. Then list any words—— thoughts, images, memories, or fantasies——that come to mind when you think of the word guilt. Do not censor anything that comes into your mind; write everything down. Sometimes it is good to start by listing recent things you feel guilty about. After that, look into your past to see if other issues emerge.

If you have trouble with this, pick key people in your life whom you feel you have hurt and cluster to these people. I have my patients cluster to words like mother, father, husband, wife, and children. The following is an example of how clustering works in actual practice.

When Tammy walked into my office, she was a severely depressed twenty-three-year-old. She had held various jobs in the previous three years, but could not find a position that tapped her real potential. Life, she told me, didn't seem to be going anywhere anymore. Tammy had taken several college courses but seemed unable to select a major.

She also had not kept a boyfriend for more than a month or two during the last several years. Tammy's relationship with her mother was cordial, but she fought with her dad a lot. "I just can't do anything right in his eyes," she complained. Tammy also was disturbed by a lack of energy, poor sleep patterns, and weight loss.

When I asked Tammy to list all the people she felt she may have hurt, either directly or indirectly, she tried, but could not come up with much. I then asked Tammy to cluster to anything she might feel guilty about. She listed several minor wrongs and then noted something she felt intense guilt over: an abortion three years before.

Tammy had stuffed her guilt into her PEST. She had tried not to think about the abortion because it was too painful. To ventilate this guilt and ease its present effects, she used letter writing (see Chapter 2), which seemed to be the best tool available. This is Tammy's letter to her aborted child:

Dear Baby,

I have to let you know why I did what I did three and a half years ago. At that time in my life things were really confusing. I had just gotten fired from a job, and had no money coming in. I was living with my parents, and they had always told me that they would not raise a child if I had one. When I told your father that I was pregnant, he said, "Well do what you want, that's your problem," and left. I felt all alone.

My mom said that she and my dad would support whatever I wanted to do, but they would not be willing to raise a small child. I felt that I would be bringing you into a world with two strikes against you.

Soon after my pregnancy, I found a new job, and my life did start to get better. Ever since the abortion, I've had a great deal of trouble forgiving myself for what happened. I realized that with a lot of effort I could have made it work for you and me.

I can tell you that never a day goes by when I don't get some reminder of what it would have been like to have you there. My sister has a three-year-old child now, and the first time I saw her I was reminded of you. I feel so much pain when I am around her baby, I can't even visit her anymore even though I'm her aunt.

The most overwhelming despair is that you'll never be able to experience the wonders of life. I know you'll never have birthdays, Christmases, carnivals, circuses, parties, friends, your own marriage, or your own children. All I can tell you is that if I could do things over again, I would never give up my pregnancy with you. I hope that some place and in some way you'll forgive me for not giving you a chance. I will never make that mistake again, and someday I know we will be together.

With love,
Your Mom

Because of the strength of Tammy's feelings, it took several days and several letters for her to fully ventilate and express them. This allowed her to turn the corner and overcome her guilt and despair. Soon Tammy gave herself a "parole" from her emotional jail. She stopped setting herself up for rejection by her father. She stopped sabotaging her relationship with her new boyfriend and they soon became engaged. She found a new job and within two months was promoted to assistant manager. Tammy stopped being victimized by her past, which she could not change, and began to grow and learn from it.

In an ironic twist to Tammy's story, she also became pregnant again before she married. She went ahead and had the baby and reported, "I feel terrific because I've had a chance to correct my mistake and prove in my life what I have learned."

Mistakes of Omission

Have you ever found yourself thinking, if only I had done _____, this whole thing would never have happened? This is a classic mistake of omission thought, guilt over something you could have done but didn't. Just like mistakes involving your actions, if you carry around guilt about things you could have done but didn't, you are being victimized by your past.

Tim was a successful, bright thirty-one-year-old accountant in a large lumber mill. He had rapidly moved up the ladder of success and was awaiting another promotion. Tim's supervisor requested that he take on the extra duty of safety supervisor for the company. He refused, initially, but continued to be badgered and pressured by his supervisor and other company officials. Tim told me in one of our early sessions, "I'm not going to take responsibility for other people's lives when I have no training whatsoever to do so."

Unfortunately, shortly after Tim's last refusal to accept the responsibility of safety supervisor, a worker fell into a paper shredder and suffered a horrible death. Tim said, "They took him out in two buckets." Tim was plagued with vivid recollections of the man's fall into the paper shredder, feeling personally responsible for his death.

Tim told me, "Every time I look out my window and see where the accident occurred, I just can't stand it and start shaking all over. All I can say to myself is, 'It would have been so easy to prevent that guy from dying. I could have stopped it from happening."

Tim was caught in a severe form of a common guilt trap, "second-guessing fate." Invariably, if you look back on events, you realize that there are things you could have done or avoided doing that would have changed the outcome. But the truth is that we were doing the best we could at the moment, and that is all that can be expected.

As part of his therapy, Tim was encouraged to express and ventilate his feelings toward the dead worker and his family. This involved much emotional material, and since Tim was a sensitive man, he spent a long time crying and expressing anger with himself. When it came time for Tim to live the lesson he had learned, he decided that he would return to work only if the company hired a qualified safety coordinator. This was Tim's retribution, and he was quite willing to undergo financial hardships until either the company responded to his request or he found another job.

FEAR

Fear is probably the most vital emotion. Fear alerts you to a dangerous situation, one in which you could be harmed. Fear also creates a nervous system "flight or fight" response.

About a century ago, William James wrote about a man who encountered a bear in the woods. Upon seeing the fierce bear, the man's heart rate increased. The blood vessels in his hands and feet constricted. Adrenaline was dumped into his blood. His pupils dilated. A light perspiration broke out all over his body and he became ready either to run or to fight for his life. In short, the man's body reacted in an emergency stress response and gave him the energy to run to escape the bear. This man's fear of being killed by the bear was highly adaptive and saved his life. Shortly after escaping, the man's body and emotions returned to normal. He also learned a vivid lesson about not walking in that particular area of the woods, at least unprotected.

Fear is composed of three elements: danger, vulnerability, and inability to overcome the danger. Danger is a situation that can produce harm, usually to you. Danger could be anything from a hungry bear in the woods to a corporate merger or layoff. Vulnerability means that you could be harmed by that danger. Inability is the feeling that you cannot overcome the danger or challenge. Take away any of these three elements and the fear will disappear.

With this principle in mind, how could our man in the woods overcome his fear? He could choose never to expose himself to the danger again. By never returning to the woods, the odds are small that he would ever again be attacked by a bear. Our woodsman also could choose to return to the woods with some friends, all armed with bear rifles. Armed and ready, he and his friends can overcome the danger. Finally, our woodsman might enter the woods with a pack of pit bulls, to intimidate bears and to prevent an attack.

It would be simple if all of the fears we faced in life were as immediate and obvious as a bear in the woods. Unfortunately, that is not the case.

Stress as Chronic Fear

In the twentieth century, our fears typically concern events like losing a job to a corporate merger or layoff, creating a tax liability, divorce or separation, failure at school, or any one of many psychosocial stressors. Our modern fears tend to be chronic, meaning that is there is no immediate action you can take to eliminate the fear and be safe. Our modern stressors require long-term problem solving.

As long as your fear remains active, your body responds with the "fight or flight" pattern of your ancestors. Your nervous system reacts in the same way to a possible divorce or job loss that it does if you face a hungry bear. The problem is that the nervous system does not turn off this response as it does when you escape the bear. You are kept at a high level of arousal and this can foster stress-related diseases, such as high blood pressure and ulcers, and lead to emotional or nervous problems.

Stress Management Principles

In the course of working with thousands of patients, with hundreds of specific stressors, I have developed a practical strategy for coping with stress. This approach is based on five principles that apply to most stressful situations involving fear.

- Clarify the stressor by listing precisely what situations make you feel afraid. Use fear in a very broad sense, including anything from being killed to social disapproval.
- Try to overcome these stressors by assertive, constructive problem solving.
- If you face a situation that you cannot overcome, consider leaving it.
- For problems you cannot solve and situations you cannot leave, learn to turn down your nervous system and relax into what is distressing you.
- Some stressful situations are long-term but can be solved if you commit a specific amount of time, daily or weekly, to

doing nothing but seeking a solution. After you have completed your set amount of time working on the problem, let go completely.

The ravaging effects of fear can take several forms. The following is an example of how what you have learned can help overcome your fears.

Alan was a forty-two-year-old, relatively successful middle manager. Alan, however, had developed some severe problems with a member of the board of directors. Alan was fearful with good cause. A key member of the board of directors was trying to have him fired. Alan stated, "I simply can't please this man. If only he would disappear, my life would be terrific." Alan realized that this man had the power to have him removed from his position and felt that the man was gradually working toward accomplishing this.

Alan tried to be assertive with the board member and voiced his concerns. Alan said that he was willing to try to change. Unfortunately, the board member simply did not like Alan and had another agenda (we found out later he wanted another man to have the job).

Alan looked closely at what he really wanted. He learned after several "why" questions that what he really wanted was not to have the board member removed, but to have a successful, productive job in which he felt happy, effective, and appreciated.

The next step in Alan's problem solving was to send his resume out to other companies. To do this, Alan had to overcome his initial fear that he was too old to get a new job. Alan's first two applications met with rejections, but the third application, for a job as a traveling representative for a large company, came through.

In short, Alan analyzed his stress-producing situation, tried to overcome his immediate problem by being assertive, engaged in time-structured problem solving to get another job, and ended up trading the stressful situation for one more fulfilling and rewarding. Today, Alan makes significantly more money and has more prestige in his new position.

Time-Structured Problem Solving. The idea of time-structured problem solving is vividly illustrated in the example of James, a fifty-year-old, highly successful real estate broker. James had created a severe tax problem over the years, and when he came in for his first session he was on the verge of bankruptcy. James admitted that there might even be criminal charges. Distress over his tax burden had leaked into virtually every area of his life. He could no longer take care of his real estate business, enjoy golf, play tennis, or even socialize with friends without thoughts of bankruptcy intruding.

When we analyzed James's fear, he realized the danger was the possible criminal charges over his tax problems and bankruptcy. James was vulnerable. At that exact moment, he was unable to overcome the danger so James and I worked out a plan.

James was to spend two hours every morning trying to resolve his tax problems. The rest of the day he would devote to his normal real estate work. He also agreed to engage in recreational activities that had given him pleasure in the past. He was also taught to relax and was encouraged to practice deep relaxation twice a day. Within three weeks, James came up with an answer to his financial problems. Along the way to a solution he: (1) clarified the danger as being his tax problems, (2) realized that he was vulnerable, (3) tackled the problem through time-structured problem solving, and (4) learned to relax and let go when he was not working on his problems.

Unrealistic Fears

Alan's and James' fears were clearly realistic. But what about fears that are based on things that happened in the distant past and are cluttering up or interfering with your life today? Or what if your fears are unrealistic, something to which the average person would not react?

Unrealistic fears include anything from a fear of riding in an elevator to a fear of flying. You already know that the purpose of fear is to protect you from harm, either physical or emotional. So once you recognize that your fear is unrealistic, you probably will wonder where it came from. Unrealistic fears usually come from earlier traumatic experiences. They may also come from observing a situation in which someone else has experienced overwhelming fear.

Bob was a twenty-year-old construction worker who feared being in small places. He also had a significant problem with anger, and felt the two problems could be related.

In Bob's case, I asked him to cluster to the word fear, and the following items emerged:

FEAR:
losing my temper
small places
being rejected
trunks

Bob proceeded to tell me of being tortured by an older brother. When he was eight years old, Bob's older brother, with the help of his friends, would tie up Bob with belts and place him in a linen chest. Bob would struggle desperately to free himself from the dark, stuffy trunk, fearing that he might smother. Bob related experiencing an overwhelming sense of helplessness and panic. Because of these earlier traumas, Bob learned to fear and avoid situations in which he might feel closed in or trapped.

Unfortunately, he overgeneralized his fear to other things. He refused to ride in elevators or airplanes and could not stand being in crowds or positions in which he felt restricted.

Bob came to realize that his fear of small places stemmed from his early childhood trauma. He saw that he was no longer a little child who could be victimized by his brother or other people. He then took the following steps to let go of the unrealistic fear:

1. He realized that as an adult, he could no longer be tied up and locked in a linen chest by his older brother.

2. He fully expressed and ventilated all the panicky, fearful feelings that were occurring while he was tied up and locked in the dark chest.

3. I asked Bob to substitute something for the unrealistic fear, something to prevent him from being trapped and victimized again, that would not interfere with the rest of his life. Bob chose not to be around people who physically abused each other.

4. Bob was taught deep relaxation and encouraged to pair up the horrible memories, fantasies, and self-talk statements of being trapped with profound physical feelings of relaxation.

I also encouraged Bob to allow his fear-producing memories or fantasies about being trapped to serve as signals for his body to become even more deeply and completely relaxed. This is a powerful process known as desensitization, which will be dealt with in detail in Chapter 10.

Fear versus Anxiety

Fear involves an unpleasant state of subjective and physical arousal that is reactive to some specific event of situation. Anxiety, on the other hand, involves the same symptoms of physiological and subjective distress (high blood pressure, constriction of the blood vessels in the hands and feet, heart palpitations, perspiration all over the body, and rapid breathing), but there is no specific event or situation that caused it. One source of anxiety is a significant fear that's been blocked out or suppressed.

A Blocked Fear. Rosanne was a shy sixteen-year-old who entered counseling when her mother and stepfather complained that she kept rejecting a father/daughter relationship with her stepfather. In our first sessions, Rosanne appeared extremely anxious around me and looked away from other men when she walked down the hall to my office.

I asked Rosanne to cluster to the word man, with these results:

MAN:
mean
scary
stepfather Jake
beatings
molest
don't trust
stay away from

In our ensuing conversations, Rosanne discussed a nightmarish sequence of events that occurred between the ages of six and twelve. Her mother had divorced when Rosanne was four years old, and in her desperate loneliness met a man on the rebound from his own divorce. The man, Jake, turned out to be an abusive alcoholic. Rosanne told me how Jake would physically and sexually abuse her and her siblings regularly. Rosanne recalls events like: being locked outside with her brother and sisters for hours in the cold rain; being lined up and stripped naked with her brother and sisters and whipped with a switch; being forced to watch her sister being sexually molested by her stepfather; and being repeatedly molested herself. She recalled that all of the children were terrified to say anything for the fear that Jake might kill them all, including their mother.

When Rosanne was twelve years old, her mother finally got the courage to divorce Jake. About a year later, she met another man and remarried. Although her new stepfather was a kind and gentle man, Rosanne could not bring herself to give him even the slightest chance to be her friend.

Her reactions were typical of people experiencing a post-traumatic stress disorder. Understandably, Rosanne had over-generalized her fear of Jake to all men. She had decided that men are scary, physically abusive, emotionally demeaning, and sexually disgusting. She knew that men could not be trusted.

Rosanne felt a strong mixture of hurt, resentment, and guilt, but the strongest emotion she suffered from was fear. I encouraged Rosanne to express fully and ventilate the fear experienced while living with her first stepfather. She was encouraged to relate vivid details of what had happened to her, all the fearful sensations she had as a small child. This was a difficult process for Rosanne and required considerable support from me. Nonetheless, both she and I believed that it was crucial for her to express her feelings not only during her sessions but also to write them out at home.

Next, I encouraged Rosanne to state exactly what she had learned from these horrendous experiences. We decided to substitute another adaptive strategy for her crippling fear of men. In Rosanne's case, the substitute strategy became, "Allowing men to earn your trust gradually, while being realistically cautious."

Finally, to get rid of her remaining fear, I taught her deep relaxation, encouraging her to recall the distressing memories of her previous trauma while keeping her body profoundly relaxed.

It took me two or three months to develop rapport with Rosanne, but once this was achieved, her progress was rapid. Her new stepfather, and mother, reported a dramatic change in her attitude toward her stepfather and toward all men. Within one month of fully ventilating her feelings, she established a cordially friendly relationship with her stepfather and began going out with friends and meeting boys. After two months she allowed herself to date again. One year later she met a naval officer and eventually become engaged.

A Realistic or Unrealistic Fear? Sometimes it is hard to tell whether or not a fear is realistic. Derek, a fifty-one-year-old corporate executive, was afraid to fly because of a near disaster on a flight. At 30,000 feet over the ocean, an emergency exit door blew off and the plane began a spiral dive toward the ocean.

Is Derek's fear of flying realistic? He nearly died in a crash, and this was real. On the other hand, his fear of flying threatened his business empire.

In his treatment, I encouraged Derek to express and ventilate by writing out all of the traumatic thoughts and experiences that occurred in his near disaster. I even told him to go further and imagine the plane going down and killing him. This is from one of Derek's letters reexperiencing the disaster:

I remember sitting in a chair next to a window and looking out into the sky. There was a carpet of white clouds several thousand feet below. I remember I couldn't really see the ocean. I picked a magazine from the envelope in front of me and began reading an article.

I remember hearing and feeling a loud thump that shook the cabin. Then I heard a loud hissing sound and a roar. I looked up and saw that papers and other objects were being sucked toward the gaping hole, about fifteen feet in front of me, where an emergency exit had been. The plane violently pitched to the right and began a slow descent toward the ocean.

During this time the oxygen masks sprang down from the ceiling above and many passengers began to scream and shriek in panic. I remember feeling my whole body go cold. I didn't even want to put the mask over my face because I was sure we were going to die anyway. I remember the dizzy feeling of spinning down in space for what seemed like hours.

I finally got the mask over my face. I remember bracing myself for a collision, with the realization that there was no way I could survive. Then it felt as if we were pulled up by a giant tether-type rope. The plane leveled out and my stomach sank. I heard the captain announce, "Ladies and gentlemen, we have regained control at 6,000 feet and will be able to make an emergency landing soon."

After he ventilated his feelings in four letters, I introduced Derek to the process of relaxation training. Specifically, he was taught the "Letting Go of Tension" exercise from Chapter 8. He was then asked to rehearse and gradually reexperience all of the traumatic occurrences in the near disaster while keeping his body profoundly relaxed. After three sessions of this desensitization procedure, Derek went back to flying again.

To summarize, there are two kinds of fears: those based on realistic, usually immediate, threats and those based on traumas or occurrences in the distant past. To deal with the former use the stress management principles outlined in this chapter. To cope with the unrealistic fears, ventilate them and learn how to desensitize or relax into them.

Remember, fear is your friend. The purpose of fear is to protect you from harm. When fear begins to interfere with the fulfillment of your life, however, it becomes an enemy. So listen to your fears, learn from them, allow them to protect you. But do not let them cripple you in situations where they are unnecessary.

GRIEF

The most helpless feeling as a clinical psychologist occurs when a patient complains of depression over losing a loved one. While the death of a loved one is perhaps the most painful type of loss a person can experience, other losses such as divorce, break-up of a relationship, unemployment, loss of physical activity level, or loss of mental functioning can all be crippling. Loss is a natural part of life, but why is it so painful?

Why Grief?

Feelings of loneliness, desolation, painful memories, and heartache associated with loss are the emotion we call grief. Since the visible behaviors of grief are represented as an attempted reunion with the lost loved one, the pain of loss may serve to motivate parents, children, or mates to look for one another as if they were lost.

When you show obvious signs of distress, despair, and loneliness, it is usually visible to other people. This allows you to be comforted or cared for by others, who help fill the gap in your life. The people, things, and activities that you find important are generally where you invest your emotional energy. When you have invested much emotional energy in a person or activity, and lose that person or activity, you become a good candidate for going through the grieving process.

When something has been taken out of your life, grief helps you find a way of putting something back into your life. Grief can be a motivator to get you to reinvest your emotional energy in something else to replace the lost loved one or activity.

Stages of Grief

Grief is a natural but painful reaction to losses such as death, divorce, unemployment, or loss of physical functioning. Elizabeth Kubler-Ross identified four stages of grieving: First, you experience the feeling of being shocked, dazed, numb, or empty inside. You also may refuse to believe what has happened and deny what has occurred. Sometimes you may think that it is "all a mistake," and that something isn't correct.

Following this denial and numbness stage, which tends to protect you, there comes a period of acute and obvious distress. You are likely to experience sharp pangs of yearning and severe emotional pain. You may have vivid dreams of the lost loved one, or illusions of seeing the person you have loved and lost. Your thoughts may be plagued by guilts of omission such as, "If only I had done something different."

The third stage of grief is characterized by depression and disorganization. You feel that life has lost much of its meaning. You may feel apathetic and submissive.

The final stage of grief is acceptance. In the acceptance phase you begin to accept the loss both mentally and emotionally. You understand that the loss is real, and although it is painful, it does make sense. You become acutely aware of pleasurable and painful memories associated with the loss. After this, you begin to build a new self-identity, which leads to what is known as the "resolution stage."

Self-Help Techniques for Coping With Loss

Foremost, you must recognize that you have suffered a loss and allow yourself to grieve. An excellent way to ventilate grief, as with other emotions, is through letter writing. As usual, go into as much detail as possible. Allow yourself to cry as much as you need to, and think of all the wonderful things you will be missing due to your loss.

Second, stop your negative thoughts. When you start hearing yourself thinking thoughts like "Life is empty," "There's no need to continue," or "I'm better off dead," try to substitute thoughts like "The loneliness is motivating me to go out and meet someone else," and "Loneliness is a natural part of life at times and I can get through this loss." Or motivate yourself even more by using such sentences as: "Before long I'll be looking forward to developing a new loving relationship."

Third, set up a daily activity schedule. Offset the depression by forcing yourself to fill your time with useful activities, such as washing your car, showering, doing laundry, cooking, studying, or working. I recommend to my patients who have suffered a serious loss that they return to work as soon as possible. This has proved effective in countering depression.

Finally, set aside a specified time each day to allow yourself to grieve. During this time you can surround yourself with reminders or signals that trigger acute pangs of grief. It is important here to allow yourself to cry as much as you need to and not hold anything back. Allow yourself to express your feelings and talk to your lost person, saying all you need to say. The open-chair technique, described earlier, is a very powerful way of ventilating and releasing grief.

Janell recently lost her husband of thirty-five years. Janell was stuck in the phase of numbness and denial, and although she showed feelings of depression, she would not allow herself to cry very much. With very strong urging on my part, Janell was able to start writing her deceased husband letters. When Janell began to allow herself to cry, through the letter-writing process, she was on the way to letting go of her grief. Here is an excerpt from one of Janell's letters:

Dear Pat,

I've just felt too much pain to be able to express my sadness to you. I can't begin to tell you how I feel right now. I just can't seem to let you go. We had so many wonderful times together and so many meaningful memories, that I just can't think of life without you. Right now I'm feeling numb, sad, lost, and disorganized all at the same time.

You were my joy in life. I did put all of my emotional energy into you, and I guess that wasn't good because now I have nothing to fall back on. How can I begin to express the lifetime of wonderful experiences we had together? Thirty-five Christmases, birthdays, picnics, the birth of five wonderful children, the realization of being grandparents, and all our activities together.

Although I have written you several letters before this one, I'm starting to wonder if you think it would be okay if I were to go on with my life and start meeting my needs. Not only were you my lover, but you were my best friend. No one will ever be able to take your place, but I hope you'll give me permission to try to find someone to share the rest of my life with. I love you, and I want to put you away in a special place in my heart where I will never forget you. I know someday I will be with you again.

Love,
Janell

In Janell's last letter to her husband, she asked for and received permission to begin living her life again. Within two years, Janell had found another friend, and begun to handle her day-to-day activities acceptably.

In the phase of numbness and denial, Janell was not feeling enough distress to experience the pains of loneliness that would force her to go out and try to find comfort and solace from friends and others. During the acute distress phase, she experienced a severe loneliness, and at that point began to reach out to others. This was a decisive moment, and during this process she eventually met someone who introduced her to a man she began to date. Janell then began slowly to reinvest some of the emotional energy she had lost when her husband died. Janell and I both realized that no one would ever take her husband's place, but at some level she had to make a kind of substitution to have her needs for attention, affection, and companionship met.

This pattern occurs with other losses such as divorce, retirement, and the empty nest syndrome. When you're divorced you will feel confused, disorganized, and lonely until you find another relationship. When you lose a job, you feel a sense of despair, distress, and upset that motivates you to find another job. When your last child moves out, mothers especially must find something to do with their previous full-time mothering energy. Loss is an essential part of life. The pain and despair you feel due to your loss is serving a purpose.

To summarize, allow yourself to express and ventilate your grief, such as through letter writing. Listen to your feelings of distress and loneliness and take the action you need to fill the gap and begin living again. If you don't reach out to others, it's going to be a very lonely road.

ANGER - "As We Forgive Those Who Trespass Against Us."

Do you ever find yourself becoming angry over something trivial? Someone cutting you off in traffic? Catching a red light when you are late for work? An innocent question by your spouse? Demands for attention by your children? A request for some extra work by your boss? If the answer to any of these questions is "yes," you probably have strong underlying anger that you are not dealing with.

Anger and its close relatives irritability, annoyance, and hostility are all caused by an underlying sense of emotional or physical hurt, disappointment, or frustration. Anger can be thought of as a doughnut. The hole in the middle is the hurt and the outer part the expressed feelings. If you look at your anger carefully, you may find the hole in the center of your doughnut is loaded with hurts or disappointments that have been stored up for years or even decades.

You may try to deal with your anger by blocking it out. You may minimize or deny the fact that you have been hurt or disappointed, or try to be "strong" and not think about it. When you continue to try to be "strong," your anger is turned inward and begins to "eat you up" inside, often precipitating various psychosomatic diseases. Furthermore, if you do not ventilate and express your anger, the hurt or frustration will continue to build.

When anger begins to build, it often leaks into inappropriate situations. You frequently find yourself looking for an argument. You may look for things to be mad at or complain about, and misinterpret other people's behavior. If you are more controlled, you may be able to block out the verbal expressions of anger yet hostile thoughts continue to run through your mind. You also may find yourself exploding over minor incidents such as dinner not being cooked quite right, an insensitive comment by a coworker, or a request by your child for a favor.

The most important problem with inappropriate anger is "displacement." Displaced anger stems from some past hurt, disappointment, or frustration. This anger gets dumped or displaced onto the wrong people—that is, someone who didn't cause the problem. Usually those who receive the displaced anger are those close to you: your husband, wife, friends, or children.

Sharon was a fifty-one-year-old school bus driver who had begun suffering from chronic migraine headaches. Medical treatment had not eliminated her pain, and she found herself with severe headaches for hours or even days at a time. In frustration, Sharon turned her anger about her physical pain against those she loved: her husband, children, and even grandchildren. Sharon confided in a session, "I'd really like to yell and scream at my headaches, but there's no person there to yell and scream at so I guess I dump it onto whoever's around me."

Generally, you get angry because someone or something has hurt you. Surprisingly, we often find that the people who hurt us feel guilty about what they have done but do not know what to do about it. This often ties in with their own guilt cycle, which was discussed earlier in this chapter.

To further complicate the problem and keep the anger cycle going, the people you hurt with your inappropriate anger are angry themselves. They often dump their anger onto other people who do not deserve it. This creates a giant spiraling cycle of displaced anger and guilt.

In my practice I often talk to people who suppress their anger to the point where they feel as if they're about to blow up. So while it is crucial to ventilate the anger built up over the past months or years, it is also important to learn assertiveness to keep new anger from reaching critical mass.

Anger Release Techniques

Many people cope with angry feelings through vigorous exercise, activities that do no harm to themselves or others but allow them to work off accumulated tension and stress. For this procedure to work it must do two things: (1) involve large muscle groups in your body, and (2) be aerobic, that is, increase your heart rate to sixty to eighty percent of its maximum. Good activities for working off anger include running, jogging, brisk walking, vigorous cycling, swimming, vigorous weight lifting, aerobics classes, chopping wood, or even hitting a punching bag.

You see, anger activates the same "fight or flight" response triggered by fear. The next time you are angry, instead of displacing the anger by fighting with someone who doesn't deserve it, let your body work out and ventilate the anger through vigorous exercise. To be effective, the large-muscle aerobic exercise must be done for at least thirty minutes to an hour at a time, although often you will want to spend a lot more time than this.

Forgiving. Unfortunately, vigorous exercise does not always release your anger completely. For a complete release of anger, you may need to go through the process of forgiving.

The process of forgiving has been detailed by family therapists Terry Kellogg and John Bradshaw and involves a five-step process:

1. Acknowledging that someone has hurt you in some significant way;
2. Acknowledging that you had feelings about this hurt;
3. Embracing and ventilating these feelings;
4. Stating exactly what you have learned from this experience; and,
5. Writing down the steps you will take to protect yourself from being hurt again.

In my practice I have discovered a sixth step, which is also essential in truly forgiving: *understanding how the person reached the point of hurting you in the first place.* Often you will discover that people who hurt you are displacing hurts from their own pasts.

Pam, a married mother of two, was successfully employed in a national company. Pam confided, "I don't know how my husband can put up with me. I feel like I'm angry and frustrated all of the time and I have this thing about men. I'm always looking and listening for an excuse to fight with them or argue."

Through clustering, Pam listed the men in her past who have hurt or disappointed her. Her stepfather's name emerged quickly. Next, I allowed Pam to express fully and ventilate her feelings by writing a letter to her stepfather detailing examples of how he had hurt her. Here is an excerpt from Pam's letter to her stepfather, John.

Dear Creep,

I can't believe the kind of person you were! You treated my mother, my sister, and me like dirt. It's like most of the time you weren't around, and when you were you were drunk. I remember the times you would emotionally and physically abuse my mom, and I remember how scared we all were of you. I remember all of the yelling and screaming, and how much my mom would cry.

Whenever you would walk into the house, everyone would get real scared and shaky. I remember whenever I saw you or heard your car drive up, I would run outside to get away from the house, and feel afraid that my mom was going to get hurt or killed. I felt this big need to protect my mom, but I knew I really couldn't do anything because you were so big and scary.

John, I know you're dead now, and all I can say is that I'm glad of it! The way you treated me and my mom has created major problems for me so far in my life. I've had a major problem learning to trust and love any man, and still find myself usually mad at men for no reason. But I can tell you this. I'm going to stop dumping my anger toward you onto men in my life who are innocent. Although you dominated and terrorized my life for years, you're not going to do it anymore.

You're no longer in my life,
Pam

Until writing this letter, Pam had been victimized by her past. She was being dominated by a dead stepfather who controlled her behavior in the here and now. Through the process of ventilating and expressing her feelings, she acknowledged that she had been victimized in the past, but refused to be victimized in the future.

In subsequent sessions with Pam, we discussed how her stepfather could have become the way he was. Pam began to entertain the possibilities that he was probably hurt and abused as a child and carried a tremendous amount of emotional pain himself.

About two weeks later, in an open-chair session, Pam began to cry again. She recovered some blocked material she knew about how her stepfather had been abused and mistreated as a child. Once Pam understood how he became the way he was, the process of forgiving was completed.

The main point: When someone is angry, obnoxious, hostile, resentful, or belligerent you can bet there is some underlying hurt, disappointment, or rejection. Remember, when you break through the surface of the anger and hostility, you are going to find tears. Then, your own protective anger quickly melts into sympathy.

Anger Options

The purpose of anger is to prevent you from being hurt again. Before you can give up your anger, you must decide how to prevent being hurt again in the same way. Here is a list of possible substitutes for anger:

- Be realistically cautious about the people you trust.
- Allow people to earn your trust gradually.
- Keep your eyes, ears, and mind open and realize when someone is starting to hurt you or let you down.
- Immediately let people know when they are starting to hurt or disappoint you.
- Be up front with people and tell them exactly what you need.
- Do not put all of your "emotional eggs" in one basket; that is, do not put too much emotional energy into one person. If you do, you risk making the person feel overwhelmed and more likely to reject you.
- Be assertive, open, immediate, and appropriate with your feelings. Express how you feel, when you feel it.

Unfortunately, the only language that some victimizers understand is the language of counterattack. This can involve anything from punching a bully in the nose to filing a lawsuit for malicious slander. Some people simply do not respond to reason. You may be assertive, appropriate, problem solving, and even forgiving. Yet if you are dealing with a true victimizer, he or she is going to continue walking all over you until you finally stand up and take action.

Some key points to keep in mind when fighting back are:

- Channel your angry energy into focused constructive results.
- Think clearly. It will not help to be angry if you have no plan for using your anger effectively.
- Implement your plan of counterattack, let go, and go on with the business of the rest of your life.

Sean was a sixteen-year-old, hyperactive, learning-disabled child who had been victimized by the public school system. Despite the best efforts by Sean's parents, myself, and other individuals, Sean never quite met the necessary criteria to get the help he needed in school. The public school system had a program for children like Sean, but because his test scores were one or two points from the cutoff, he was not allowed to participate.

Sean's mother made sincere efforts at local, city, county, and even state levels to get her son's educational needs met but ran into a closed door at every turn. Finally, in total frustration, she hired an attorney who filed a civil class action lawsuit against the public school system. Granted this action was drastic; but she could no longer watch her son continue to be victimized. She won the suit, and Sean responded beautifully to the extra help he soon received.

IN SUMMARY . . .

Realize that your past only haunts you when there is a lesson you have not yet learned from it. Strong and unpleasant feelings like guilt, grief, fear, and anger serve a clear purpose and exist for a reason. Don't run and hide from them. Embrace them; experience them; learn from them. Then set your sights straight ahead for the future and get on with the business of living.

5 | What You Need

and How to Get It

You already know what you want. But, do you know what you really need and how to get it? It does not matter how good a situation you are in, how good you are at recognizing and expressing your feelings, how assertive you are, or how well you have cleaned out problems from your past. If you are not getting your needs met you are not going to be a happy camper.

Every day in my practice, I see patients who seem psychologically well-put-together, but who are unhappy because something seems missing. After a few simple questions what is missing usually becomes obvious.

A good example is Katrina, a sales manager with an eight-year-old son. Katrina's job performance is good. She has her bachelor's degree with a major in psychology and knows quite a bit about staying mentally healthy. She has a nice three-bedroom home and is well thought of in the community. Unfortunately, Katrina's husband of ten years just left her for her best friend. She suddenly experienced a double loss. While the emotional consequences of such a devastating event are far reaching, at a basic level, Katrina's needs for love and companionship are no longer being met.

Sometimes what's missing is less obvious.

Debbie is a social service eligibility worker. She is happily married, has two lovely children, a nice home in the country, and a few good friends. But Debbie feels chronically frustrated and helpless about her job. Often she is unable to help families who really need it, but more often she is the target of verbal assaults and threats from people who are out to con their way into receiving welfare benefits. The people whom Debbie does help clearly take her for granted. The appreciation she gets from the people she serves is near zero and Debbie starts to feel bad about herself. Debbie is not getting her needs for self-esteem and respect from others met.

So, let's begin our examination of how to meet your needs by first taking a close look at what your needs actually are.

Psychologist Abraham Maslow believed that human needs formed a pyramid-like structure, with basic needs at the bottom and higher-order needs at the top. He contended that before higher-order needs could be recognized and met, the lower, more basic needs, must be satisfied. For example, your need to find a warm, loving relationship quickly takes a back seat if you don't know where your next meal is coming from.

SURVIVAL NEEDS

At the base of the needs pyramid are survival needs which are basic to all human beings. Survival needs include: oxygen, water, food, shelter, sleep, and sex. If you look closely at survival (physiological) needs, you realize that they too form a pyramid. If, for example, you are extremely hungry and desperately searching for food and suddenly have your oxygen supply cut off, your need for food will quickly be replaced by a clear need for breathable air. When your basic physiological needs are frustrated, they scream for fulfillment. You may even become obsessed with them.

Sleep and Sex Deficits

In modern America, our needs for food, water, and shelter are typically met. That leaves two survival needs that are often unfulfilled: sleep and sex.

Individuals vary in the amount of sleep they need and typically need less sleep as they get older. But research has shown that the average adult needs about 7.6 hours of sleep per night. If you fail to get enough sleep, you may have trouble concentrating during the early afternoon hours. You think about a relaxing situation and may even nod off. Waves of sleepiness come over you and you have to struggle to stay awake. Fatigue and lethargy resulting from lack of sleep impair virtually every area of your life. You are unlikely to be sharp on the job or at school. You will lack the energy to devote to your relationships. And you will not pursue stimulating or creative activities.

Although humans are sexual beings, our sexual needs are often unfulfilled. Many patients report severe frustration over not having their sexual needs met, yet feel guilty when they engage in a "meaningless, one-night stand" to satisfy them. The problem surfaces whenever the fulfillment of human sexual needs is regulated by society, which is nearly always. Western cultures, like ours, stress sexual contact only within a loving relationship.

Although there may have been a sexual revolution, many people are either aware of it or are reactionaries. The recent AIDS crisis has reemphasized the importance of monogamy. The problem is that, while sexual needs are basic, the higher order needs for love and bonding are more complex and difficult to meet. It is difficult for many people to postpone sex until they are in a position to fulfill these higher-order complex needs.

SAFETY NEEDS

Safety and security needs are the next level of the pyramid above survival. Child psychologists have noted that children need a predictable world in which there is consistency and routine. To some degree this is also true for adults. If you live in an unpredictable world, characterized by violence, crime and threat, you become preoccupied with safety and security. Insecure people have a compulsive need for order and stability and will go to great lengths to avoid the unknown and the unexpected. Your needs for safety are often directly related to your living situation.

LOVE AND BELONGING NEEDS

People develop a hunger for affectionate relationships, a hunger comparable to the physiological hunger for food. It is important not to confuse love with sexual needs. The need for love involves both the ability to receive love and the ability to give it. Carl Rogers, a major force in twentieth century psychology, defines love as a "state of being deeply understood and deeply accepted." Although love and belonging are not considered survival needs, there is scientific evidence of their extreme importance. Early in the twentieth century, Dr. Henry Chapin found that in nine-out-of-ten children's asylums in the United States, every infant under the age of two years died. These babies did not die from lack of food, shelter, clothing, or nutrition, but from a deprivation of physical contact and love. Research by Harry Harlow found that the need for affection and love is basic, even to primates (monkeys and apes). Infant monkeys deprived of maternal affection became social and psychological misfits. Developmental psychologists note that when children are abandoned or neglected they will often wrap their arms around themselves and rock themselves, emulating the maternal hug and gentleness they so deeply desire.

ESTEEM NEEDS

Esteem needs—feeling good about yourself—are divided into those involving esteem from within and esteem from others. Self-esteem needs include the need for competence, confidence, adequacy, mastery, and independence. Esteem from others includes receiving prestige, recognition, status, appreciation, and reputation.

One of the best ways to develop self-esteem is to do a strength bombardment exercise I call "I am." The "I am" exercise involves beginning a sentence with "I am" and following it with every positive thing you can think about yourself.

Martin, a medical resident, had recently moved to Northern California from Chicago. He felt completely alone. He knew virtually no one in his new community, and was feeling very insecure.

I had Martin do an "I am" strength bombardment exercise, and he came up with the following items:

- *I am young and healthy.*
- *I am free from physical or emotional disease.*
- *I am intelligent.*
- *I am friendly.*
- *I am helpful.*
- *I am a physician.*
- *I am a member of a family (although far away) that loves me.*
- *I am capable of working effectively.*
- *I am athletic.*
- *I am filled with energy and vitality.*

After doing the strength bombardment exercise, Martin felt better. Gone was the wavering sense of insecurity, and it was replaced by a sense of confident, self-assured well-being.

There is always something positive to say about yourself. One severely physically and emotionally abused young boy I worked with began his "I am" statement with "I am alive." When doing your own "I am" strength bombardment exercise, keep the doors wide open to every positive event or attribute about yourself. If you feel bad about yourself and can think of nothing to feel good about, go back to something fundamental like "I can read" or "I can walk and talk." Be sure to include what you have accomplished educationally and occupationally, successful past relationships, your past and present friendships, and your physical and mental attributes.

An important point to realize with respect to self-esteem is that when you feel competent and confident about yourself you will be much more likely to gain the respect and admiration of others. Accepting the respect and admiration of others will, in turn, build more of a sense of competence and confidence.

STIMULATION

Next on the pyramid are needs for stimulation, excitement, and novelty. If your basic needs are being met, and your self-esteem is good, the next unpleasant emotion you are likely to experience is boredom. This feeling is telling you that your life is too predictable and you need to stir things up a little. Most of us fall into the rut of a routine, predictable, boring job. When this occurs, you have to look outside the office to find a sense of stimulation.

One of the biggest obstacles to meeting your needs for stimulation is the sense of safety and security you get from living out your life in a routine, predictable, dull set of behaviors and experiences. But human beings are meant to be more than predictable little robots.

Think back to the times in your life when you felt the most challenged and stimulated. Those high school football, basketball, or baseball games. Competing for the one you love. Striving for your degree. Working your way up the corporate ladder. If you are like most of us, when you feel stimulated and challenged, you feel the most alive. So make it happen. Create challenges, stimulation, and novelty in your life.

SELF-ACTUALIZATION

Human beings have a basic need to fulfill their potential and become all they can be. This highest order need is known as the need for self-actualization. Maslow found that people functioning at the highest level were self-actualizers and exhibited a consistent set of traits. They felt a compelling need for wholeness, perfection, justice, beauty, goodness, uniqueness, and truth. They were invariably focused on not only helping other people, but helping humanity.

The Reality of the Dollar

Although Maslow does not mention it, you and I both know that there is a definite reality with respect to how much money we make, and our financial situations. Certainly, financial security is not a higher order need in the sense of truth, beauty, or justice, yet its impact on your everyday behavior is compelling.

In my work as a clinical psychologist, I usually ignore financial situations and focus on helping people change their feelings and behaviors, but the reality of the dollar became apparent to me while I was working with a twenty-nine-year-old chronic pain patient named Jim. Jim had been referred to me when he suffered a herniated cervical disc while working at a construction site. His physician had noticed that Jim had become depressed and lethargic, and had mentioned suicide on several occasions.

Upon interviewing Jim, I found a tall, slender man who was extremely depressed. He spoke in monosyllabic words, and his emotions were flat. I quickly realized, consistent with other chronic pain psychologists, that Jim's depression was due to his lack of employment and activity. Yet, Jim did not complain as much about his chronic pain as he did about his financial situation. He had gone from making $2,000 a month to a $400 per month social security disability check. Jim had retained a worker's compensation lawyer, but his court date wouldn't be coming up for over a year. In the meantime, Jim had to move out of his apartment into a small trailer, and get by with as little as possible. Even with his very basic lifestyle, Jim was having serious problems making financial ends meet, and on a couple of occasions missed appointments because he simply didn't have enough money to buy gas.

Then, in an unexpected development, Jim received a significant amount of money from a relative to help him get by until his trial date. I remember, in our next session, Jim looked like a new man. He told me he was able to keep enough food on the table, pay his utility bills, and have enough gas for his truck. He said that he even had enough money to occasionally take his girlfriend out to a movie or dinner. Jim still had his pain and distress, yet the compelling reality of the dollar dramatically lifted his mood.

HOW TO SATISFY YOUR NEEDS

Many authors have tried to describe our basic needs, but few have tackled the question of how to go about satisfying them. The subspecialty of problem solving, in the general area of cognitive psychology, has a tested method to help us get what we want. If needs are relabeled goals, the Six-Step Problem-Solving Method will help us get what we need.

The Six-Step Problem-Solving Method

1. Write out the problem clearly using positive, goal-directed terms. Clarification of the problem, need, or goal is essential for developing a workable plan. When describing the problem, include the exact outcome or goal you wish to achieve. Your goals should be measurable, that is, something you can see or hear or touch. Be sure that your goals are stated positively, not a negatively. For instance, if you have an unmet need for love and companionship say "I want a warm, loving, affectionate relationship" instead of "I don't want to be lonely anymore." If you set your goal as a negative instead of a positive, you will have no clear direction to achieve what you want.

2. Assess your situation. As you recall from the chapter on situational engineering, situational constraints and opportunities play an important role in determining whether you can meet your needs and achieve your goals. If you are in the unfortunate situation of facing a corporate merger, takeover, or layoff, you will undoubtedly feel insecure regarding the stability of your job. This is a realistic feeling about a stressful situation, and the feelings of insecurity are compelling you to take action to correct the situation or find a job somewhere else.

3. Assess your strengths, weaknesses, and resources. For instance, Dave was a shy, insecure nineteen-year-old who had a great deal of difficulty initiating relationships with women. After

doing a strength bombardment exercise, Dave recognized that he was an expert bowler and worked at a bowling alley where several eligible females bowled. He decided to use his strength as an expert bowler for initiating relationships with women, offering them tips on how they could improve their games.

4. Develop three or four alternate plans. Once you have specified your goal, assessed your situation, and have a good idea of your personal strengths and weaknesses, you are ready to develop alternative plans. Your plans, just like your goals, should be clearly defined. This will be illustrated in the later section on real life examples.

A technique called brainstorming is an effective way of developing unique and creative plans. Brainstorming produces many quality ideas for solving problems. Although brainstorming is a technique designed to be used with a group, it can be used alone. Once you get the little voice inside your head to stop criticizing the number and adequacy of your ideas, you will find yourself coming up with many unique solutions. There are four simple rules to follow in brainstorming:

Rule 1: Create as many solutions to the problem as possible; the more solutions the better.
Rule 2: Absolutely no criticism. All evaluations should be postponed until after the brainstorming session.
Rule 3: Encourage creativity, uniqueness, and originality. As you are generating ideas, don't consider whether the idea is practical, just go for a high number of unique answers.
Rule 4: Try to build upon previous ideas.

5. Implement your plan. No matter how many unique, creative, or original ideas you have, they will do nothing to solve your problems or meet your needs until you implement them. As you learned from the technique of time-structured problem solving, it may take continuing effort to achieve your goal. Be realistic and give your plan enough time to work.

6. Evaluate your progress. Once your plan has been implemented and given a reasonable chance to work, evaluate the results. To evaluate the results, you need to go back to Step 1 and see if your plan has led to the outcome you wanted. If, in the evaluation phase, you realize that your needs have not been met and your goals have not been achieved, it is time to go back to plan development and try your second or third choice plans.

People have found the six-step method to be extremely effective in helping them achieve their goals and meet their needs. Nonetheless, some still get stuck and go nowhere when trying to create and act on a plan to improve the quality of their lives. These are the people who are unable to transcend the barriers to successful problem solving. Often, they do not know these barriers exist or how to overcome them.

Barriers to Successful Problem Solving

Problem Solving Set. Problem solving set occurs when a person repeatedly tries only the same old method instead of considering several different approaches to a problem. An example of problem-solving set is the case of Edward, a recently divorced man who was obsessed with getting his ex-wife back. After assessing Ed's needs, it became apparent that his needs for sexual fulfillment, love, and affection were frustrated. He had satisfied these needs in the past with his wife, and he saw the logical solution to his problem as getting his wife back. Ed tried several plans and techniques to get her back, yet nothing seemed to work.

With some work, Ed realized that there was nothing particularly magical about his relationship with his wife, and that she simply met his needs for love, affection, and sexual satisfaction. Then Ed became aware that what he wanted was not his wife back, but a warm, loving, affectionate relationship with a woman. Once Ed realized this, he was no longer stuck in the problem-solving set of trying to meet his needs solely by getting his wife back.

Functional Fixedness. Functional fixedness is a barrier to problem solving that occurs when you see only familiar uses for well-known objects and fail to see unique, novel, or creative uses for them. Functional fixedness applies not only to objects, but also to relationships.

Go back to our example of Ed. After he got over his problem-solving set, he became aware that there were many attractive eligible females where he worked, some of whom were interested in him. He had been stuck at a level of functional fixedness by seeing these women simply as friends or acquaintances. He had never considered an emotional involvement with any of them because he was married. As a single person, Ed had to break through his functional fixedness barrier and become open to the possibility of developing meaningful relationships with other women.

Spinning Your Wheels. Spinning your wheels is a problem-solving barrier whereby people spend much time and energy trying to solve a problem, or meet a need, and never achieve their goal. They are consoled by their furious problem-solving activity, but never get the brass ring. To these perpetual problem solvers, it seems like the harder they try, the farther away the goal becomes. What they seem to fail to understand is the need for an incubation period, a break in which the mind can do its work. Cognitive psychologists have discovered that when you temporarily give up trying to solve a problem, a solution may arise spontaneously.

So when trying to solve a particular problem or meet a specific need, spend a reasonable amount of time working on the problem, then relax, let go, and do something else. Cognitive psychologists have discovered that the optimal span for human concentration is about ninety minutes. If you continue to try to force answers beyond this time, you may actually undo any progress you have already made.

Not Goals. Some people have a "not goal" for every goal. Not goals consist of all the reasons, explanations, fears, and excuses they can come up with for not succeeding. Little goals have little not goals, and big goals have big not goals. The way to overcome dealing with not goals is to avoid accepting the not goals as excuses for not getting what you want. Instead, channel your energy into finding alternative ways of getting there. In short, focus and act on what you want, not what you don't want.

Unrealistic Expectations. If your goals are unrealistic, you will become chronically frustrated and dissatisfied over never achieving what you want. Although it is good to aim high, if you aim too high you are setting yourself up for failure and frustration.

What seems obvious to outsiders is sometimes invisible to those whose expectations are distorted. Susan was a lonely California waitress, whose goal was to have a relationship with a major league baseball star whom she had never met. Given Susan's location, social standing, lifestyle, and the fact the baseball star was married and lived near Atlanta, the likelihood of her achieving a romantic involvement with him was near zero. Susan could not feel good until she accepted this reality and adjusted her expectations accordingly.

Tip: Equifinality. In working with my patients to meet their needs and achieve their goals, I have found the *equifinality* concept extremely effective. Equifinality refers to the idea that a goal can be achieved through a number of different means or routes. There are going to be numerous opportunities for jobs, friends, relationships, and other events and occurrences that can fulfill your needs. Try not to get stuck in the trap of thinking that one way is the only way to meet your needs. Keep your mind open and be aware of the numerous opportunities that will present themselves to you throughout your lifetime.

REAL LIFE EXAMPLES

Need satisfaction, problem-solving barriers, successful problem solving, and equifinality are all crucial when it comes to achieving your goals and becoming happy and fulfilled. To see how they really work, let's look at some real examples of the application of these principles.

Leif: Unmet Security Needs Lead to Extreme Behaviors

Leif was a shy twelve-year-old boy who was referred to me after his release from a state psychiatric hospital. Leif's problems started when he was ten, when his parents divorced. Leif idolized his father and chose to live with him after the split. Leif's father had a severe alcohol and drug problem, and Leif was consistently exposed to his dad's erratic behavior, violence, and persistent threats. More than once Leif described his dad's fighting with other drug dealers, being arrested, and having to be physically subdued and handcuffed by the police.

Due to his dad's alcohol and drug problems, Leif was frequently the target of senseless beatings at home. Leif learned that he had little safety and security in his day-to-day life, and no sense of predictability or routine.

Leif's behavior at school became bizarre. He began scratching on his wrist with pens, threatening classmates with a stolen pocketknife, and talking aloud to himself. School officials recommended that Leif be placed in a psychiatric hospital.

After testing his limits, Leif became aware that the state hospital offered a lot more safety, security, routine, and structure than living with his dad. After a year, Leif's behavior became less bizarre. He no longer reported hearing voices without knowing where they came from, nor did he make any gestures to harm himself or anyone else. He began looking forward to an opportunity to go live with his mother and younger brother.

Before Leif's return to his mom, she and I discussed how we could make his situation as safe, secure, and predictable as possible. She told me that one of Leif's biggest fears was that the kids at school would learn that he had been in a mental hospital and would ridicule and harass him. Once Leif's need for safety and security were met, he rapidly progressed from being an institutionalized mental patient to a typical twelve-year-old boy.

Kathy: Looking in the Wrong Place for Love, Affection and Belonging

Kathy was a twenty-five-year-old woman who came into counseling devastated after being dropped by Greg, her boyfriend of three years. Greg had left Kathy for a woman named Sherry, and Kathy was obsessed with getting Greg back or making Sherry disappear from his life. Kathy accumulated mounds of evidence showing what a bad person Sherry was, and continually tried to convince Greg of this. Kathy was very nice to Greg, took good care of herself, and tried to give Greg everything he wanted. Kathy let Greg know that she was on call for anything he needed, and diligently waited for something to go wrong between Sherry and Greg. Yet, despite her best efforts, Greg now belonged to Sherry.

Kathy hoped that sooner or later Greg would come to his senses and return to her, the one who truly loved him. Unfortunately, after a year of trying, Kathy was no closer to a renewed relationship with Greg then she was at our first meeting. Kathy had struck the barrier of problem-solving set. She saw the only solution to her need for love, affection, and belonging as the relationship with Greg.

Eventually, Kathy accepted the idea that what she wanted was not a relationship with Greg, but a relationship in which she felt love and belonging. A new dimension opened up for Kathy with this understanding. She knew several attractive eligible men who were interested in her. She began to accept dates and after dating several different men, Kathy had an opportunity to vacation in Alaska with one of them. About two months later I received the following letter from Kathy:

Dear Doctor,

I just wanted to let you know things are going great. My relationship with John is better than anything I ever had with Greg. He's a real outdoors type of person, and we spend a whole lot of time hiking around and fishing. Through some friends of his, I recently got a job up here with the National Parks Service, and just love it. When I think back to how I was stuck on Greg, I wonder how I could have put up with him for that long. I guess I had an idea in my mind of what I really needed, and refused to consider other options.

- Kathy

Darren: Exploring Options for Meeting Esteem Needs

Darren was a robust twenty-nine-year-old husband and father of three who had taken a leave of absence from his job as a prison guard. Darren worked at a prison four hours from his home and only got to see his wife, children, family, and friends on weekends. Despite five years of asking, he was not given a transfer so he could live near his home.

This situation might have been tolerable to Darren were it not for the fact that his supervisors and most of the other people at the prison were nonsupportive and unappreciative of his efforts. He reported consistently receiving "fair" to "adequate" evaluations despite doing his best.

After some exploration, Darren became aware that his problem was not having his esteem needs met by others: respect, appreciation, and admiration. This was leading to a serious decrease in Darren's self-esteem, which had once been high. Darren's only plan to meet his needs was to get a transfer, so he could interact daily with his supportive family and friends. From them he would get the respect, love, and appreciation he needed. Unfortunately, despite Darren's best efforts, he was unable to achieve his goal.

I encouraged Darren to do some brainstorming, and he came up with the following fourteen possibilities for fulfilling his needs:

- *Be assertive and tell the boss my problems.*
- *Go over the boss' head and tell his supervisor about the situation.*
- *Get help from my union.*
- *File a grievance.*
- *Get job stress counseling.*
- *Exercise daily to work off frustration.*

- *Practice relaxation training.*
- *Use as many sick days and as much vacation time as possible.*
- *Apply for a transfer to another department.*
- *Look for another job.*
- *Try to befriend the boss and get him to like me and transfer me.*
- *Try to get a friend of the boss to get him to ease up on me.*
- *Have the boss kidnapped.*
- *Win the lottery.*

As far as implementing his plans, Darren reported that he had already tried several of the techniques he listed during our brainstorming session. He had tried being assertive with his boss, gone over his boss's head, filed a grievance, tried to get help from his union, and even contacted an attorney. He had gone through job-stress counseling, exercised daily to work off his frustration, and was using as much sick and vacation time as possible. He had already asked for a transfer to another department and done the best he could to befriend the boss. He realized that it was absurd to have his boss kidnapped and knew that the likelihood of winning the lottery was near zero. He found the relaxation training to be effective and also started to consider looking for another job.

Due to Darren's job stress, he did qualify for a medical leave of absence for one month. During this time, Darren noticed that his sleep improved, his gastrointestinal problems ceased, and he was no longer bothered by headaches. Darren was feeling better because he was receiving love, respect, appreciation, and attention from his family and friends.

Darren was willing and eager to return to work, but not to the job he left. When trying to get Darren to apply for another job, it became apparent that the $50,000 a year he received as a prison guard far exceeded the pay for any other job he could get, given his qualifications. I jokingly confronted Darren with the reality of deciding whether his lack of appreciation, respect, and recognition on the job was worth a $25,000 a year pay cut. My hunch is that it will not be, and that Darren will return to his previous job and have to learn to tolerate the frustration of his esteem needs, at least on the job.

Linda: A Brilliant Convenience Store Clerk

Linda was referred for counseling due to depression and pain reactions to an auto accident. Despite having an IQ of 150 and a bachelor's degree in English, Linda had been working as a clerk at a convenience store.

After experiencing emotional ventilation and learning relaxation techniques, Linda's pain and depression disappeared. A much more formidable issue emerged. Linda was keenly aware that there was a terrible mismatch between her intellectual and creative potential and her position in life. Linda was a gifted child, but, in her desire to fit in with the other children, had developed into a tremendous underachiever. While the underachieving helped her fit in better during junior high and high school, it was now interfering with her fulfillment.

During therapy, Linda became aware that she was not even beginning to tap her potential. She realized that she had a tremendous love for arts and the theater and had a great desire to direct and produce plays, and also to write them. With minor encouragement, Linda began helping to rewrite and direct a community play. In one of our sessions Linda commented:

> I feel like for the first time in my life my mind is really alive. I love to get into the intricacies of rewriting and directing my interpretation of Hamlet. Al (senior director and instructor) and I have a very close working relationship, and he told me that he's learning from what I have to say. I've got enough taste of the theater to make me want to really pursue this as a career.

Once Linda became aware of her new-found creativity and talent, her mind opened up to the many opportunities available to pursue her tremendous potential. She accepted the opportunity for extended study in theater at Stratford-upon-Avon in England.

This past Christmas, Linda brought me some photographs she had taken of Stonehenge and told me that her life was working out beautifully.

IN SUMMARY . . .

Since your higher-order needs cannot be recognized and fulfilled until your lower-order needs are satisfied, you have an obligation not only to yourself, but also to other people and to society to meet your basic needs. It works like this. If you are preoccupied with your survival needs, you will be unable to achieve your needs for safety and security. When consistently insecure, you will probably be unable to develop a good loving relationship. Without a loving relationship, you will experience little esteem——the respect of others——or self-esteem. Without esteem, you will be unable to address your self-actualization needs for meaningfulness, beauty, truth, justice, and perfection. You will remain preoccupied with yourself, unable to help improve the conditions of others or the world around you.

Know your basic needs, use the power of problem-solving techniques, overcome the barriers, and allow your unlimited potential to unfold. When functioning at your highest level, you will experience a sense of effortlessness, aliveness, and excitement in your life and work.

6 | Your Emotional

Investments

What Hooks
Do You Hang Your Life On?

What matters in your life? Your husband? Courage? Your children? Honesty? Your friends? Your spirituality? Although it is necessary to know what you value, it isn't enough. You must show these values consistently in your behavior.

THE EMOTIONAL INVESTMENT OCTOPUS

Early in the twentieth century, Sigmund Freud developed an idea called *object cathexis*. Freud's idea was that human beings have a certain amount of psychic energy, which they invest in objects or relationships. A way to understand Freud's object cathexis is through what I call the "emotional investment octopus." Imagine for a moment that you are an octopus with eight arms. You can put one arm around each of eight different things, all eight arms around one thing, or any combination. If you think of yourself as an emotional investment octopus, what do you hold in your arms? To understand this better, consider how Stanley and Barbara invest their emotional energy.

Stanley and Barbara: A Case of Extremes

Stanley is a hard-working "octopus." He typically works sixty hours a week, either in the office or at home. Stanley thinks he spends his time working to provide and care for his wife and children. Unfortunately, his wife and kids rarely see him. When they do, he is busy at his desk working for the family's good. Stanley has six arms wrapped around his job, and his two remaining arms around his wife, four children, and himself.

Things start out good for Stanley, but over the years his children begin to get in trouble; one develops a drug problem, another is busted for shoplifting, and a third is held back a grade in school for not working up to his potential. His wife, in loneliness, becomes depressed. Finally, Stanley's wife has enough, and decides to take the children and leave.

Stanley is upset and decides to throw the two arms he had around his wife and children around his work. He puts all his emotional energy into his job. This works for a year or so, until Stanley hears a rumor that his company has become a takeover target and he is likely to be laid off. Now, Stanley develops some serious stress-related problems including high blood pressure and ulcerative colitis. When the takeover finally occurs, Stanley is left holding the work bag——with nothing in it.

Barbara's emotional investment octopus is different from Stanley's. She put two arms around her husband, one arm around each of two children, one arm around several friends, two arms around her job, and her remaining arm around several personal recreations, hobbies, and herself.

After her separation, Barbara's life runs more smoothly. Her children receive the attention they need from their mother. Barbara maintains good performance at work and earns regular promotions. She continues to do things she enjoys in her free time, recharging her emotional batteries. She has close friends who are there for her whenever she needs them.

Unfortunately, Barbara's company also becomes a target of a hostile takeover but Barbara does not develop stress-related disorders. Instead, she channels her surplus emotional energy into sharing her feelings with her family and friends and spends more time pursuing recreations and hobbies. When the hostile takeover occurs, and Barbara loses her job, she feels disappointed but not devastated. While looking for another job, she accepts support from her family and friends, and is buoyed by the good feelings she receives from her recreations and pastimes.

What You Say and What You Do. Stanley continued to tell his wife and children that they were the most important thing in the world to him——right up to the time they left. So Stanley was confused about the family's break up, until he looked at how he spent his time each day. He would spend sixteen hours working, five and a half to six hours sleeping, and about two hours doing miscellaneous things around the house. The most interaction he had with his family was an occasional nod, asking "What's for dinner?" or telling his wife and children, "I'll see about that later."

In short, Stanley was a hypocrite. He valued one thing and did another. The most important thing to realize about your emotional investments is this: *You are what you do with your time.* If you spend six hours a day thinking about your wife and children but never let them know it, it is a wasted emotional investment. If you spend eight hours a day working and six hours worrying about the elimination of your job, this is another wasted emotional investment.

Consider again the fundamental question: What's really important to you? Although this is not a workbook, it is essential in understanding yourself to write out the things that you feel are important to you. Be sure to include your husband/wife or other significant relationships, children, friends, recreations, hobbies, and pastimes. Once you've done this, rank them in the order of their importance. You may rank your husband/wife first, your children second, and your job third. Or you make rank your job first, children second, and a relationship third. Be as honest as you can in ranking the importance of the people, situations, and activities in your life.

I have found it useful with my patients to ask them to note especially the top ten on their personal importance list. After you select your top ten investments, look at how you're taking care of them.

How You Spend Your Time

Are you living your values? The only way to answer this question is to take an honest, clear look at your everyday behavior. How do you spend each hour of a typical day? List each of the twenty-four hours of a day. Next to each hour note what you usually do at that time.

When you analyze how your time is spent, you will see that your two most time-consuming activities are sleeping and working. Most of us take these for granted. But to get an idea of what matters to you, focus, instead, on the remaining hours on your list. You will have about eight hours a day to work with, plus your weekends, days off, and vacation. In a typical day, you will find essential activities that are not important to you, such as commuting and errands. List everything you do and the amount of time you spend doing it. Honestly estimate how you spend your free time. Count the number of minutes or hours you spend talking or playing with your spouse and children, exercising, talking with your friends or acquaintances, or pursuing your hobbies.

Are you spending three hours watching your favorite football team play, and ten minutes with your children? Is that professional football game more important to you than your children? Is the four hours you spend shopping in the mall reflective of what you really care about and what makes you feel good? "Of course not!" you say. Then look at how you spend your time. Are you translating your values into behavior?

UNWISE EMOTIONAL INVESTORS

The Workaholic

Larry is a thirty-one-year-old married father of two who spends a minimum of sixty hours a week pursuing his career. Larry gets home from work so frustrated and tired that he has very little emotional energy for his wife and children. Larry has also become caught up in a common myth. He feels that some critical mass of money will solve all his problems and lead to happiness. At the pace Larry works, he could become financially independent at fifty. With his stress and fatigue, the odds are higher that he will have a cardiac arrest or other stress-related disease first.

When Larry's job is going well, he feels good, and develops a strong sense of self-esteem, about being a good engineer. When business slacks off, Larry has surplus emotional energy and nowhere to put it. He spends much of his time worrying over jobs that do not exist, and figuring ways to pursue his career. In one sense this is adaptive, because it may lead to other ways of making money. On the other hand, it is an extension of his workaholic mentality.

Most workaholics approach leisure and recreations with the same work-related ethic. They view a tennis match as a war. They consider a steep ski slope an opponent to be defeated. In short, the workaholic applies the competitive work ethic to almost every arena of life. You often find such people on vacations looking like they are working harder at winning at their recreational pursuits than they work at making money on the job.

There is a final problem for Larry, and other workaholics who invest most of their time and energy in one thing. Not only are they in a bind if a chosen occupation fails to meet their expectations, but other areas of life suffer as well. The conversations of children of workaholics best illustrate this. These children usually come from upper-middle-class families and have a traditional value system. Usually both parents work and have little time to give individual attention to the children. The children hunger for parental attention, and when they don't get it, they do things to gain attention, even if it's negative.

Aaron, a fifteen-year-old with a recent bout of shoplifting and pot abuse, is a good example. Aaron's father was a dyed-in-the-wool workaholic who spent more than eighty hours a week at his job or work-related activities. Aaron knew very little about his father, since he had little interaction with him, and when he did see him, dad was glued to his desk.

I worked with Aaron for about two months. He started to respond favorably simply from the one hour of undivided attention I was giving him every week in counseling. He finally confided:

It seems like nothing I do ever matters to my dad. I often need to talk to him, but he's always busy. There were a few times when he let me go to work with him, but when we're there all he talks about is the job. I think we've gone fishing once in the past ten years. I really need time and attention from my dad, and I really feel like I don't know who he is. I have to admit, when I got in trouble for shoplifting, Dad did start to notice me. He was really mad at me, but at least he was giving me some attention. At least it makes me feel like I exist in his life.

The workaholic's unwise investment not only leads to personal pain and suffering, but also to family dysfunctions. A quick prescription for workaholics is: Write down all the things that are important and meaningful to you. Recognize that your job is one part of your life, not all. If you overidentify with your job, you may receive the rewards of a successful performance. You also risk devastation if the job turns sour. Treat your family, personal relationships, recreations, and hobbies with respect. Show what is important to you in your everyday behavior. If you value your family, prove it by giving your undivided attention to your spouse and children every day. If you value physical health and exercise, prove it by spending time each day in physical activities. By enjoying pleasurable activities with those you care about and love, you'll get a double emotional dividend.

The Codependent

Another example of an unwise emotional investor is the codependent. Codependents are so absorbed in other people's problems that they lack the time or energy to identify and solve their own problems. They care deeply about other people, yet do not appear to know how to care for themselves. They often spend hours trying to control events, situations, or people around them and have little time or energy left for themselves. In short, a codependent is a personalized version of a workaholic. A codependent's job is to take care of another person (often an alcoholic) who is creating problems.

Diane was a forty-five-year-old mill supervisor. She had some workaholic characteristics, channeling a tremendous amount of her time and energy into her job. Unfortunately, when Diane was not at work, she spent nearly all her remaining time trying to control the consequences of her twenty-six-year-old alcoholic daughter's acts. She found herself consistently making phone calls to her daughter's employers. She offered excuses why her daughter did not show up for work and reminded her of job interviews when she was unemployed. She made frequent excuses for her daughter's drunken behavior at family get-togethers and constantly explained her daughter's shortcomings to her husband. Like many codependents, Diane was unaware that she was enabling her daughter to continue her self-destructive alcoholic behavior. Since Mom was there to pick up the pieces, her daughter had no worries about the consequences of her actions. She had no incentive to be responsible for herself.

For Diane, the situation was extremely stressful. She found herself emotionally buffeted by circumstances beyond her control, by her daughter's behavior. The best Diane could hope for was a few consecutive days when her daughter was not drunk, facing DUI charges, or creating other problems. When things were going smoothly, she waited with a sense of dread for the next crisis.

Diane had allowed herself to be a victim. Despite Diane's best efforts to take care of her daughter, no improvement could occur until she decided to let her daughter take care of herself. Eventually, Diane examined the return on her emotional investment in her daughter and saw that the most she could possibly receive from it was temporary relief.

Diane's story has a satisfying conclusion. Through counseling, she learned to support her daughter's appropriate goal-directed behaviors and to ignore or extinguish her inappropriate and irresponsible behaviors. When Diane's daughter made moves in the right direction, she earned attention, support, and approval. Diane learned to ignore her daughter's irresponsible behavior and let her learn from her mistakes. Diane learned to shift the energy she had unwisely invested in her daughter's behavior into people and activities that gave her a sense of fulfillment and meaning. She began to spend much more quality time with her husband, taking up cycling, golf and skiing.

The Chronic Worrier

Ruth was a chronic worrier who spent much time worrying about her children and grandchildren. Like most chronic worriers, Ruth's motto was "To worry is to live."

Ruth's problem was that her constant worrying about her children and grandchildren provided little sense of emotional fulfillment or happiness. When she solved one problem she immediately worried about a new one. Her life consisted of an endless series of potential crises. By constantly waiting for the next problem she developed a pessimistic outlook. Life to her was a series of fires to extinguish.

Through counseling, Ruth learned that her returns on her emotional investments were putting her in the red. Ruth then decided to start focusing on things she could control, and she and her sixty-nine-year-old retired husband began to travel. She still made herself available to her children and grandchildren, but she stopped waiting for the next crisis. Ruth developed an "out of sight, out of mind" philosophy and spent no time worrying about her children or grandchildren while she and her husband were traveling. The returns on Ruth's new emotional investments were good. She said, before leaving for an extended three-month vacation:

> I was wearing myself out worrying about those kids. I still love them as much as ever, but I guess I realize that I can't control everything that happens to them. I had let my marriage go to pieces, spending all my time worrying about the kids, and

hadn't taken good care of myself. I realized that these kids have their whole lives ahead of them. My husband and I probably only have another ten or fifteen years at best. I really feel my husband and I have done a good job in life, and deserve the rewards of an exciting, fulfilling retirement."

The Drug Addict

Mark was a twenty-six-year-old cocaine and crack addict. He began using cocaine socially with friends at weekend parties and for a while kept things under control. He enjoyed the accelerating high of cocaine, but did not feel addicted. One night he tried some crack, a potent form of cocaine, and experienced "the rush of my life!" He quickly began to seek more crack and soon found himself doing everything he could to get a supply of the drug.

Mark is an extreme example of unwise emotional investing, but his case illustrates an important principle: *the law of diminishing emotional returns*. Many people like Mark see their emotional investments as a quest for extremely positive feelings, even perpetual euphoria. The law of diminishing emotional returns, however, alerts us to a debit side of any extreme emotional investment. It says that over time, your highs get lower, while their negative aftereffects increase.

Mark's initial experience with crack gave him that incredible euphoric rush he described as "the rush of my life!" But as Mark continued to use crack, it took a little bit more each time to approximate that same euphoric rush, never quite reaching it. Mark also noticed that the letdowns he experienced after his highs began to get progressively worse. Soon, Mark was no longer taking crack to reach a high but to escape a crashing low. Mark had been suckered into a bad emotional investment and was continually in the red. We will take a closer look at the underlying principle operating here a little later.

WISE EMOTIONAL INVESTORS

The high-rolling winner is an emotional investor who has put all his or her eggs in one basket. A classic example of a high-rolling winner is tennis star Ivan Lendle. Lendle reportedly spent more time working on his game than anyone else on the tour. Fortunately for Lendle, the work and effort paid off when he was ranked number one in the tennis world for two straight years. Examples of high-rolling winners, and losers, can be found in all areas of life. Although the rewards are gratifying, the potential risk of being an emotional high roller is high. You have to consider how many people strive to be number one at what they do and never reach their goal, resulting in disappointment and despair. A safer, happier, yet less-dramatic emotional investor is the diversifier.

A Diversifier

Chris, a thirty-eight-year-old marriage, family, and child counselor, has diversified his emotional investments. He is married and the father of two children. He devotes at least a half hour a day to quality time with his wife. He dedicates at least a half hour a day to each of his children and often spends more time with them on the weekends. Chris engineers situations so that his personal needs and values, such as downhill skiing, can be realized while his family shares these activities with him.

Chris has a busy and active practice as a marriage and family counselor and typically spends forty hours a week working. He has learned to draw the line, though, and refuses to see patients on the weekend or after hours, devoting this time to his family. Chris has highly diversified recreations and pastimes. He enjoys seasonal sports, such as downhill skiing, wind surfing, mountain biking, tennis, racquetball, and soccer.

Despite what you might think, Chris's diversified emotional investment gives him increased energy for his job, more than that available to workaholics. He finds the extra time needed to work

on a highly successful professional project involving underprivileg-
ed children.

My interview with Chris was not a therapy session, since he is
doing extremely well in life. Here are some of his comments:

Well my typical day goes something like this: I get up about
seven a.m., go downstairs, and make some fresh-brewed coffee.
I sit and look at *The Chronicle*, while enjoying my coffee on
our patio. Usually after about ten minutes of reading the
paper, I get a little distressed about what's happening in the
world. Next, I go for a three-mile jog. When I get back, I'm
feeling better and I shower and shave. Next, I have a healthy
breakfast, kiss my wife and kids goodbye, and go off to work.

I see patients from nine until noon and take an hour and
a half off for lunch. Three days a week my lunch time is free,
and I work out at the gym. The other two days a week I
usually have some type of meeting and spend my lunches
handling business. About one-thirty I start with my afternoon
patients. I see four people in a typical afternoon. I get off at
five-thirty or, sometimes, six-thirty.

Next, I get home and spend about thirty minutes just
winding down from the day. During this time, the kids are
pretty hyper and everybody is hungry for dinner. I help my wife
with a few kitchen chores, and we all sit down for dinner
around seven o'clock. After dinner, I spend a half hour to an
hour of quality time with my children. Our activities depend on
the time of the year. For instance, in the summer I'll be out in
the back yard swimming with them, or going for bike rides. In
the winter, when it's dark and rainy, we usually spend time
playing some games, working on gymnastics, or watching
movies together. The kids get put to bed about eight-thirty.
This is always an ordeal.

My wife and I don't get to sit together until after nine.
Typically from nine or nine-thirty till ten o'clock or so, my wife
and I spend quality time together. This includes talking about
how our respective days went and about projects in the future,
handling the children's issues, and doing other things together.

Usually about ten, my wife and I spend some individual time reading together. During this time I sneak in some extra work on my project. We both hit the sack between eleven and eleven-thirty.

Weekends are special. Our family has made a commitment to have as much joy and excitement during the weekends as we possibly can. We believe having fun on the weekends recharges our batteries, helping us to be better members of the community, better workers, better students, and better human beings. Therefore, in the winter, we spend nearly every weekend snow skiing. In the summer and spring, we spend most of our weekends going to amusement parks, wind surfing, or camping. I've got to admit life is pretty darn good. Our family has been following this pattern for about five years now, and so far we've not had complaints from anyone.

Chris has diversified his time and energy between his family, his wife, his job, his special projects, his recreations, and his hobbies. Chris's life is not one-dimensional. He is tasting the different flavors that the menu of life has to offer, and is enjoying life to its fullest. Chris is not without problems. When problems do arise, Chris uses constructive problem-solving behaviors, learns to let go, and puts his time and energy into other things. When I asked Chris to rank order the ten most important things in his life and compare these to how he spent his time, there was a pattern of consistency. His actions were consistent with what he said he valued.

EMOTIONAL REINVESTMENT

What happens when the person or activity you have put much emotional energy into is removed from your life? Some examples of the complete loss of emotional investments include children growing up and leaving home, retirement, divorce, and bereavement. There is a principle in physics called the *conservation of energy*. When applied to psychology, it implies that the emotional energy once invested in people who are no longer with us, or in activities we can no longer do, does not disappear or evaporate. It remains with us and must be directed into something else. There is a big gap in your life when you lose something in which you have invested emotional energy, and now you must rechannel this energy.

You will recall from Chapter 1 that Robert, the retiree, reinvested his emotional energy in a new leisure interest, sailing. Fran, the victim of the empty nest syndrome, reinvested her emotional energy in her husband and hobbies such as gardening, fishing, and traveling.

The best example I know, of wise emotional reinvestment, comes from the case of Katherine, a seventy-year-old woman alone.

Katherine and her husband never had children, and she was an only child. Many of her friends had died. Although financially secure, Katherine felt a tremendous void in her life when her husband died. Wisely, she went about reinvesting her emotions.

First, Katherine made some phone calls to people in her neighborhood. She discovered a sixty-year-old single man who had been lonely for many years. Through a mutual friend, they met and developed a close and lasting friendship.

Second, Katherine became involved with her church. Although raised as a Catholic, she had been inactive in the church for several years. She was happy to find that the church welcomed her back with open arms and had several programs for senior citizens. Katherine received such a warm welcome from her Catholic friends that she decided to try this strategy with other churches.

Before she knew it, Katherine became involved with four other church programs for senior citizens and was on half a dozen committees. Through her acquaintances in the church programs, she also became politically active and got involved working for a state congressman's reelection.

In one of our conversations, Katherine told me she felt like her new friends were a family. She said, "We all take good care of each other, and stay active."

PROCESS AND TERMINAL VALUES

Is there some magical state of existence that represents the pot of gold at the end of the rainbow? In my opinion, there may well be. But only if you consider the pot of gold as a process and not a product. To understand this more fully, you must distinguish the two types of values that psychologist Milton Rokeach discovered: *terminal values*, the results you have achieved; and *process values*, the means by which you go about achieving your goals.

Whenever you achieve a goal or complete a project, it can give you a temporary sense of satisfaction, pleasure, energy, and power. The emotional energy you have invested in your goal has paid off. These terminal values mainly serve as way stations in life, to let you know how you are doing. But once you achieve them they begin to fade. For instance, how long can you bask in the glory of receiving your high school or college degree, or in the reality that you are now married?

Process values are more important because they represent the essence of what it means to be a living human being. If you value being a loving, creative, friendly, and exciting person, you have to demonstrate these process values in your behavior day in and day out. Or, metaphorically, it is not enough just to be invited to the grand ball at the castle. You have to go, sing, dance, and be merry all night long.

The Opponent Process Theory of Motivation

Here is a final perspective to consider when thinking about your motivations and emotions and how they change. In 1974 psychologists Richard Soloman and John D. Corbitt reviewed existing facts on motivation and emotion, and developed what they called an *opponent process theory of motivation*. The idea is that many emotional states are automatically opposed by central nervous system mechanisms that reduce the intensity of both pleasant and unpleasant feelings. The opponent processes for most hedonic states are strengthened by use and weakened by disuse. Here are some examples of how this works.

In Soloman and Corbitt's first example:

A woman discovers a lump in her breast and immediately is terrified. She sits still, intermittently weeping, or she paces the floor. After a few hours, she slowly regains her composure, stops crying, and begins to work. At this point she is still tense and disturbed, but no longer terrified and distracted. She manifested the symptoms usually associated with intense anxiety. While in this state she calls her doctor for an appointment. A few hours later she is in his office, still tense, still frightened; she is obviously a very unhappy woman. The doctor makes his examination. He then informs her that there is no possibility of cancer, that there is nothing to worry about, and that the problem is just a clogged sebaceous gland, requiring no medical attention. A few minutes later, the woman leaves the doctor's office, smiling, greeting strangers, and walking with an unusually buoyant stride. Her euphoric mood permeates all her activities as she resumes her normal duties. She exudes joy, which is not in character for her. A few hours later, however, she is working in her normal, perfunctory way. Her emotional expression is back to normal. She once more has the personality immediately recognizable by all of her friends. Gone is the euphoria, and there is not a hint of the earlier terrifying experience of the day.

This woman's initial feelings of panic and terror, were counterbalanced a few hours later by a feeling of joy and euphoria.

You can get a better idea of how the opponent process theory of motivation works by reexamining the case of Mark, mentioned earlier. Mark's first few episodes with crack gave him an incredible euphoric rush, which he described as "the rush of my life." Mark began to notice that, as he continued to use crack, it took a little bit more each time to approximate that same euphoric rush. And he never quite achieved the original high. More importantly, Mark noticed that the letdowns experienced after his highs became more severe. As time passed, Mark's euphoric highs became lower and his negative aftereffects became more severe. Soon, Mark is no longer taking crack to achieve the high, but to escape the crashing low. At this stage, the most Mark can hope for is to return to his normal state.

The opponent process theory of motivation can also be applied in a favorable and healthy way. Darleen, a thirty-six-year-old bungee jumper experienced her first few jumps as terrifying. The aftereffect of the first jump was a feeling of joy and contentment. With subsequent leaps, her initial terror gradually lessened to a feeling of exhilaration and excitement, while the aftereffect of her bungee jumps became a peaceful sense of joy and serenity.

The point is that when investing your emotions in looking for those magical highs, remember this: With time, your highs or rushes will decline, while the negative aftereffects will become stronger.

IN SUMMARY . . .

Consider the vital question, what hooks do you hang your life on? Your terminal values or goals represent way stations in the course of your life to let you know how you are doing. Process values involve showing what you stand for and believe in your ongoing behavior.

Do a careful examination to discover the people, activities, ideas, and events that are important to you. The resulting pattern of emotional investments represents the hooks upon which you hang your emotional life. Once you recognize these emotional hooks, take an honest look at what you actually do in life. If your behavior does not coincide with what you claim to be important, you are a hypocrite and are likely to be in constant conflict with yourself and others. The happiest people are those whose values show in their everyday behaviors.

You can review your emotional investments in people, activities, ideas, and events to see if they are producing emotional rewards or losses. Although putting all your emotional eggs in one basket has led to some dramatic positive outcomes—the winners—this is a risky policy that courts catastrophic failure—the losers. A more diversified emotional investment pattern is safer and many times more enjoyable. If you lose an important activity, person, or hook in which you have invested a lot of emotional energy, you must rechannel that energy into something or someone else.

Finally, remember that intense emotional experiences are followed by an opposite emotional aftereffect that tends to grow stronger with time, as the primary emotion grows weaker. Although this opponent process theory of motivation can be applied in positive ways, usually it leads to the principle of diminishing returns on unwise emotional investments such as drug induced highs.

You are what you do, so do what matters to you.

7

Behavior

Dynamics

How Your Actions Can Lift
Your Moods

Have you noticed how difficult it is to stay depressed or upset while you are doing something you love? A key to emotional strength and well-being is to overcome your behavioral inertia ("a body at rest tends to remain at rest") and become active—even if you don't feel like it.

Many of us have acquired a belief I call the *motivational fallacy*. It goes like this: "I should only do the things I feel like doing when I feel like doing them." If humanity ran on this principle, the world would quickly come to a grinding halt. Have you gone to school or work when you did not feel like it? Have you taken out the garbage, mowed the lawn, washed clothes, or washed dishes when you would have preferred to rest on the couch? A close look at our responses to the requirements of living reveals that feeling like doing an essential task is not a necessary condition for getting it done.

My point is that the motivational fallacy is applied selectively, usually to those times when you are completely free to choose your activities, and especially when you are in a low mood. This is understandable because when you are most depressed, or upset your activity level declines. Then a vicious cycle begins. The less you do, the more depressed you become.

Few people are aware that depression and bad moods can be relieved by behaving as though they do not exist. Some research-ers—*attribution theorists*—have accumulated evidence indicating that if you do certain behaviors, you begin to believe that they are part of you. If you are severely depressed, but adopt an erect posture, an expressive voice, show physical exuberance, and put a smile on your face, you will come to believe that is the way you are or feel. This may sound like a simple answer, but the inertia that accompanies bad moods may make even simple things hard to do.

The fact that it is nearly impossible to be depressed when you are having a good time served as a starting point for a series of fascinating research studies by Dr. Peter Lewinsohn and his colleagues at the University of Oregon. Dr. Lewinsohn noticed that when people are depressed, their activity level becomes low, which in turn leads to more depression and less activity. In short, when people are depressed, they do not do the things that make them feel good, and this leads to deeper depression.

Lewinsohn believed that we can break this depression cycle at a behavioral level. That is, when you are feeling your absolute worst and do not want to do things that would make you feel good is the time to force yourself to do them. To help break the inertia of low moods, I have developed a process I call *behavioral autopilot*.

BEHAVIORAL AUTOPILOT

It was one of those Sundays when I just did not feel like doing anything. I had attended a party the night before and chatted with some friends until about 2 a.m. I woke on that Sunday morning at my usual 6:30 a.m., after only a few hours sleep. First, I tried to go back to sleep. Then, I got up and tried to start my usual day, but I was too tired. I was unable to concentrate on my writing and picked up a book to read. My mind started to wander; I could not seem to keep my attention on anything for very long.

As a last resort, I picked up the TV remote control and began scanning for some entertainment. I found nothing even mildly interesting; I felt stuck in a bad mood. More than once during the day I tried to take a nap, but for some reason I just could not go to sleep. Then, behavioral inertia set in. The less I did, the less likely it became that I could get going.

I decided to try an experiment. I remembered reading Dr. Lewisohn's work at the University of Oregon. It stated that when depressed people are forced to do enjoyable activities they tend to break out of their depression. Granted, I was not clinically depressed, but I sure felt bad. I decided to try this strategy to see if I could snap myself out of my bad mood.

I loaded my mountain bike on top of my car and drove out to Whiskeytown National Forest to a mountain bike trail. All I could think of on the drive out was how I needed three more hours of sleep and how I really did not feel like doing this. When I got to the trailhead, the temperature was about fifty degrees; the air seemed hazy. It was early November, and although the season's first frost had turned the leaves to beautiful colors, I really didn't appreciate them. Although I felt a little better, I still did not want to go on that bike ride. The first thing I would have to cope with was a two-mile climb up a narrow dirt trail. This requires much energy, even when feeling good, and at this point I knew I just didn't have it.

I got the bike down and started to mount it, thinking things like: "When you're this tired you won't be as sharp and could have an accident and get hurt. If you're feeling this bad you might overexert yourself and have a heart attack or a stroke. It's not good to go bike riding by yourself. The bike's rear tire doesn't seem properly inflated. The chain is not adequately oiled."

Despite these thoughts I decided to plow ahead with my plan, on behavioral autopilot. Whether or not I felt like it, I would go through the motions and ride the bike. I jumped on and began a torturous climb through some loose gravel. At several points I wanted to quit, and I came close to stopping, turning around, and coming back. But I continued to keep my legs moving, climbing up the hill. Within the first five minutes I knew my heart rate had reached an aerobic level. I continued to climb the hill. Thoughts went through my mind like, "This sure isn't any fun. I want to go back. I really don't like this. I feel worse than before."

Within twenty minutes, things started to change. I began to appreciate the beauty around me and to notice how my body was working. After about a half hour I reached the summit of the mountain and felt nearly exhausted, yet a sense of euphoria came over me. My heart rate was at the upper end of the aerobic level, and I felt a sense of accomplishment. Then, a new source of energy kicked in.

Now came the good part: a winding five-mile stretch of downhill terrain with exciting jumps, dips and curves. About forty-five minutes later I rolled back to the trailhead and hopped off my bike. I felt euphoric—a sense of excitement, joy, relaxation, and peace all rolled into one. I felt like there was nothing I had to do and I was content just to be there.

Driving back home, my consciousness was still altered. The same mountains and trees I saw on the way out to the trail had taken on a different meaning. Everything was so much more vibrant and intense, like a Van Gogh painting. I found that not only had my fatigue disappeared, but I felt revitalized and alive! The good feeling lasted the rest of the afternoon and on into the evening. That night I slept like a log.

What I did at a neurochemical level was to use my behavior to give myself several shots of some powerful, natural, safe chemicals to alter my consciousness. These chemicals, endorphins and norepinephrine, resemble opium and amphetamines in their chemical structure but are much more powerful. At a motivational level, I went on behavioral autopilot and completely overrode my lack of will to act.

While strenuous large-muscle activities are established methods for reducing depression, anxiety and stress, any enjoyable activity can help pull you out of the blues.

Mood-Altering Activities Options

Review the following list of activities that many people have rated as pleasant. See if you can find some that you might enjoy.

Highlight or underline the pleasant activities that you have enjoyed in the past or think you might enjoy in the future. Next, put a check by the activity if you have engaged in it during the last month.

Mood-Altering Activities

Acting
Attending a concert, ballet, or opera
Beachcombing
Being coached by someone
Bird or animal watching Boating
Bowling
Camping
Caring for your plants
Clothes shopping
Collecting things of interest interest
Collecting driftwood, rocks, or other objects
Collecting antiques
Contributing to your church or other religious group
Counseling someone
Creating a song or writing music
Dating someone
Developing ideas to make money
Doing volunteer community work
Doing scientific work or experiments
Doing craft work like jewelry or pottery
Doing favors for someone else
Drafting or designing
Driving skillfully
Fishing
Gardening or landscaping

Getting or giving back rubs or massages
Giving a speech or lecture
Going to a restaurant
Going to lectures
Going to the races (horse, car, motorcycle, etc.)
Going for a leisurely walk
Going to a sporting event
Going to a rock concert
Going on picnics or barbecues
Going to the movies
Going to an amusement park
Going to church
Going to auctions or garage sales
Going to comedy clubs to hear jokes or comedy routines
Going to a play
Going to a civic or social gathering
Going to a social club
Having lunch with friends
Having a lively discussion
Having sexual relations
Horseback riding
Learning a foreign language
Listening to music
Making preserves
Making people laugh
Making gifts for others
Meditating
Motorcycle riding
Painting or sculpturing

Performing well on a test or an examination
Playing party games
Playing frisbee or catch
Playing with your pets
Playing ping pong
Playing lawn sports like horseshoes, badminton, or volleyball
Playing a musical instrument
Playing with your children
Playing golf
Playing chess, checkers, or backgammon
Playing cards or board games
Playing with your grandchildren
Playing pool
Playing tennis
Reading magazines
Reading
Reading the paper
Sewing
Sharing something
Singing with other people
Solving problems or puzzles
Snowmobiling or riding dune buggies
Sunbathing

Supervising others
Taking photographs
Talking to old friends
Talking on the phone
Talking about your hobby or project
Talking about politics or other public events
Talking about your grandchildren
Teaching someone something
Traveling
Visiting or comforting people who are having problems
Visiting with friends or relatives
Watching movies or TV shows
Working for a political movement
Working with computers
Working with others as a team
Working on a project
Writing papers or essays
Writing letters or cards
Writing in your diary

Most people find enjoyable and mood-altering activities on this list. Remember, when you feel most down or depressed, you are least likely to be engaging in the activities that make you feel better. Go through this list. Highlight the items that have made you feel good in the past or that you think may make you feel good in the future. Get out there and start doing them.

The Ambitious But Unhappy Surgeon

Don was a thirty-eight-year-old general surgeon, husband, and father of two. Don had become rundown during his medical practice, and came into my office wondering if he should give up his medical career. As Don and I talked, he described for me a typical day:

> Well I get up about six o'clock in the morning and make a pot of coffee. I look at the paper, and that usually puts me in a bad mood right off the bat. Then, I go over to the hospital and sign off my charts. Usually I have to make rounds, and by the time I'm done, it's around 9:30 or 10 a.m. If I'm scheduled for surgery, I will either do this or assist another doctor's surgeries later in the morning. I usually grab a bite to eat, in 20 minutes, at some fast food place, and then get back to my office for my private patients. Between 6:30 and 7 p.m. I get home. Then, the phone often rings and I have to go back to the hospital to see other patients or to deal with crises. Now and then I get a crisis call at 2 or 3 in the morning. I'm on call all weekend twice a month. This really puts a damper on what I can do. I do love to help people and feel a sense of accomplishment in my work. I'm so burned out and tired of it I don't know if I can take it anymore. Sometimes I feel like I'm losing my mind.

I asked Don to describe the last time he had any fun. He said that two years ago he and his wife went to the Bahamas for two weeks. They had a good time and found themselves doing things that he had done as a teenager, like swimming, water skiing, and sunbathing. After this vacation he and his wife both came back refreshed and revitalized.

In Don's haste to make up the earnings he lost while on vacation, he became dominated by his ambition to see many patients, work competently, and earn some indeterminate amount of money that would be "enough." After two years of a frantic grind, seeing patient after patient, Don began to burn out.

As many of us would, Don turned his mind toward himself. He tried to figure out what was wrong with him. When Don completed the list of enjoyable events and activities, it was apparent that all he was doing was working, eating, and sleeping.

After doing the pleasant activity checklist, Don discovered that activities he used to enjoy greatly included fly fishing, playing tennis, and jogging. Yet, he had not done any of these for two years.

The next step was to develop a plan to get Don out of the work routine, at least for a little while, and into some enjoyable activities. Although Don was certain there was something wrong deep within his mind or some secret he needed to figure out, he reluctantly agreed to schedule enjoyable activities regularly. At first, he agreed to play tennis three times a week after work, and to go fly fishing at least one day every weekend.

Six weeks after beginning these enjoyable activities, Don reported a definite change in his mood. During one of our last sessions Don confided:

> I don't know what has changed, but I'm feeling okay about my medical practice. Things are the same, but I am taking a little more time off from work. The only real difference is that I'm playing tennis, and going fly fishing on the weekends. It's hard to believe that these simple things could have such a strong effect on my feeling, my thoughts, and my life. I have to admit the regular enjoyable activities do make a huge difference. I feel like when I go fly fishing on the weekend I come back with my batteries recharged and my spirit refreshed. When I'm feeling my best, I'm more effective with my patients, and I have a lot more energy and vitality to devote to the people I love the most, my wife and children.

Two years later I had the opportunity to speak briefly with Don's wife. I asked her if he might be willing to go for a mountain bike ride with me. She said he would probably love to, but doubted that he could find the time, because he was in a tennis league, jogging frequently, and fly fishing every weekend.

Enjoyable activities and events can involve anything from large-muscle aerobic activities to sedentary activities. The less strenuous activities are crucially important in helping people with severe medical problems, injuries, or other physical limitations.

A Case of Chronic Lethargy

Brenda was a highly successful fifty-five-year-old senior executive with a large company. She lived an active life and beautifully blended her enjoyable events, exercise, job, and family into a high-quality existence.

Brenda began to complain of severe headaches and had to undergo a series of extensive medical tests. After three months of severe anxiety and uncertainty, Brenda was finally diagnosed as having chronic fatigue syndrome. This is an illness that strikes with different degrees of severity. It can last from six months to years. The severity of Barbara's chronic fatigue syndrome was intense. When it struck, she would find herself lying in bed for two or three days at a time without the energy to get up. Then, the symptoms would decrease, and she would experience mild to moderate fatigue for one to three weeks. This dramatic interruption in Brenda's schedule caused her to eliminate the things she previously loved to do, like snow skiing, aerobics classes, and jogging.

Brenda, like many other patients with chronic pain and severe physical problems, was a prime candidate for *substitution therapy*. This involved Brenda's learning to reinvest her energy into things that she was able to do and that had a high potential for producing a sense of well-being.

After completing the enjoyable activity checklist, Brenda became fascinated with the game of chess and began to take lessons. Before long, she was competing at a high level. She became actively involved with photography and soon showed me some excellent photographs. I encouraged her to pursue this, and before long she was selling some of her photos for postcards. Finally, she channeled a significant amount of her talent into running adult children of alcoholic groups, since she was an adult child of an alcoholic herself. This gave her a great sense of accomplishment and a feeling that she was helping other people.

In my work with chronic pain patients, I have found it often helps if they learn to enjoy high-quality passive activities as a replacement for their previous high-energy aerobic and large muscle activities. The more passive activities and events are particularly useful for people, many elderly, who have major physical problems, or suffer from overwhelming pain. Physically passive activities that my chronic pain and older patients have found delightful and enjoyable include:

- Being entertained
- Developing cooking into an art
- Doing volunteer work
- Drawing
- Fishing
- Going to concerts, ballet, or theater
- Going on cruises
- Learning a foreign language
- Learning to play a musical instrument
- Making stained glass
- Photography
- Quilting
- Singing in a choir
- Social group with similar interests
- Taking classes at a college
- Traveling
- Writing poetry
- Writing novels or short stories

HOW AEROBIC ACTIVITY AFFECTS YOUR MOOD

A sequence of neurochemical reactions occurring in our brain determines our emotions. Neuropharmacologists tell us that our brain operates on a lock-and-key principle. Nerve impulses run down to the end of one cell and send chemical messengers across a tiny gap called a synapse. On the other side of this gap, receptor sites pick up the chemical messengers and transmit them into another nerve impulse.

Research in neurochemistry and brain physiology has taught us that certain neurotransmitter chemicals fit into special receptor sites like a specific key fits into a lock. In my mountain biking excursion, I had triggered my body to activate these neurotransmitters, releasing them into the special receptor sites in my brain. People who take drugs or alcohol to get high are altering their neurotransmitters in these synapses, which are taken up by the receptor sites, leading to "highs."

The logical implication of this lock-and-key principle is that any high you can get from drugs or alcohol can be gotten naturally by using your neurochemistry. This is because the receptor sites are specific to certain chemicals. Why would the receptor sites exist to serve as chemical locks that can be opened only by a substance foreign to the human body? In short, every high you can get from a drug can be mimicked by your brain's own neurochemistry.

Scientists have just begun to unravel the mystery of our brain's chemistry. We already know that naturally occurring chemicals called *endorphins* or *enkephalins* can imitate the effects of opium and are much more powerful than opium itself. In fact, endorphins are hundreds of times stronger per unit than opium.

You may have experienced an "adrenaline rush" sometime when you were extremely excited. I have worked with many amphetamine and cocaine addicts who reported that the adrenaline high from naturally occurring excitement is close to, but more intense than, the rush from amphetamines or cocaine. What do we know about producing these "feel good" neurochemicals in your brain?

It begins with oxygen. *Aerobic capacity* is your body's maximum capacity for oxygen consumption. It is unquestionably the single most important measure of physical fitness, but your aerobic capacity also has a tremendous influence on the level of vigor in everyday life. Consider some recent research findings on aerobic activity. Several studies have shown that aerobic exercise, besides being important for cardiovascular conditioning, has a powerful antidepressant and antianxiety effect. It is also beneficial to self-esteem and creative thinking. The effects of large-muscle aerobic exercise on mental health are compelling. The following are some of these benefits:

- Reduced muscular tension
- Reduced fatigue
- Reduced anxiety
- Reduced or eliminated depression
- Reduction or elimination of stress
- Improved self-concept
- Improved self-esteem
- Improved cardiovascular functioning
- Improvement in creativity

To develop your large-muscle aerobic activity into a powerful key that can release the feel-good chemicals in your brain you must first determine your present aerobic level.

The Important Numbers

The first thing to do in learning to calculate your aerobic level is to find your pulse rate. There are many ways to do this. The easiest is to take the two middle fingers of your right hand and place them along the left side of your windpipe. Move your fingers around until you feel a rhythmical pulsing sensation. This pulse is called your *carotid pulse* because it originates in the large carotid artery in your neck.

Next, using the second hand on your watch, or ideally a digital second display, count off the number of beats in your carotid pulse over a six-second period. Then, add a zero, and this will give you an estimate of your heart rate over a one-minute period. For instance, if you count seven beats over a six-second period, your estimated heart rate is 70 beats per minute.

This method is extremely handy when doing large muscle aerobic activities because you only have to take a six-second pause to measure your pulse. Therefore you can keep your heart rate in its optimal training range.

The next important number to calculate is your *never-exceed pulse rate*. Do this simply by subtracting your age from 220. For instance, a fifty-year-old woman would have a never-exceed pulse rate of 220 minus 50, which equals 170. For a twenty-year-old man, the never-exceed pulse rate would be much higher: 200.

The next step is to figure out your *optimal aerobic heart rate training zone*. To do this you will need to find two numbers. The lowest level heart rate, over a one-minute period, to receive aerobic benefits is your never-exceed heart rate multiplied by .60. For our fifty-year-old woman, this number would be:

$$220 - 50 = 170$$
$$170 \times .60 = 102$$

Your *maximum aerobic training level heart rate* would be your never-exceed heart rate multiplied by .80. Again for our fifty-year-old woman this number would be:

$$220 - 50 = 170$$
$$170 \times .80 = 136$$

This fifty-year-old woman would need to keep her pulse in a range between 102 and 136 to receive optimal aerobic training.

The following table is a to give you an estimate of your optimal aerobic training level, your target zone, based on your age. This chart can give you a quick estimate of the heart rate needed to reach your aerobic level of conditioning.

min = Minimum Aerobic Heart Rate
max = Maximum Aerobic Heart Rate
never exceed = Never Exceed Heart Rate

age	min	max	never exceed
20	120	160	200
30	114	152	190
40	108	144	180
50	102	136	170
60	96	128	160
70	90	120	150
80	84	112	140
90	78	104	130
100	72	96	120

Research done in physiology laboratories shows it is necessary to maintain an ideal aerobic training level for a minimum of twenty to thirty minutes per session, at least three-to-four times per week. You would be aerobically fit if, for example, you jogged for a half hour every Monday, Wednesday, and Friday.

Recent research suggests that more intensive long-term aerobic activity can have a pronounced effect on your psychological well-being. Studies have found that natural opiates—the "feel good" chemicals—triggered in the body by prolonged rhythmic exercise, are likely to enhance your mood, improve pain tolerance, and suppress appetite. These recent studies corroborate what marathon runners have known for a long time. After intense levels of large-muscle aerobic activity—usually about ninety minutes of sustained activity—these individuals experience what they call a "runner's high." They describe this as a euphoric feeling, and many even develop a positive addiction to running regularly.

Following is a sample list of a few widely-available large-muscle aerobic exercises you might consider doing regularly:

- Brisk walking
- Jogging
- Running
- Vigorous cycling
- Stairmaster exercise
- Stationary bike or ski machine

- Swimming
- Rowing
- Full court basketball
- Aerobics classes/Jazzercise

You might wonder why I left out activities such as tennis, racquetball, volleyball, and football. These activities can be very vigorous and lead to an increase in your heart rate. Unfortunately, your heart rate is not likely to remain as consistently high as it should for aerobic benefit. When playing tennis, for instance, in the middle of a point you run about trying to chase down the ball until the point is over. Then you rest for between thirty seconds and a minute before the next point is put into play. Tennis is good physical conditioning and can be enjoyable, but it may not keep your heart in its target zone. The same is true for racquetball, volleyball and football. The purpose of aerobic activity is to get your heart rate into the optimal training zone and to keep it there for at least twenty to thirty minutes.

WARNING: Before engaging in a large-muscle aerobic activity program, consult your personal physician.

Aerobics in Treating Depression

The powerful healing effect of large muscle aerobic activity was recently demonstrated to me by Jane, a fifty-two-year-old former administrative director. About a month before her visit, Jane was in a serious auto accident and diagnosed with: brain stem injury, soft tissue damage, herniated cervical and thoracic vertebras, and degenerative disk disease in the spine. Jane's subjective complaints included headaches, vomiting, and an inability to walk for more than five minutes without falling.

Jane told me, with much emotion: "I was so depressed. I was completely convinced I was dying. I was anxious, frustrated, and devastated over being unable to do the only thing I really knew how to do, work. I truly considered suicide when I thought nothing could help." Complicating the problem, Jane reported a history of abuse as a child. She could no longer escape into her work to get away from these memories. Without her work to escape into, Jane soon began to experience general anxiety and panic attacks.

I consulted with Jane's physician. We both believed it important that she pursue an adequate level of physical activity to prevent a phenomenon called *disuse atrophy*. This occurs when lack of muscular activity leads to a shrinking of muscle tissues and a significant increase in pain. With her physician, I discussed research indicating that large-muscle aerobic activity has a profound influence on reducing and eliminating depression, anxiety, and stress.

Jane began an intensive program of physical activity and therapy. At the start of her program, she could only stay on a treadmill for about three minutes, swim for four minutes, and work on a stationary bike for five minutes. The training consisted of working out six days a week for a minimum of one hour a day for the first week. Jane reported that at first she was exhausted, but soon she began to enjoy her workouts.

After ten weeks, Jane was up to two and a half hours at a six-degree angle on the tread mill. She could jog on the stairmaster for thirty minutes, ride a stationary bike for an hour and a half, or swim for two miles without resting. She had tapped into the powerful, natural, feel-good chemicals in her brain and experienced a near-miraculous recovery.

What was most noticeable was the change in Jane's emotional state. She told me, "I'm so totally relaxed; I've never been this relaxed in my life. I don't feel any stress, anger, or depression. I have pain sometimes, but it doesn't really bother me. I'm making decisions so much more easily now. Even my relationships with other people have improved. I feel like after about thirty minutes of working out I go into a meditative state, and nothing at all can disturb me."

Jane is delighted with her present life and is looking forward to vocational rehabilitation. She has learned to use a powerful key to well-being: regular large muscle aerobic exercise.

ADRENALINE HIGHS

Another set of behaviors and experiences that offers a unique blend of excitement, fear, joy, and clear danger are popularly called "adrenaline highs." Although not for everyone, adrenalin highs can provide an escape into excitement and thrills that is frequently missing in our often routine, mundane, and sometimes boring existence. Adrenalin highs are especially important for people called *sensation seekers*, who persistently crave feelings of excitement and novelty. Although some adrenalin highs are dangerous, many are not, such as riding a roller coaster. Adrenalin highs are produced by potentially enjoyable events that may or may not involve large muscle or aerobic activity. A few sources of adrenalin highs are:

- Car and motorcycle racing
- Competitive sports
- Extreme skiing
- Freestyle skiing
- Hang gliding
- Surfing
- Mountain biking
- Rock climbing
- Martial arts
- Sky diving
- Wave sailing
- White-water rafting or kayaking
- Bungee jumping

Some of the typical benefits of adrenalin highs include:

- Reduction of perceived stress
- Reduction of anxiety
- Elimination of depression
- Feelings of revitalization

Through my interviews with people who pursue adrenalin highs I have learned that it helps many stay the course of a difficult and stressful life. For others, adrenalin highs provided a way out of a disastrous pattern of self-destruction.

Philip, a thirty-two-year-old account executive for a major manufacturing company is bombarded daily with many important decisions and demands. Philip is struggling to make his way up the corporate ladder, and finds himself working until eight or nine o'clock at night. He finds it difficult to create time during the week to routinely exercise, yet has kept his weekends special, using them to recharge his batteries.

In Philip's words:

> I routinely put in at least sixty hours of work a week at the office and sometimes more. More times than not, I leave home before the sun rises and get back long after it has set. The demands of my job are compelling. I know that I've got to perform or I won't be here very long. But the real scary part is the fact that a number of corporate mergers have been sweeping the country and I realize that even if I do perform better than anyone else in my position, a corporate decision at a higher level could leave me out in the cold.
>
> My big escapes occur on weekends when I go snow skiing. It's a completely different world when you're on top of a nine-thousand-foot mountain overlooking a majestic panorama of snow-covered peaks and valleys. Then, when you ski down an extremely steep face between rocks and boulders, or jump off cornices into light fluffy powder, everything else completely disappears. I find myself immersed in the here and now and my work world is a million miles away. Within a matter of minutes after I start skiing extreme or difficult terrain, my body feels alive and my spirit is free. When I return to the office Monday morning, I feel refreshed and revitalized.
>
> This works really well four months out of the year, but until I discovered wave sailing, I had no outlook for the other eight months. Fortunately, I am within two hours of the coast, and discovered I could get an equal, if not greater, adrenalin high

on weekends the other six to eight months of the year by wave sailing. Wave sailing is a mixture of surfing and sailboarding. Probably the most exhilarating part is hitting an eight-foot wave face at twenty miles an hour, launching over twenty feet into the sky, and floating back down to the water. Although it is incredibly exciting, the risk of being injured while wave jumping is really quite low.

Before you put on your skis and leap off a cliff or go launching off a wave face on a sailboard, remember that it takes months, and sometimes years, to develop the skills necessary to produce the adrenalin highs we have just talked about. No, you don't have to be a death-defying daredevil to take a few risks and stimulate yourself. You can find reasonably safe activities to produce adrenalin highs.

While it is clear that adrenalin highs can provide you with relief from a stressful and difficult world, I have also seen adrenalin-high behaviors rescue patients from paths which were certain to lead to self-destruction.

Karen was twenty-two years old when I saw her in the in-patient psychiatric unit after she attempted suicide. Karen had a history of amphetamine abuse and was working part-time as a stripper when she overdosed.

Through Karen's counseling, we learned that she was a sensation seeker, craving a high level of stimulation and excitement. After looking over a list of potentially enjoyable high-stimulation behaviors and activities, Karen decided to give sky-diving a try.

Here are some of Karen's descriptions of her first and subsequent sky-diving episodes:

After ground school and training, I was really excited about going up for my first jump. I remember getting in the plane and taking off. While we were climbing up to our jump altitude, my instructor was asking me about how I felt and wondering what was going on with me. I got a sense that he was trying to calm my nerves, but as the time to jump got closer, I began to get really scared. Once we reached 10,000 feet it was really neat because the sky was a lot bluer than it was at ground level. When I walked up to the edge of the door and looked out of the plane I could see a checkerboard pattern of fields, roads, and streams below. The sun was back off to my right, and seemed small in the deep blue sky. It was about 10:30 a.m. and the temperature was fifty-five degrees. The instructor asked, 'Ready?' I nodded my head, and he said, 'Ready or not here we go!'

I had learned to do a tandem jump with my instructor, allowing him to free-fall with me until my chute opened. I guess the biggest thing I had to overcome was the initial jump. Although I knew in my mind my parachute would work and I trusted my instructor, there was something very deep in me telling me not to jump. When I stepped out of that plane I felt the most incredible acceleration I've ever had in my life. My heart raced, I felt my stomach go into my throat, I gasped for a breath, and every muscle in my body felt an electrical charge!

I heard my instructor say pull, and as I pulled my ripcord he peeled away. I felt an upward pull, then a tremendous sense of relief. I felt as if I was gliding or floating down, but my heart rate and breathing were still rapid. I remember after landing, I felt stunned, and kind of numb. After about a half hour, things were back to normal.

By the time I did my sixth jump things had changed. When I jumped I was no longer terrified, but had an incredible degree of excitement and eagerness to experience the free-fall. After landing, I felt a joyful sense of euphoria and exhilaration. This feeling would sometimes last for three or four hours.

For several hours before, during, and after her jumps, Karen completely escaped her problems. Her mind had been consumed with the fear of making her first jump. Soon she eagerly anticipated the exhilarating effects of jumping. Karen looked forward to her weekend sky-diving and cultivated a new set of friends who also enjoyed the sport.

In Karen's words: "To my new friends, doing speed or being a stripper wasn't cool, so I quit doing them." Karen substituted a naturally occurring adrenaline rush-producing behavior for the previous high she got from amphetamines and stripping.

IN SUMMARY . . .

Your behaviors can alter your moods, your neurochemistry, your self-esteem, and change the course of your life. The most difficult question is, "How do you get people to undertake a behavior that is good for them when they don't feel like it?" The best answer I can give to this question is to go on what I call *behavioral auto-pilot*. When you feel your worst, your activity level is likely to be at its lowest, which will increase your distress. You know you need to go to a dentist when you have an abscessed tooth, regardless of how you feel about going to the dentist. When you are severely distressed, upset, or depressed, you need to do activities that are good for you even if you do not want to do them.

Research has clearly shown that regular large muscle aerobic exercise can reduce or eliminate depression, alleviate anxiety, improve cardiovascular functioning, reduce excess body weight, and promote creativity. Research has shown that engaging in enjoyable activities, whether passive or active, can reduce or eliminate mild to moderate depression.

Research in neurophysiology and neurochemistry suggests that alcohol and drug highs can also be achieved through natural activities or behaviors. Neurochemical receptor sites in our brains are "locks" that can be released by neurochemical "keys" that are a by-product of engaging in certain natural activities. When unlocked, these neurochemical receptors produce intense feelings of pleasure, well-being, and euphoria. A challenge for each of us is to discover and pursue the natural activities and events that will unlock these feelings.

8 | Getting Back in Control

The Power of Relaxation and Imagery

Do you often feel tense, anxious and unable to relax? You will recall that emotions, or feelings, arise through your body's physiological reactions to your behaviors and thoughts. Feeling tense and anxious signals that you are in a state of heightened readiness. We all experience these feelings in response to serious external threats. The problem is that after a threat recedes, some people are unable to regain a natural state of calm relaxation. Their tension is constant. They do not know how to release and relax.

In this chapter I will show how you can achieve a state of profound relaxation, using relaxation scripts and multisensory imagery. Then, in chapter 10, you will learn that when your body is profoundly relaxed, you cannot be upset—no matter what you think or experience.

There are two types of relaxation scripts: the first to relax your body, and the second, to calm your mind. You should memorize the scripts eventually, but to get started, tape-record them. Read the script aloud, slowly, in a calm and relaxed tone of voice. If this is difficult, you might ask a friend or loved one with a pleasant voice to help you record. With practice, you will not need to rely on the tapes. You will be able to release and relax any time, anywhere.

Giving yourself permission to relax is always the first required step. Make this permission tangible by carefully structuring your relaxation environment. When you practice relaxation you will need an uninterrupted twenty-to-thirty minutes, so arrange for someone to answer your phone and door for you. Select a relaxation environment where there is little or no noise or distraction. Lie or sit comfortably. Loosen any tight or restrictive clothing.

Giving yourself permission to relax also means censoring thoughts such as, "I really should be doing something else." Substitute the thought, "Relaxation will enhance my performance in every area of my life." Think of focused relaxation as a way to boost your energy and vitality, so you can better cope with the stresses of life and reach your goals.

PROGRESSIVE RELAXATION

The following script is based on an established relaxation technique developed by exercise physiologist Edmond Jacobson. He called it *progressive relaxation*. The multisensory imagery journeys in this and the other techniques presented later in the chapter are patterned on a series of excellent multisensory imagery scripts developed by psychologist William Fezler.

WARNING: Never do the exercise contained in this chapter while you are driving, operating machinery, or doing any other activity requiring sustained concentration.

Relaxing Your Body - The Script

Begin by assuming a comfortable and relaxed position. Realize there is nothing else you must do, no other place to go, and no problem to solve. You are in a completely safe, totally secure situation. Nothing can disturb you. Nothing can bother you.

In a moment you will be asked to tense and hold and then relax different muscle groups. This will teach you the difference between muscle tension and relaxation. Each time a muscle group is tensed and then relaxed the relaxation will be deeper. If your thoughts are distracting, say two words to yourself: "safe" and "secure." Each time you inhale say "safe" and each time you exhale say "secure."

Hands and Forearms. With your arms at rest, make a tight fist with both hands and hold for a count of ten seconds. Feel the tension and tightness in your fists and forearms. Notice details like the feeling of your fingernails in the palm of your hands, your thumbs pressing tightly on your fingers, the skin pulled tight and taut across the back of your hands, and the tension and tightness in your forearm. After the count of ten, take a deep breath. As you exhale, release, relax, and let go. Sense the surge of relief that flows into your hands and forearms.

Upper Arms. Without lifting your arms, tighten the muscles between your elbows and shoulders for a count of ten seconds. Feel the tension and tightness on the top and the bottom of your upper arms. Hold it. Focus on it. Now take a deep breath and as you exhale, release, relax, and let go. Feel the surge of relief flow into your upper arms and forearms.

Shoulders. With your arms hanging loose and relaxed, lift your shoulders up toward your ears, as high as you can, and hold them for a ten count. Feel the tension and tightness in your shoulders and the muscles of your upper back. Hold it. Concentrate on it. Feel it. On the count of ten, take a deep breath, and as you exhale drop your shoulders. Release and let go. Feel the surge of relief flow into your upper back and shoulders as the muscles relax completely.

Scalp. With your eyes closed, lift your eyebrows as high as you can and pull them together, feeling tension and tightness in your forehead. Hold it for a count of ten seconds. Feel the tension. Focus on it. On the count of ten, take a deep breath. As you exhale, release, relax and let go. Feel the surge of relief flow into your forehead as the muscles relax completely.

Brow. Pull your eyebrows down and together, holding them tightly. Focus on the tension and tightness in your brow for a count of ten. Then, take a deep breath and release, relax, and let go. Enjoy the relaxed comfort that flows into your brow and through your forehead.

Face. Now, squint your eyes and wrinkle your nose . . . tighter and tighter. Feel the tension and tightness around your eyes and nose. Hold it for a count of ten seconds. On the count of ten, take a deep breath, exhale, release, relax and let go. Sense the surge of relief that flows through your eyes and around your nose.

Pull the corners of your mouth back as far as you can, using your cheek muscles. Make an exaggerated smile until the muscles in your cheeks strain. Hold it for a count of ten seconds. Then, take a deep breath. As you exhale release, relax, and let go. Once more, concentrate on the surge of relief that flows into your cheek muscles.

Jaw. Bite your teeth together firmly, creating tension and tightness in your jaw. Hold it for a count of ten seconds. Feel the tension and tightness and hold it. On the count of ten, take a deep breath, and as you exhale, release, relax and let go. Let your jaw go loose and relax. When your jaw muscles are completely relaxed, you will notice that your mouth is open just a little.

Tongue. Push the tip of your tongue up against the roof of your mouth, creating tension and tightness in the muscles under your chin and in front of your throat. Push hard, and hold it for a count of ten seconds. Feel the tension and tightness. On the count of ten, take a deep breath, and as you exhale, release, relax, and let go. Feel the surge of relief stream down the sides of your face, under your chin, and into your throat.

Neck. Push your head back firmly against the surface behind your head, and hold it. Don't cause pain, just tension and tightness in the muscles in the back of your neck. Hold it for a count of ten seconds. Feel the tension and tightness and focus on it. On the count of ten, take a deep breath, and as you exhale, release, relax, and let go. Feel the surge of relief flow into the back of your neck as the muscles are deeply and completely relaxed.

Pull your head down and forward, touching your chin to your chest, and hold it for a count of ten seconds. Feel the tension and tightness in the back of your neck and hold it. Then, on the count of ten, take a deep breath, and as you exhale, release, relax, and let go. Let your head return to its normal comfortable position and feel the surge of relief that flows into your neck muscles.

Chest. Take a deep breath. Fill your lungs and hold your breath for a count of ten seconds. Feel the tension and tightness throughout your chest and your upper body, and hold it. On the count of ten, release, relax, and let go. Feel the surge of relief through your chest and body as you release and relax. Breathe easily and effortlessly. Take another deep breath. Fill your lungs and hold your breath for a count of ten seconds. Feel the tension and the tightness. On the count of ten, exhale, release and relax. Let your breathing return to an easy effortless pace. When you breathe in, let your stomach rise and when you breathe out, let it fall.

Concentrate on the little pause at the end of each breath out, and let it be a point where your body becomes even more deeply relaxed. Let your breathing occur at your own pace and in your own way.

Stomach. Now, tighten up your stomach muscles as if you are preparing for a blow. Hold it tightly for a count of ten seconds. Feel the tension and tightness in your stomach. Hold it. Concentrate on it. On the count of ten, take a deep breath and as you exhale, release, relax, and let go. Feel the surge of relief flow into your stomach muscles as they become deeply and completely relaxed. Let your stomach muscles become soft and loose.

Double back for a moment and allow your arms to be loose and floppy like dishrags, your face smooth and serene, your neck muscles relaxed and comfortable, and your breathing easy and effortless.

Lower Back. Now roll your hips down and forward stretching your lower back. Do not cause pain, only create tension. When you roll your hips down you will notice your stomach pushing out. Focus on the tension. Stretch in your lower back and hold it for a count of ten seconds. Now take a deep breath, and as you exhale, release, relax, and let go. Focus on the surge of relief that flows into your lower back as the muscles become loose and relaxed.

Hips and Buttocks. Now, tighten the muscles in your hips and buttocks. Let your upper body remain completely relaxed. Tighten your hips and buttocks and hold it for a count of ten seconds. Feel it. Focus on it. On ten, take a deep breath and again release, relax, and let go as you exhale. Focus on the surge of relief that flows into your hips and buttocks as these muscles become deeply and completely relaxed.

Thighs. Tighten your thigh muscles and hold them tense for a count of ten seconds. Focus on the tension and tightness in the top and bottom of your thighs, the inside and outside. Hold it. Feel it. Focus on it. On the count of ten, take a deep breath, and as you exhale, release, relax, and let go. Feel the surge of relief flow into your thighs as the muscles become deeply and completely relaxed.

Feet. Point your toes straight ahead, creating tension and tightness in your calves and the arches of your feet. Hold it for ten seconds. Feel it. Focus on it. On the count of ten, take a deep breath, and as you exhale, release, relax, and let go. Again focus on the surge of relief that flows through your calves as the muscles are deeply and completely relaxed.

If you notice any part of your body is still tense, go back and repeat the procedure for that area, holding the tension for a ten count, taking a deep breath, and letting the tension go.

Now that your body is relaxed, allow your breathing to take you to an even deeper state of relaxation. Do this by concentrating on releasing, relaxing, and letting go with each of your next ten exhalations. As you do this, count backward slowly from ten to one, allowing yourself to be in a much deeper state of relaxation when you reach one.

Your body is relaxed, so it's time to clear your mind.

Calming Your Mind

Imagine that any disturbing thoughts you have are words written on a chalkboard. Some words representing disturbing thoughts might be: money problems, relationship problems, job pressures, or family problems on your imaginary chalkboard. Take a moment and concentrate on what is written there.

Imagine you are sweeping the chalkboard clean with an eraser. As you sweep the chalkboard clean, imagine the thoughts being erased. Spend a few more moments making sure you have erased everything from your chalkboard, until your mind is completely blank.

Give yourself permission to take a beautiful multisensory imagery journey, a daydream that will become vivid, personal and real. Let your imagination blend my words with your fantasies, movies you have seen, other images you recall. Fill in the details in your own personal way. Just let yourself imagine:

You are walking out from a grove of shady palm trees onto a warm sandy beach. You are on a beautiful tropical island where nothing can disturb or bother you. It is the middle of the afternoon and it's hot, over ninety degrees. The sun is a fiery yellow, and the sky is a deep blue. The sand is a dazzling shimmering white, in the sunlight.

Feel the hot sand shift beneath your bare feet as you walk toward the shore. Feel the warm sun bathing and caressing the front of your body. See your body from the chest and shoulders down as you walk toward the shore. Notice the roar and hiss of the ocean waves. Notice how the sound of the waves gets louder as you approach the shore.

Arrive at the shoreline and feel the cold, wet, firm, packed sand and the angle of the shore beneath your bare feet. See the beautiful shades of aqua, green, turquoise, light blue, and deep Mediterranean blue with whitecaps rolling in. Walk into the surf and feel the next wave wash over your feet as it crashes against the shore. Hear the hissing sound as the water goes back out, and feel a sinking feeling as it pulls the sand from under your feet.

Turn to your right and begin walking up the shoreline, noticing the warm sun against the left side of your body. Every step you take makes you feel better. Feel a light mist of ocean spray blow against your skin. Smell the salt air. Lick your lips and taste the salt left there by the ocean spray. See a piece of driftwood half-buried in the sand, and strands of green and brown seaweed sprawled lazily on the shore. Notice a sand crab dart out of a hole and run under a log. Notice the high screeching call of sea gulls. Look up to your left, and see five gulls circling overhead. See them fly back down the shoreline and hear the sound of the screeching fade away.

You come to a beautiful dome of sand. Covering the sand are brilliant yellow buttercups and deep purple violets. You stretch out in the warm sand, and smell the soft sweet flowers, and look out at the ocean. The sun is beginning to set, and it is reflecting off the ocean with a brilliant white light.

With the gradual setting of the sun into the sea, your mind becomes more calm and your body more relaxed. When the sun has completely set you will be in a profound state of relaxation. Look at the sky; it's turning crimson . . . scarlet . . . amber . . . gold . . . orange . . . and the bright red ball of the sun sets at an angle beneath the deep blue sea. You're engulfed in a velvety purple twilight.

You look up at the sky and it's a dazzling starry night. You can even make out the Big Dipper. Hear the roar and hiss of the ocean. See the velvety blue-black sky. Feel the warm sand beneath your body. Smell the salt. Notice how the breeze shifts from the ocean to the land. You are completely calm and relaxed on your tropical island this summer night.

Bring this calm relaxed feeling back with you. You will come back feeling not only calm and relaxed, but also refreshed, with a revitalized sense of well-being. Now, take five deep breaths. As you do, imagine you're picking up a handful of that sand. Let the sand gradually run out of your hand, one . . . two . . . three . . . returning to the here and now . . . four . . . and now, at your own pace and in your own way, when you're ready to come back feeling calm, clear, relaxed, and refreshed . . . five . . . let your eyes open, stretch, and reorient yourself.

If you practice this relaxation technique twice daily for two weeks, you'll discover a growing sense of serenity.

Relaxing Your Nervous System

Relaxing you nervous system involves *autosuggestion* a technique used in self-hypnosis. I will discuss self-hypnosis later, but first I would like to introduce you to a German mind-control technique developed by J. H. Schultz. He called it *Autogenic Training,* a relaxation method used to heighten the concentration and performance of East German athletes. Autogenic Training is based on the assumption that if you repeat the same suggestions to yourself (autosuggestion), and imagine certain sensations within your body, your body will begin to produce them.

Schultz's autosuggestions involve the physiological sensations of heaviness and warmth in the limbs and abdomen, coolness of the forehead, a calm and regular heartbeat, and easy and effortless breathing. I have added two autosuggestions based on psychologist Paul Eckman's research on facial expressions, emotions, and biofeedback, which shows that people under stress maintain high muscle tension in their necks and backs.

Make sure that you're in a completely safe and secure environment. Realize that there is nothing else you must do, nowhere else to go, and no problem to solve. Give yourself permission to spend an uninterrupted twenty-to-thirty minutes allowing your mind and body to return to their natural state of calm relaxation. If your attention wanders off during this relaxation exercise, just bring it back gently to the suggestions and imagery.

Begin by allowing your breathing to become easy and effortless, slow and deep. When you breathe in, let your stomach rise, and when you breathe out, let it fall. As you give the autosuggestions, don't do it with a "prove it to me" attitude. Make the autosuggestions as if you're allowing them to happen, and imagine that they are happening. Synchronize your autosuggestions with your breathing. Repeat each autosuggestion ten times, on ten breaths, concentrating on the statement and the sensation each time you exhale. Also, imagine the supplemental images as you repeat the autosuggestions. In short, you are doing two things: repeating an autosuggestion ten times, and imagining the supplemental image as you do this.

1. My hands and arms are becoming loose and heavy.

Supplemental image: My hands and arms are starting to feel exactly and precisely like a couple of heavy wet towels.

2. My feet and legs are becoming loose and heavy.

Supplemental image: My feet and legs are starting to feel exactly and precisely like two heavy wet towels.

3. My neck and back are becoming loose and relaxed.

Supplemental image: The muscles of my neck and back feel exactly and precisely like a plate of boiled noodles.

4. My face is getting smooth and serene.

Supplemental image: My face is getting as smooth as a baby's behind.

5. My hands and arms are getting comfortably warm.

Supplemental image: My hands and arms feel exactly and precisely like two towels that have just been fished out of a steaming hot spa.

6. My feet and legs are getting comfortably warm.

Supplemental image: My feet and legs feel exactly and precisely like two towels that have just been fished out of a steaming hot spa.

7. Warmth is flowing into my abdomen.

Supplemental image: My abdomen is beginning to feel just like it does when I drink a cup of delicious hot chocolate.

8. My heartbeat is slow and regular.

Supplemental image: My heartbeat is as calm and regular as the tick-tock of a grandfather clock.

9. My breathing is easy and effortless.

Supplemental image: The air is breathing for me, as a gentle breeze blows into and out of my lungs.

Next, focus on the pause after each time you exhale. Allow each pause to represent a step downward to even deeper levels of relaxation. With your next ten breaths, count back from ten to one, and go deeper and deeper into relaxation. At the count of one, your body is deeply and completely relaxed.

Imagine that any distracting thoughts or feelings are coming from a noisy radio or stereo. Whatever phrases or thoughts are going through your mind, imagine that they're being blared at you by this stereo. Imagine that you are reaching over to the volume knob on the stereo, and turning it down . . . quieter and quieter.

Imagine the distressing phrases or thoughts becoming less and less noisy, and finally, completely silent.

Now, using your own life experience, your fantasies, things you have read about or seen, and my words, allow yourself to drift into a beautiful multisensory imagery journey to a place where nothing can disturb you and nothing can bother you. Just let yourself imagine.

You are in a safe, secure cabin in the mountains. It is late at night in the middle of January. Outside, the wind is howling. Hear it whistle under the door. You are sitting in front of a blazing fireplace. See the dancing, flickering orange, red, and blue flames. See the darting shadows on the wall. The only source of light is the orange fire. The rest of the cabin is in a purple darkness. Hear the crackling and popping of the logs as the sap hits the fire. Smell an occasional whiff of smoke from the burning oak logs. Get up and stand next to the fire. Feel the intense heat, the prickly, itching sensation on the front of your body because the heat from the fire is so intense.

Walk over to the window of your cabin. See your body from the chest and shoulders down. Feel your arms and legs moving as you walk to the window. Reach up and pull back the curtains. Look out the large dual-pane window. There is a lacelike pattern of ice around the edge of the upper window pane. Place your warm fingertips on the cold, icy glass. Feel and see the heat from your fingers melt the frost, leaving little fingerprints in the icy frame. Your fingertips now feel cool and moist.

Look outside. The moon is full and silvery blue, the snow a creamy, silent blanket of bluish white in the moonlight. Tall, dark, green fir trees sway and whistle in the wind, casting deep purple shadows across the serene whiteness. Close the curtains. Walk back over to your chair and sit.

On the table next to you is a cup of steaming hot chocolate. Place the hot chocolate to your lips and smell the flavor. Feel the steam rising up against your face. Sip the chocolate and feel the heat. Taste the chocolate flavor. Feel the warm hot chocolate go down your throat and into your stomach. Feel the glowing warmth within your body.

Stretch out in front of the fire on a thick, furry, black bearskin rug. Pull a heavy, homemade, red and blue patchwork quilt over you. Notice the pattern in the quilting. Pull a pillow, just right for you, under your head. Hear the crackling of the logs, the howling wind, the whistle of wind under the door. Smell an occasional whiff of smoke. See the darting shadows on the wall. See the dancing flickering orange, red, and blue flames against the purple darkness. Feel the soft, furry rug, the heaviness of the quilt, the gentle warmth of the fire. That fire will be burning for hours. You are completely safe and totally secure in your mountain cabin this January night.

It's now time to bring the safe, secure feeling of your mountain cabin back to the here and now. You will find, in a few moments, when you come back, that you are not only feeling safe and secure, but refreshed and revitalized with a powerful sense of well being.

So begin counting to yourself, from one to five, with each breath in one, getting more refreshed; with each breath in . . . two . . . three . . . returning back to the here and now . . . four . . . and now, at your own pace and in your own way, when you are ready to come back feeling safe and secure, relaxed and refreshed . . . five, let your eyes open, and gently stretch and reorient yourself.

A reported effect of autogenic training is a reduction in blood pressure. I wouldn't recommend substituting this exercise for your blood pressure medication, but it can have a useful adjunctive role. It has eventually led to blood pressure control for many of my patients.

Self-Hypnosis

They say that one picture is worth a thousand words. If you say to yourself, "I will be confident," the message must be accompanied by a mental picture of yourself as the confident person you want to be. If you keep fortifying this image with the appropriate suggestions, eventually these images and suggestions will create the self-assured feelings you seek.

The idea of self-hypnosis is simple. If you keep implanting positive images and suggestions in your mind, they will become part of your behavior, experience, and personality. All that is necessary for self hypnosis is the ability to (1) concentrate, (2) relax, (3) give yourself suggestions, and (4) use your imagination.

Do not think that you must enter another world to be in a hypnotic state. This idea has been created by motion pictures, novels, and TV. You will only be in a very deep state of relaxation and heightened concentration. Since your concentration is more heightened, you clearly cannot be asleep. You may go into this state whenever you wish, and come out of it whenever you desire.

Anyone can learn self-hypnosis, but to get the best results you must carefully consider what you want to accomplish. Through self-exploration establish reasonable goals. No, hypnosis won't make you taller, or more attractive, or change the color of your hair, but it can lead to some dramatic changes in how you feel about yourself and others. Reasonable goals such as improved confidence, patience, diligence, and tranquillity are common, achievable goals using self-hypnosis. It is also effective for habit removal such as smoking or overeating. You may develop a feeling of detachment, or you may experience a pleasant sinking feeling. You are likely to get a feeling of deep peace and serenity as you continue to practice.

Once you have achieved a self-induced hypnotic state, you may deepen it through autosuggestions if you wish. At each new attempt at self-hypnosis, imagine yourself going deeper and deeper into a relaxed state. However, it is not essential to reach a profound level of self-hypnosis during your first few tries. What you want to establish is a "reflex" that will cause you to react instantly to a preselected signal. With frequent repetition, the signal will trigger the self-hypnosis. For instance, if you are dealing with a difficult boss, you might autosuggest that the moment you see your boss you will take a great deep breath, your body will become completely relaxed, and your mind perfectly calm and clear.

The following self-hypnosis script is based on an excellent autohypnotic procedure developed by William Kroger and William Fezler.

Begin by selecting a quiet place and arranging your schedule so you can practice self-hypnosis for an uninterrupted ten to fifteen minutes, two or three times a day. Sit in a comfortable chair with your hands at rest. Recline, if you can.

Fix your eyes on a spot on the ceiling directly above the level of your eyes, so that you feel some strain in your eyelids. Then begin counting very slowly from one to ten, allowing several seconds between each count. Start counting slowly.

On the count of one, sense your eyelids. Between the numbers one and three, tell yourself repeatedly that your eyelids are getting very, very heavy——that your eyes are getting very, very tired.

My eyelids are getting heavier and heavier. The heavier my eyelids get, the more deeply relaxed I'll become, and the better able I'll be to follow all suggestions I give myself. My eyelids are getting very heavy. In a moment it will feel so good to close my eyes.

When you have counted three and you're sure that your eyelids feel heavy, let your eyelids close. Roll your closed eyeballs up as if you're looking onto the darkness of the back of your forehead and then say:

My eyelids are locked so tightly that I don't feel like opening them. My eyelids shut tighter . . . and tighter . . .and tighter. As they lock tightly, I am more deeply relaxed.

As I count, I feel a soothing, calm, relaxed feeling beginning in my toes and moving into my legs. I notice a comfortable heaviness in my legs. I can feel them sinking farther into the chair each time I breathe out. As I become more deeply relaxed, my legs begin to feel very loose——loose and floppy like dishrags. As I become more deeply relaxed, there is a comfortable numbness starting in my toes and moving up . . . up . . . up from my toes into my legs. It's a numb, tingling feeling, like when my dentist injects Novocaine into my jaw; like the feeling when I sit too long in one position; the same feeling I would have in my legs if I sat cross-legged for very long.

On the count of four say:

By the time I count to five, my legs will be completely relaxed, from my toes through my thighs . . . heavy, loose, and numb.

On the count of five say:

My legs are so comfortably relaxed now that I don't want to move them. My eyelids are sealed so comfortably that I don't even try to open them. My legs are relaxed from my toes through my thighs.

Each time you retrace the suggestions and images, you stamp in the learned relaxation pattern. You continue in this way:

By the time I count six and seven, my fingers, hands, and arms will feel very, very heavy. I feel them sinking into the arms of my chair or my lap. I can feel my shoulders sag a little more with each breath. A heavy, detached feeling is moving up from my fingers through my forearms, past my elbows, and through my shoulders. Both arms, from my hands through my shoulders, feel looser and looser with every breath. As I become still more deeply relaxed, I begin to notice that same numbness developing in my arms——the same feeling I have in my arms when I fall asleep on them.

By the count of seven, when you finally reach the point where your arms and legs are completely relaxed, repeat all the suggestions you've given yourself thus far, adding:

My legs are so relaxed and comfortable I don't even think of moving them. My eyes are sealed so comfortably tight that I don't even want to open them. My arms are so heavy and comfortable I don't even think of lifting them. When I've counted from seven to eight, my torso will be relaxed, too.

Then go back to your eyelids, legs, and arms and say:

By the time I count eight and nine, my chest will have relaxed. With each breath, I feel myself going deeper and deeper into a relaxed state. My upper, middle, and lower back are getting very, very loose. Very comfortable. I can feel the muscles in my chest relaxing and letting go with each breath.

Eight . . . My entire body from the neck down is releasing, relaxing, and letting go.

Nine . . . I am completely relaxed. I don't even want to open my eyes, move my legs, or move my arms. I feel my whole body relaxing thoroughly and deeply. It's so refreshing to drift into this deep quiet state.

I will now relax my neck and head so that on the count of ten I'll be completely relaxed from head to toe. I can feel that with every breath out I'm becoming calmer and more deeply relaxed, calmer and more deeply relaxed . . . into a safe, soothing, refreshing state. I feel like I'm floating away . . . falling deeper and deeper . . . not asleep, just thoroughly relaxed.

Ten . . . I'm completely relaxed now. My eyes and limbs are incredibly comfortable. My whole body feels heavy, loose, or numb as I drift deeper and deeper.

You may deepen your level of relaxation by imagining that you are a large maple leaf, floating down from the top of a tall tree toward the soft, green grass. With each breath, in and out, you float back and forth, going deeper and deeper into relaxation. Since you're a leaf, there's nothing to think about or worry about. You just drift down slowly and gently, closer and closer to the soft, green grass . . . floating down deeper and deeper into relaxation, and finally, landing softly on the soft green grass. When you touch that grass you'll be completely calm and totally relaxed.

Using a combination of your life experiences, memories, fantasies and my words let yourself imagine:

You are in the midst of a vast orchard. It is late at night. The moon is full and yellow. The air is warm and balmy, about eighty-five degrees. You are walking barefoot on a warm, dry, two-foot-wide dirt path, on either side of which are orange trees. The yellow moonlight is bathing the trees, and the oranges are brilliant orange against the deep green of the leaves. There are ripe oranges on the ground, and the smell of ripe orange saturates the air.

You see your body from the chest and shoulders down and feel your arms and legs moving as you walk along the path. Reach up with your right hand and pick an orange. Feel its weight, shape, texture, and temperature. Using your thumb, you begin to peel the orange. Notice the pattern of skin as it comes off the orange. Peel off a plump juicy section of orange. Place it in your mouth, and bite into it. Taste the delicious pulp and juice. Feel your jaws working as you chew, taste, and swallow the orange. Continue eating the rest of your orange as you walk along the path.

You come to a little wooden bridge arched over a babbling brook. Hear the babbling water beneath the bridge. You cross the bridge and come to a place where two paths cross. You turn to your right, walking down a path on either side of which are peach trees. Yellow and red peaches hang heavily from the branches, shimmering in the yellow moonlight. Pick a peach from the branch. Feel the smooth, fuzzy, outer surface of the peach. Bite into the peach and taste the sweet, juicy flavor. Continue walking, the taste of peach lingering in your mouth.

Suddenly, to your right, you see a long descending white marble stairway, rolling down the hillside. You begin to descend the steps, and with each step of your bare feet on the cool, smooth marble, your mind becomes more calm and your body more relaxed. As you reach the base of the steps, you will be in a profound state of calm relaxation . . . walking down now . . . getting more and more relaxed . . . about half-way down . . . feeling as if you're floating now.

You're standing at the base of the steps. There before you is a huge white, marble, kidney-shaped swimming pool. Surrounding the pool are gardenia bushes in full bloom. The smell of gardenias is heavy in the air. Reach over and pick a gardenia. Put it to your nose. Smell the deliciously sweet scent of gardenia.

Now you glide into the pool. The water is warm, and filled with thousands upon thousands of gardenia petals. You find yourself floating effortlessly in the warm, soft water, gazing at the full yellow moon. You drift and float and dream, not a care in the world.

You will find it easy and effortless to bring the carefree feelings back to the present. In a few moments you will come back feeling carefree and suffused and saturated with a feeling of peace and serenity. Count from one to five with each of your next five breaths. With each breath you feel more refreshed and revitalized. One . . . two . . . allow the orchard to gradually fade away. Three . . . return to the present. Four . . . and now at your own pace and in your own way, when you're ready, come back feeling carefree and filled with an overwhelming sense of peace and serenity.

Let your eyes open, stretch, and gently reorient yourself.

The principles of making self-hypnosis work are simple: (1) Select a trait or quality which you would like to develop, such as self-esteem, patience, or courage. (2) Use the self-hypnosis induction procedure. You can record it at first, and eventually memorize it. (3) Always use this procedure or one of the other multisensory imagery journeys described in this chapter. (4) At the end of the multisensory journey, imagine or visualize yourself displaying the trait or quality you are practicing. For instance, visualize yourself at work, completely calm, confident, and relaxed. See yourself being assertive and courageous with your supervisor and handling yourself extremely well. (5) At the end of the procedure, repeat the quality you want, five-to-ten times. For instance: "I am confident and self assured . . ."

To make your hypnotic exercise more powerful, it is useful to focus on all five sense modalities. Be sure to embellish your imagery by noticing the details of what you see, hear, smell, taste, and feel. Don't be surprised if some of these details appear to you spontaneously.

Basically, self-hypnosis can be thought of as another type of relaxation exercise, but it is more. Using the principles of self-hypnosis, imagery, and autosuggestion, you can, with diligent practice, bring improvement to virtually every area of your life.

Your Special Space Meditation

The previous relaxation exercises encourage feelings of looseness, heaviness, and warmth. *Special space meditation* brings a feeling of lightness. It is particularly effective in helping people acquire a revitalized sense of well-being. Special space meditation is particularly effective when you face extreme physical or mental demands requiring high performance. I often use special space meditation with amateur and professional athletes who are preparing for competition, or with those who need an energy boost. A special space meditation script is as follows:

Imagine your body surrounded by light, cool, relaxing, refreshing space. This space is like a refreshing and revitalizing blue cloud or a vapor. The light, cool, relaxing, refreshing blue space is between your fingers and surrounds your hands.

Imagine the space within your hands, beneath the skin. The space within your fingers, thumbs, and hands is starting to feel exactly like that light, cool space between your fingers. Your fingers, thumbs, and hands are light and hollow inside.

Imagine that same light hollowness within your forearms and elbows. That light hollowness between your fingers is flowing up through your forearms, elbows, and upper arms.

Your arms feel like balloons. There is a light hollow space within your shoulders. Allow the lightness to become more noticeable with each inhalation. Sense your shoulders rising slightly with each breath, as they feel lighter and lighter.

Let yourself imagine this light cool space within your ears . . . within your mouth . . . a light, cool space within your nose and sinuses as you inhale and exhale. Notice how the space within your nose and sinuses seems to expand each time you inhale.

Let yourself imagine light, cool round space within your eyes . . . between your ears . . . between your eyes . . . the light cool space within your throat as you inhale and exhale. Notice how that space expands with each breath. Imagine the light coolness in your throat expanding out to saturate your neck. Your neck is starting to feel exactly like that light cool space within your throat.

Let yourself imagine the space between your ribs. Notice how that space expands with each breath. Think of the space within your lungs and bronchial tubes. Notice how that space expands with each breath. Allow the lightness to fill your chest with each breath.

Imagine the space within your stomach. As you breathe, and your stomach rises, allow that lightness to develop with each breath. Imagine the space within your backbone and spinal cord. Your backbone is a rubber hollow tube, filled with light, cool air. Imagine that light coolness saturating all of your upper, middle, and lower back. The lightness within your chest and lungs is flowing gently through your whole upper body. Allow the upper half of your body to become lighter each time you inhale, without even having to think about it.

Now imagine the space between your toes and around your feet. That light refreshing space is flowing into your toes and feet. Your toes and feet are beginning to feel exactly like the space between your toes. As you relax and experience the lightness, you can no longer feel where one toe ends and the next begins. That light space flowing into your ankles and lower legs. Imagine the delightful light space within your knees and thighs. You may feel a sudden hollowness within your legs and thighs. You may experience a gradual lightening of your legs, as if the lightness were flowing into your legs from between your toes.

Concentrate on the boundary of your body and the light refreshing space surrounding you. Imagine that your body's boundaries are blending and merging with the space around you, as you become lighter and lighter . . . lighter with each breath in . . . and more relaxed with each breath out . . . drifting and floating and dreaming into a beautiful sensory journey . . . to a place where nothing can disturb you, and nothing can bother you. . . .

You are sitting by the ocean. Notice the smell and taste of salt. It is two o'clock in the afternoon. The air is still. A half-dozen gulls fly overhead screeching loudly. They land twenty yards up the shore to your right. Notice the black, grey, and white of their feathers. Far out to sea dark, thick, storm clouds are gathering. On the beach, the sun is shining brightly, bathing you in a comfortable warmth. A grey and black mist is rolling in as the storm clouds move toward the shore.

A great gust of wind comes, blowing a fine mist onto your skin. Feel the light coolness against your body. The sun filters through the clouds, sending huge beams of light out from a central core. The entire sky is an intense rainbow of purple, red, orange, yellow, green, turquoise, and blue light.

Each time you inhale you feel lighter and lighter. The fine mist constantly ascends. With your next breath in you float with the mist up into the spectrum of color, your body completely weightless. You feel lighter and lighter as you continue to float upward.

Look back down on the shore as you pass through purple . . . then red . . . then orange . . . then yellow . . . then green . . . then aqua . . . then light blue. . . . You are now saturated by a light, cool, blue mist. Your mind, body, and spirit are bathed in a cool, light blueness.

It will be easy and effortless to bring the light, refreshed, revitalized feelings back to the present with your next five breaths. . . . One . . . focus on breathing in . . . two . . . staying calm and relaxed . . . three . . . refreshed and revitalized . . . four . . . lighter and better than ever. . . . And now, at your own pace and in your own way, when you're ready to come back feeling light, refreshed, calm, and totally revitalized . . . five. . . . Let your eyes open, gently stretch, and reorient yourself.

A Brief Relaxation Exercise

The relaxation techniques I have described thus far are effective but require a block of time. If you are like me, though, there will be times when you need to relax but do not have the twenty to thirty minutes required for the whole procedure. For those occasions, there is an alternate procedure that takes less than three minutes. This brief relaxation exercise is as simple as taking ten deep breaths, giving yourself a few suggestions, and using your imagination.

First, pick two words to describe how you want to feel. For instance; safe and secure, calm and relaxed, refreshed and revitalized, light and loose, clear and focused, or healthy and vigorous.

Then, take ten slow deep breaths. Synchronize the first word of the pair with inhaling, the second with exhaling. For instance, autosuggest "light" each time you inhale, and "clear," each time you exhale. Do this for ten consecutive breaths and you will find yourself becoming much more focused and relaxed. If there is time, allow yourself a brief multisensory imagery journey: the beach, the orchard, or any place you like. Finally, allow yourself to bring the optimal feelings you have created back to the present by focusing on five deep breaths.

On the fifth breath, when you are ready to come back feeling your best, open your eyes, stretch, and reorient yourself.

IN SUMMARY . . .

Your mind and body were meant to be in a state of calm relaxation, but the stresses of everyday living cause many of us to become chronically tense. Through daily practice of the relaxation exercises I have described, you can alleviate this tension.

You must practice relaxation regularly. To realize the greatest relaxation effects, practice any of the first four exercises at least once a day for thirty days. After you have completed your thirty-day relaxation program, you must follow up with frequent "booster shots" of brief relaxation training. The time to practice relaxation is when things begin to get stressful and out of control, not afterwards. If you practice relaxation training and imagery regularly, you and those around you will notice a profound difference in the quality of your life.

9 | Your Sphere of Influence

What You Can and Cannot Control

God, give us grace to accept with serenity the things that cannot be changed, courage to change the things which should be changed, and the wisdom to distinguish one from the other. - R. Nieburh

Do you often find yourself spending hours worrying about things over which you have no control? How do you feel when you listen to the news or read the paper?

U.S. GOES TO WAR WITH IRAQ
JUMBO JET EXPLODES 36,000 FT. OVER SCOTLAND
FREEWAY COLLAPSES IN QUAKE
ASSASSIN OPENS FIRE IN SCHOOL YARD

Each of these headlines issues a call for action. For instance, the schoolyard massacre in California served as a rallying point for antigun lobbyists throughout the nation. The explosion of the jumbo jet over Lockerbie, Scotland became a stimulus for tighter airport security. Thousands of people responded to the cry for help from the disastrous earthquakes in China and the San Francisco Bay area with donations of food, clothing, and money. Millions more simply read the headlines, felt distressed, but took no action. These people, at some level, felt a call for help, but chose to do nothing about it.

Not too long ago I asked my friend Phil how he felt about life today. He replied in a cynical tone, "I think it's a mess. Although I enjoy the things I do, I feel society is phony. Politicians manipulate people who in turn are manipulated by money. There is constant strife in the Middle East. Child abuse and neglect continue. Drugs and drug-related crimes are increasing. The ozone layer is being eaten away. The AIDS epidemic is killing thousands of people. All our national resources are being depleted."

"Well, Phil, what are you doing about these things?" He replied, "Nothing. There really isn't anything I can do." Phil had fallen into the trap of feeling manipulated by events over which he has little or no control.

But just how do you know what you can and cannot control or influence?

YOUR PERSONAL SPHERE OF INFLUENCE

I have found a useful way of conceptualizing what you can and cannot control, which is to think of it in terms of a sphere of influence which surrounds your actions and beliefs. I often find it useful with my patients to use the metaphor of the "tractor beams" on the *Starship Enterprise* in the *Star Trek* television series. For those unfamiliar with *Star Trek*, tractor beams are used by the *Starship Enterprise* to influence other ships or objects in surrounding space. Things closer to the Enterprise are strongly influenced by the tractor beam, while things farther away are weakly influenced. At a great distance, things can no longer be affected at all. It is useful to think of the things you want to control as being a certain psychological distance from you and under varying degrees of control by your personal tractor beam.

A good way to learn the limits of your sphere of influence is to look at what I call *central versus peripheral spheres of influence.* To use something basic as an illustration, something within your central sphere of influence or immediate control is what you prepare for yourself for lunch today. This is completely within your control. You can make yourself a salad, a tuna fish sandwich, a turkey sandwich, a bowl of soup, a TV dinner, or go out for lunch. At an interpersonal level, your small children are probably clearly within your sphere of influence. If they begin running about the house you can pick them up, stand them in a corner, and make them take a time-out.

Things within your peripheral sphere of influence illustrate gradations of your control. Examples of peripheral influence are asking your husband to meet you for lunch, trying to get a raise from your supervisor, or writing a letter to your congressional representative urging legislation against environmental pollution. It is much more likely that you will succeed in making your tuna salad sandwich or getting your husband to meet you for lunch than in persuading your congressman to enact legislation to prevent pollution.

Other things are completely outside your sphere of influence, such as the ebb and flow of the tides, the behavior of sun spots, and weather patterns which influence our climate. Unfortunately, many of us spend a great deal of our time and energy trying to control the things we have little, if any, control over while neglecting to take care of important business that we should be handling.

PATTERNS OF CONTROL

In working with people who are learning to discover their limits of control and to clearly discern their sphere of influence, I have discovered five common patterns of control: (1) learned helplessness (2) overcontrolling (3) passive worrying (4) obsessive avoidance and (5) self-deception.

Learned Helplessness

In 1975, psychologist Martin Seligman wrote a book on what we can control, our expectations, and how these influence depression and distress. Seligman's theory implicated helplessness as the source of depression. He summarized his theory as follows:

> The expectation that an outcome is independent of responding (1) reduces the motivation to control the outcome; (2) inter-

feres with learning that responding controls the outcome; and, if the outcome is traumatic, (3) produces fear for as long as the subject is uncertain of the uncontrollability of the outcome; and then (4) produces depression.

Seligman contends that when we learn our efforts have no effects on reality, we develop an expectation of helplessness, followed by depression. Perhaps the best example of learned helplessness is called the *Golden Boy effect*.

Paul was a fifteen-year-old son of a multimillionaire. When he first came to see me he disclosed that he had everything he wanted: two dirt bikes, a quad runner, a large house with a pool, many friends, all the money he could spend, video games, tapes, compact discs, stereos, horses, boats, jet skis, and frequent travel. Despite all he had, Paul was deeply depressed.

Upon close questioning, I saw that no matter what he did, or did not do, he would always receive the benefits of his father's work. Paul received a large sum of money every week for his allowance. He frequently received surprise gifts that would leave him temporarily ecstatic.

At a deeper level, however, Paul had fallen into the expectation that events and outcomes in his life were completely independent of his efforts. He was a "Golden Boy" in his father's eyes. He was rewarded just for existing. While Paul's father's intentions were good, he had created an emotional invalid. Paul felt that his existence on this planet made no difference.

Treatment for Paul was uncomplicated. Paul, his father, and I agreed upon a set of chores and obligations that Paul would have to complete to receive his benefits. For instance, Paul had to earn at least a B average in his classes to have the privilege of riding his dirt bike. He had to start taking care of the yard and mowing the lawn for his weekly allowance. Pairing up Paul's privileges with these simple obligations proved to be effective in breaking this young person's cycle of learned helplessness.

On the opposite side of the spectrum was Milton, a sixteen-year-old severely abused child who also was deeply depressed. Milton had learned that no matter what he said, did, or thought, his reality was completely out of his control. Milton was the son of an abusive, negligent, crack-addicted couple. The frequent target of physical and emotional abuse, the best Milton could hope for from his parents was to be ignored. Before being removed from his home, Milton showed me scars where his father had burned him with cigarettes. In one of our sessions Milton explained, "It doesn't matter how well I do my chores, or how good my grades are, or how good I am in sports. Dad and Mom just keep being mean."

While at different ends of the socioeconomic spectrum and vastly different in parental love and support, Paul and Milton both are classic examples of learned helplessness and depression. Paul, Milton, and all of us want and need to feel a sense of control and influence in our lives. But how do you know what you can and cannot control?

Overcontrolling

On the opposite end of the continuum from the person who has learned to be helpless is the overcontroller. Overcontrollers are a resourceful people who have learned that by putting their mind to it, they can get what they want. Their thoughts and actions are meant to manipulate and control the people and events around them. They love to call the shots.

Mickey, a fifty-five-year-old multimillionaire, real estate investment banker, is a good example. Mickey is on top of virtually every aspect of his job. He is constantly making demands on subordinates and coworkers to produce. At home, Mickey continues his high-pressure tactics. He is controlling about where his wife goes and what she does, what they have for dinner, who his children associate with, what kinds of recreations and sports they are involved in, and even what kind of clothes they wear.

While bright, successful, and influential, Mickey has bitten off more than he can chew. His incessant efforts at overcontrol begin to alienate those around him. As his children start to dislike him, his wife is nearly ready to apply for divorce, and his subordinates begin to sabotage his business deals. Mickey's health begins to suffer. He develops ulcerative colitis, hypertension and migraine headaches.

Mickey is a man who has tried to overextend his sphere of influence and completely control and dominate many things over which he has only some influence.

Passive Worrying

The passive worrier has a slightly different problem with respect to his or her sphere of influence. The passive worrier wants to control everything, yet does not engage in the overcontroller's manipulation and dominance. The passive worrier essentially worries about things and wants desirable outcomes, yet does not take action to make things happen. Passive worriers can be seen throughout all levels of life. The most common example is the mother who incessantly worries about the behavior of her grown children, yet does nothing about it.

Obsessive Avoidance

The emotional ostrich practices obsessive avoidance by burying himself in two or three distractions, while ignoring the rest of the world. The emotional ostrich has locked into his personal tractor beam the two or three things that are important to him, but ignores everything else. This is fine until everything else comes crashing down.

Jarod, a thirty-six-year-old safety consultant practices obsessive avoidance. He distracts himself with downhill skiing, basketball, and hunting. He goes through the motions of doing his job, yet really isn't interested in the quality of his work. Jarod has been married for two years and cares little about the happiness of his wife, as long as she does not interfere with his skiing, basketball, and hunting.

Jarod does not notice important things that are clearly within his control and demand attention: his supervisor's poor evaluation of his job performance in the past month, his wife's constant complaints that he neglects her, and the rattling sound in his truck's engine that indicates he has neglected to check the oil. Jarod seems to be happy as long as he skis forty days a year, gets his bucks and ducks during hunting seasons, and maintains his starting position on the B league basketball team he has played on for five years. But, if Jarod does not take control of things that need to be handled in his life, he will soon find himself unemployed, divorced, without a truck, and wondering what happened.

Self-Deception

A different type of error in recognizing and handling control issues is made by the self-deceiver. This person is convinced of having complete control over essential aspects of life, but in reality is powerless.

Pamela, a 22-year-old amphetamine addict is a self-deceiver. In my interview with Pam, she told me that she had been using amphetamines heavily for five years, but knew that she could cut down or quit whenever she wanted. She just never got around to it.

Pam is clearly deceiving herself. When she experiences the slightest signs of amphetamine withdrawal, Pam begins searching desperately for a supply source. Pam's self-deception regarding her sphere of influence generalizes to her boyfriend, Doug. Doug, also addicted to amphetamines, is unpredictable and physically abusive. On two occasions, he has beaten her to the point of requiring hospitalization and police intervention. Yet, Pam chooses not to press charges or to leave Doug although she believes she could at any time. Pam's illusory control of her drugs and her relationship have no basis in her reality.

RECOGNIZING YOUR SPHERE OF INFLUENCE

We all want to control the important people, situations, and events of our lives. But to what extent are these things actually under our control? The degree to which we control important people, events, and objects is a matter of our perception, so we should examine specific areas which might be important to us and get some sense of the amount of control we can exercise.

Your Feelings

You already know from Chapter 2 that your feelings are extremely important in helping you recognize and act on your values. Your emotions or feelings are based on underlying assumptions you have about the way the world should be. When you find yourself experiencing events that cause feelings such as anger, guilt, joy, sadness, fear, or surprise, it is important to recognize and express these emotions. One of the biggest control errors you can make is trying to manipulate, minimize, deny, or suppress your feelings.

It's important to consider, when trying to sort out how to control your feelings, what underlying assumptions or ideas they are based on. At the simplest level, if you smile at a passerby on the street and he or she looks away or shuns your greeting, you may feel rejected. If you examine your ideas and beliefs closely, you may discover an underlying assumption that everyone should like you, and whenever you make a friendly gesture to someone they should respond in kind. We already know that this assumption is irrational and unrealistic.

An excellent way to check out the assumptions and beliefs upon which your feelings are based is to look at the irrational beliefs listed in the chapter on self-talk. If your beliefs and assumptions are irrational, you may find yourself being victimized frequently by feelings that are not helping you adjust and adapt to life. The question of personal control over feelings involves listening, recognizing, and expressing what your feelings tell you. If you find yourself being dominated or manipulated by your emotional reactions to events, take a close look at the underlying beliefs and assumptions upon which they are based.

Your Health

In assessing how much control or influence you have over your health, you may be surprised to learn that you have a lot more control than you think. We know that habits such as smoking, excessive alcohol consumption, drug abuse, obesity, and lack of exercise contribute significantly to heart disease, stroke, and cancer. On the positive side, we know that a healthy, balanced diet, regular exercise, and the ability to relax and enjoy life all improve your physical health and longevity.

Conversely, there are aspects of your health that are less controllable or even uncontrollable. For instance, do you know if you are going to inhale a virus or contract a bacterial infection through a handshake with a friend? Do you know if another car will run through a stop sign and broadside you? What can you do if heart disease is hereditary? Should you worry about exactly when you will die?

For most of us, our health is somewhere within our peripheral sphere of influence. We have significant, but not total, control over it. So, use the information you have with respect to maximizing your health, physical fitness, and well-being. Don't spend days or weeks worrying over aspects of your health that you have little or no control over, and above all, don't waste your time worrying about the inevitable.

Your Spouse or Significant Other

Does what you say to your husband or wife make a difference in their behavior? If you need something truly important to you, can you get it from them? If they are doing something to hurt you, can you make them stop? Do you feel neglected or ignored?

Applying Seligman's principle of learned helplessness to relationships, if you feel you have no influence over your spouse or significant other, you are likely to feel helpless and depressed. In terms of advice, it is up to you to take the bull by the horns. If you give up control of your life to those close to you, they will continue to victimize and manipulate you until you let them know they can no longer get away with it. An excellent way of regaining control and asserting your sphere of influence in your relationships are the assertiveness techniques described in chapter 3.

Your Children

One of the most important things to consider when determining your sphere of influence over your children is their age. While writing this manuscript, my thoughts are often interrupted by the shouts of my seven-year-old daughter and five-year-old son battling over a video game. I go downstairs, talk to them, give each a ten minute "time-out". Fifteen minutes later they are playing together without conflict, at least for a while. They are within my central sphere of influence while they are in the house with me. But, when my children are twenty and eighteen years old, my sphere of influence will have shrunk considerably. If, however, your children love and respect you, you are likely to exercise a moderate amount of control over them even into adulthood.

Last week I received a call from Sam, the father of a nineteen-year-old chemically dependent young woman. He told me that he loved his daughter but would no longer pay her college tuition until her drug problem was under control. Sam's stipulations regarding drugs and tuition had a considerable impact on his daughter's decision to stop using. She wanted to stay in school, and realized that to do this she would have to treat her recovery as a priority. However, there were other compelling influences that were clearly beyond Sam's control. His daughter confided, "Coincidentally, when I quit using drugs was when my boyfriend . . . a dealer . . . and I broke up."

Your Job

If you are like most of us, your job consists of a number of important aspects: your supervisor, coworkers, working hours and conditions, present income, and upward mobility. To what extent do you feel you have control over them? When trying to determine your sphere of influence with respect to important aspects of your job, listen first your feelings. Are you afraid of your supervisor? Intimidated by coworkers? Do you disdain your employees? Do you find your job conditions unbearable? Is your job tedious and boring? Remember, your feelings are there to serve a purpose. After you have clarified what your feelings are, you need to take control of the situation by assertively trying to solve the specific problem. The moment you begin to take action, regardless of the outcome, is the moment you begin to get back in control.

A STRATEGY FOR TAKING CHARGE

The extent to which you can influence important issues within your life is broad reaching and multifaceted. Consider some of the major problems facing our generation: the AIDS crisis, drug abuse and addiction, the depletion of the ozone, crime, pollution, overpopulation, the plight of the homeless, abortion, recession, skyrocketing college tuition fees, nuclear power, disposal of nuclear waste, elimination of the South American rain forest, preservation of endangered wildlife species, civil rights, women's rights . . . and the list goes on and on.

When looking at the broader, more crucial issues facing our generation, apply the following same simple strategy that works for crises of control closer to home:

- Recognize and listen to your emotional reaction to the event in question, e.g. newspaper heading about the war in Yugoslavia, a phone call from your daughter asking for money, or a rumor that you will be laid off.

- Ask yourself to what extent you can realistically improve or solve the problem or situation, e.g. lending your daughter $200 to help her through a semester of college is a lot more likely to resolve that situation than calling the president of your company and trying to convince him that a layoff is not the solution to his troubled company's problems, or personally requesting a cease fire in Yugoslavia.

- Take assertive action to correct the problem or situation if you think there is a realistic chance of influencing it. If you actually think a phone call to the company's president might result in a delay or elimination of a layoff, you had better make it.

- Recognize that many distressing experiences and events are on the outer limits or beyond your sphere of influence. Allow yourself to recognize and express your emotional reactions to these occurrences, but do not let them continue to victimize you emotionally. For instance, you cannot eliminate the problem of world hunger, but you certainly can make a donation. No, you cannot single-handedly end sex discrimination, but you certainly can become an advocate for women's rights in the workplace.

- While constantly being perceptive and aware of issues and problems that need to be addressed on a broader level, do not neglect the work to be done in your own psychological backyard. There are many things that are clearly within your immediate sphere of influence that you are likely to neglect. For instance, are you giving your husband or wife enough quality time and attention? What about your children? Are you really putting forth all you could be on the job? Are you doing all the things you should be doing to take care of yourself?

More Tips on Applying Your Sphere of Influence

Time-structured problem solving has a lot to do with helping you learn what you can and cannot control. What about those problems or projects that require years of persistence or even a lifetime's work? For decades, diligent medical research scientists have been working on a cure for cancer. Many have lived their lives dedicated to stopping this great killer, with no clear victory. The most difficult problems facing you and humanity may require extensive, dedicated efforts to solve. How do you maintain your commitment, continuing to work on chronic or difficult problems or projects, without spinning your wheels and eventually burning out?

We discussed earlier the principle of time structured problem solving, a technique many already practice in their daily lives to gain control. Time-structured problem solving involves committing a set amount of regularly scheduled time to working on a problem and then quitting temporarily and going on to something else.

Time-structured problem solving can give you a sense of control when applied to everything from giving your children a half hour a day of undivided attention, to committing three hours a week to working with an environmental group. The most important thing to realize about time-structured problem solving is that when you commit a certain amount of time to working out a problem, you must follow through. Then, acknowledge that you feel good about your efforts, no matter what the outcome, let go, and go on to something else. Often, when attempting to solve a difficult problem or project, you will find that after you relax and let go the answer appears spontaneously. And, when the answer appears, you are completely back in control.

Finishing versus completing. To feel a sense of control in what you are doing, you need to recognize that when you finish a problem or project, it disappears and you are free to go on to the next problem or project. When dealing with projects that require extensive, long-term efforts, it is crucial to develop a psychological sense of completion for the work you have done so far, even though the project or problem as a whole remains unfinished.

A good example of feeling completion versus finishing a project might have to do with the raising of your children. You may feel a sense of pride that you have been a good father or mother for a particular day or week, while realizing that you still have fifteen years to go before your child is raised.

Temporal windows of influence. Temporal windows of influence are opportunities for action that can result in a significantly changed outcome. You can quickly get back in control. These opportunities are time limited; you must seize the moment and strike while the iron is hot. The following are examples of temporal windows of influence wherein you might quickly regain control over a situation that makes you feel helpless:

- Your refrigerator completely breaks down and you are low on cash.

    Temporal window of influence: You read in the paper of a sale in which refrigerators are half-price for one day. Go down and buy one.

- You are trapped in a miserable job working for a disgusting supervisor who continues to deny you promotions and makes lewd sexual comments.

    Temporal window of influence: You read in the paper that a new company is recruiting for managerial positions in your city for one day. Go for an interview; and get the job.

Events change quickly. At critical times, you are likely to exercise a significant amount of control over these events. If, in the above examples, you had not acted on the refrigerator sale or tried to get the new job that was advertised you would still be saddled with the problems.

RESPONSIBILITIES AND HOW TO HANDLE THEM

Responsibilities represent a special set of considerations within your personal sphere of influence. Responsibilities refer to things that you are accountable for and answerable for, and they assume a knowledge of right and wrong.

In 1938, a brilliant German psychologist named Wolfgang Kohler wrote one of the most important, yet little-understood books of the twentieth century. In his work, *The Place of Value In a World Of Facts*, Kohler addressed the possibility of the scientific study of human values, with a closely reasoned analysis regarding responsibilities. Central to his position, and essential to our understanding of your sphere of influence, is the concept of *situational requiredness*. Kohler proposed that, given a certain state of knowledge and abilities in a given person, there are situational requirements that, if perceived by the individual, compel an action. Let's look at how this works in a real-life situation in determining what you can and cannot control, and your responsibilities.

While dining in a restaurant three years ago, my conversation with my wife and friends was interrupted by the sound of a woman choking. Her gasp became weaker and weaker, and my sense of obligation to help her became stronger and stronger. Upon reaching the booth where she and her daughter were sitting, I found an obese woman in her fifties, slumped over the table. One of her daughters recognized the seriousness of her condition and ran to the manager for assistance.

Realizing the emergency, the manager immediately dialed 911 for an ambulance. Meanwhile, I shouted, "Is there a physician in the house?" There was no reply. I immediately pulled the woman on to the floor, tilted her head back, and determined that she had a totally obstructed airway. After three slaps between the shoulder blades failed, I applied Heimlich maneuvers, the second of which cleared the obstruction.

In terms of situational requirements, three individuals on the scene took action to the extent that their knowledge and abilities allowed. The woman's daughter got the manager for help, the manager dialed 911, and I applied the Heimlich maneuver. It would have been unfair to expect the daughter or manager to apply the Heimlich maneuver since neither of them knew anything about it. Given their knowledge and abilities, they took the most responsible course of action available to them. It was also unfair to expect restaurant patrons dining in another part of the restaurant to respond, since they had no perception of the actual problem. In short, in this crisis situation, several people felt a call to action. There was an emergency that needed to be resolved. The extent to which this crisis could be resolved was more within the control of some people in that situation than others. But the key point is that people took action to the extent that they were able to resolve the crisis.

Ingredients of Responsibility

The first component of responsibility is your perception of the situation. Should you be held responsible that your child is failing in school if your child's teacher or your child never alerts you to the problem? If your wife never complains but suddenly one day just leaves, is this your fault? You see that to feel an obligation or responsibility, you must first have some perception that your action is required.

The next component in understanding responsibility or situational requiredness is the idea of knowledge and ability. It is indeed a helpless feeling to recognize a desperate situation without the ability to correct it. I remember feeling a true sense of helplessness when the 1989 earthquake hit the San Francisco Bay area. I felt that, though many people were injured or dying, there was little I could do about it. The most realistic course of action I could take was to send some money or food to help those in need. On the other hand, when a patient comes into my office suffering from a panic attack, I clearly have the skills necessary to exercise my control, eliminate the panic, and help the patient feel better.

After perceiving that something in a situation needs fixing, and determining whether or not you have the knowledge and/or ability to correct it, the third component of responsibility involves deciding to take action. If you perceive a situation that needs correcting, have the knowledge and ability to do so, and decide to take action, you must then make it occur in your behavior. This is a decision involving a right and wrong. We know the nagging uneasy feeling when, while Christmas shopping, we walk by and ignore the bell ringer for the Salvation Army. On the contrary, we know the sense of moderate self-satisfaction we feel when we make a donation.

According to the ideas presented so far, you might think that if you're a bright, perceptive, intelligent, capable person, you should spend your entire life trying to correct personal or social injustices or problems in order to be responsible. This is impossible. What is required is a balancing of your obligations and preferences.

Balancing Your Obligations and Preferences

In wrestling with the issue of responsibilities and obligations, you should be aware of four important points:

1. In order to meet your obligations, you must take good care of yourself. If you spend all of your time trying to correct problems, but severely neglect yourself, you will soon become burned-out and unable to fulfill your obligations to others.

2. You can learn to balance your obligations and preferences. Speaking from personal experience, I can guarantee you that it is not always fun to be a clinical psychologist. I often spend hours dealing with people who are severely distressed or upset. Undoubtedly, this has a strong effect on my emotions and feelings, and I often find myself feeling drained. To balance this sense of duty that I show in my work, I commit myself to

recharging my batteries through highly enjoyable recreation and exercise when I'm not at work. I view it as a trade-off. I spend all of my working hours giving my best efforts to helping other people, and devote a lot of my free time to recharging my batteries and helping myself and my family feel good.

3. Learn to make your responsibilities meaningful, enjoyable, and even fun. In my Ph.D. dissertation, I investigated the extent to which people's obligations and preferences influenced their mental health. The significant finding was that the happiest people are those who enjoy their obligations. These people find intrinsic pleasure in doing what they "should do" or what is right.

   Examples of people who enjoy their obligations can range from a dancer who delights in the artistic beauty of creative movement, to a minister who is ecstatic over serving the Lord, to a contractor who takes great joy and pleasure in providing families with their first home. These people are the luckiest people in the world because they have learned to enjoy what their conscience tells them is right.

4. Once you perceive a situation that needs correcting, and you realize that you can do so, this awareness will remain at some level of your mind urging you to take action. Perceived responsibilities do not go away, they just hang out until you take care of them. We can relate this to daily duties—doing the laundry, washing dishes, mowing the lawn, or an obligation that seems more serious, such as visiting a seriously ill parent.

Psychological completion of your responsibilities will yield a significant increase in energy and vitality. Think back for a moment on how you feel after fulfilling obligations. Everyone I have talked to about this feels a profound sense of relief and completion, and a surge of energy. The people who feel the most fatigued and overwhelmed are the ones who haven't gotten around to washing the clothes, shopping, cleaning out the garage, or visiting their sick mother.

Now that you have some idea of your sphere of influence, what you can and cannot control, and how these apply to your responsibilities, consider how these principles apply in some real cases.

Using Spheres of Influence

Caring for a Diabetic Husband. Eileen was a thirty-seven-year-old married mother of two whose husband, Richard, was a late-stage juvenile diabetic. Richard suffered from blindness, frequent seizures, and total disability. Saddled with the responsibility of her husband's previous chores around the house, her job, and the care of her two preadolescent children, Eileen became overwhelmed. She found herself frequently panicking over the reality that Richard might soon die, and spent her time waiting for his next medical crisis. At the time I saw Eileen, Richard had just gone in for a kidney dialysis and had nearly died.

In exploring the sphere of influence idea, I simply asked Eileen what she could do to help Richard in the last couple of years of his life. In several sessions, Eileen discussed Richard's condition with his doctor and learned how to take care of him, handle his seizures, give him medications when necessary, and make his life as comfortable as possible. I taught Eileen how to support Richard's efforts at seeking independence and enjoyment of life. The quality of their life dramatically improved for his last two years.

The turning point in Eileen's therapy was the realization that she was not a medical expert in the treatment of diabetes, nor an internist or a specialist. She became aware of what she could and could not control and decided to do the best she could and let go of the rest. When a condition with Richard arose that she could not handle, she immediately took him to the hospital. Their two teenage children also learned how to comfort and care for their father. Several months before his death, Eileen reported that she and Richard went to a concert together and to his favorite professional football team's game. Although Richard died very young, Eileen felt no guilt or resentment. She knew she had gone as far as she could to help and comfort her husband. She realized where her boundaries lay.

A Repressive Supervisor. Bill was a fifty-two-year-old tax accountant for the State of California. During his ten years in that position, Bill had seen many expert supervisors come and go. Unfortunately, his most recent supervisor had put the clamps on Bill's extra work and would not allow him to do anything outside his job description.

Bill knew all the work that needed to be done. Realizing that his department was falling far short of its goals, he began to feel extremely frustrated. Despite many run-ins with his supervisor and direct complaints to his supervisor's boss, Bill was getting nowhere. He noticed that his department continued to get further and further behind, and he felt powerless to do anything to help it.

Bill was another candidate who responded beautifully to the idea of discovering and accepting his sphere of influence. Bill became aware of the precise description of his job. He had to learn how to set clear and distinct boundaries between what he was required to do and what he was not allowed to do. Using office partitions Bill set up physical barriers around his desk to screen out the distracting information that disturbed him. During one of our sessions, Bill and I discussed the metaphor of taking care of your own yard and not trying to control the things in your neighbor's yard.

When Bill put up the office partitions around his desk, he was questioned by his supervisor. He replied, "I'm going to take care of the things that come to me through my phone and my desk and not allow myself to be distracted and frustrated by what other people are not accomplishing." In short, Bill learned how to say and believe, "That's not my job."

A Son on Probation. Jill was a forty-five-year-old mother of an eighteen-year-old who had had several brushes with the law. While on probation, Jill's son Mike was required to maintain residence at Jill's house. Given Mike's rebellious nature and Jill's over-protectiveness, this made for a volatile situation. While Mike was living at home on probation, Jill had the leverage to have him sent to jail if he did not abide by her demands. When Mike completed his probation, that leverage disappeared.

Jill felt frustrated and upset because Mike no longer planned to tell her where he was going, what time he was coming home, or with whom he was associating. At first, Mike was unreasonable and wanted no controls. After counseling he agreed to provide his mother with enough information to give her a sense of security.

Nonetheless, Jill had to learn where her control began and ended. Mike was now eighteen, had his own car, a full-time job, and a girlfriend, and was no longer her little boy. Although she could offer him help and advice, she could no longer control his behavior. When Jill realized her sphere of influence with Mike, it came as a jolt. She then realized that she could still love and support her son, yet could not control everything he did or did not do. In short, Jill learned to give her son the freedom to be responsible for his own decisions and behaviors.

Surprisingly, when this occurred, Mike made a few mistakes but learned from them very quickly. His behavior rapidly shaped up when he realized that he would be responsible for his own actions or inaction. His boss would not accept excuses when he was late for work, and his mother couldn't bail him out. When he didn't turn in the homework or make the grades in his night class at college, the professor was not forgiving either, and he quickly learned that his actions had direct consequences on his life. Jill's recognition of the limits of her sphere of influence over her son, prompted him to accept responsibility for his own behavior. He learned to accept the consequences of what he did and did not do.

IN SUMMARY . . .

Your sphere of influence, what you can and cannot control, is one of the most important issues that you will ever deal with. There are many things you can control, yet many other things that you have little, if any, control over. You must learn your boundaries, affecting the things you can and letting go of the things you can't. Don't fall into the trap of illusive boundaries, like the people who have learned to be helpless, the overcontrollers, the chronic worriers, the emotional ostriches, and the self-deceivers. Be a reality-based controller. Listen to your feelings and take action when you know that the action may have a significant effect. Above all, don't be emotionally victimized by things you cannot control. If you want to control something, start with yourself —your lifestyle, behaviors, diet, and emotional reactions.

Realize that your responsibilities represent a special aspect of your sphere of influence. If you perceive a situation that needs correcting and have the ability to correct it, it is your obligation to do so. But life is more than obligations. You must balance your obligations with your preferences, and take care of yourself——at least as well as you take care of others.

In general, take care of the business in your sphere of influence and let go of the rest. As one patient put it, "I do the best I can with what I have and let God make up the difference".

10

Neutralizing

Distress

Finding the Emotional Strength
to Survive and Overcome

What do you do when your worst nightmares become real? The best thing to do is to combine three keys to emotional strength you have already learned: (1) ventilating and learning from your feelings, (2) relaxation training and imagery, and (3) discovering your sphere of influence. The idea is this: Once any distressing emotion is fully ventilated and expressed, any thought, memory, or perception that might rekindle this emotion can be neutralized by pairing it with a deep level of relaxation. Once you have ventilated your feelings, and know what they are telling you, you can relax into them and they will no longer bother you.

Going back to the ingredients of your emotions, you will recall that your feelings consist of three things: (1) your body's physiological responses, (2) your behaviors, and (3) your thoughts and cognitions.

When you eliminate your body's physiological responses and the behavioral components of distress through relaxation training, it is impossible to be upset no matter what you think about or perceive. The key is to learn how to relax more deeply into distressing thoughts or perceptions.

Systematic Desensitization

Physician Joseph Wolpe developed a technique whereby he taught patients to relax deeply and then to imagine situations of gradually increasing anxiety. In preparation, each patient developed what Wolpe called a personal *anxiety hierarchy*. This involved making a personal list of several anxiety-provoking situations, graduated from mild to severe. For example, being in a large room with a few people might induce mild anxiety in someone with claustrophobic tendencies. At the other end of the scale, being trapped in an elevator cram-packed with people might be intensely anxiety producing for this same person. Several situations of varying levels of anxiety, between these extremes, would be identified and listed in order of strength.

Next, Wolpe taught the patient to relax his or her muscles beyond the level of normal tonus through relaxation training (progressive relaxation). After learning how to achieve a state of extreme relaxation, the patient was instructed to imagine the mildest anxiety-producing scene in the sequence. The patient was trained to lift a finger upon feeling any anxiety whatsoever. Then Wolpe would help reestablish a deep level of physiological relaxation. Eventually, through repeated exposure, the mildly anxiety-producing situation would elicit no anxiety. The patient would then go on to the next image in the sequence.

Through repeated pairings of anxiety-producing images with deep physiological relaxation, patients learned to *countercondition* anxiety or fear responses. When the claustrophobic's image of a cram-packed elevator stuck between floors was repeatedly paired with a profound sense of physiological relaxation, fear and anxiety subsided.

NEUTRALIZING DISTRESS

After seeing the power of systematic desensitization in the treatment of fears and phobias, I began to wonder just how far this technique could go. I wondered if it could help patients neutralize or overcome crippling sadness, guilt, envy, jealousy, anger, frustration, and despair.

I began working with my patients to see if I could relax them to a profound level and then have them imagine situations that triggered feelings of anger, grief, remorse, guilt, despair, or frustration. Would their strong feeling diminish? To my surprise, I found that when I tried to relax patients, before allowing them to fully express their feelings, they could not achieve deep relaxation. Their unexpressed emotions might burst forth in the midst of the relaxation training. Patients would often become angry, begin to cry, or show other symptoms of internal distress.

To deal with these fundamental emotions, I went back the principle of ventilating and expressing feelings. You will recall from an earlier chapter that this principle states that once a feeling has been fully expressed and ventilated, it disappears. At this point, I began giving my patients an opportunity to fully express, ventilate, and learn from their feelings before practicing relaxation. After the patients had fully expressed and ventilated their feelings, and had listened to their message, they were willing and eager to learn about relaxation training and imagery. In short, it seemed that patients needed to learn a lesson from their feelings before they could relax into them and let them go.

The best way to understand the power of systematic desensitization in neutralizing distress is to see how it works in real cases. The examples I am about to describe represent some of the most nightmarish events that could occur in a lifetime. My purpose in presenting these horrifying examples is to give you an idea of the extraordinary power of neutralizing distress. Every case is true.

A Mother's Grief

The patter of cold rain and darkness of winter night was pierced by a shrill siren and flashing red and blue lights. Despite the frantic efforts of two EMTs, the nineteen-year-old boy who lay unconscious next to a crumpled motorcycle would never awaken. Back at home his mother and sister waited as the minutes turned to hours. Then the doorbell rang, the policeman entered, and every parent's worst nightmare became real.

In the aftermath of this tragedy, the young man's mother, Pam, developed serious sleep disturbance, poor appetite, and low energy. She withdrew from people and lost interest in her hobbies and activities. Her son's favorite songs on the radio, the park where he had hung out with his friends, his room, and countless other reminders triggered acute grief pangs long beyond the customary six-week period of mourning. Eventually Pam's grief deteriorated into a severe depression.

During counseling, Pam disclosed that her relationship with her son had been rocky. "There are so many things I need to tell Dave (her son) but can't," she confided. She regretted that she had continuously urged Dave to make something of himself, thinking he was going nowhere with his life. The day of the accident, they had had a falling-out. Pam had told her son to leave the house.

In Pam's case, I used the open-chair technique described in Chapter 2. I asked her to close her eyes and visualize her son in the room with her, encouraging her to tell him whatever she needed to say.

Once she began, after two or three sentences, her emotional expression crested. Tears flowed as she told her son how much she loved him and how she regretted the last things she had said. She continued by second-guessing fate, saying things like, "If only I hadn't told you to leave that day, you wouldn't have been on the motorcycle that night."

I then asked Pam to free her imagination and take the perspective of her son, responding to what his mother had just said. With extreme emotion, Dave responded that the accident was not his mother's fault, that he loved her, and that he regretted not being with her anymore. This dialogue between mother and son continued through the rest of that session and into the next and became an important milestone in Pam's recovery from grief and depression. Pam had held onto her guilt and remorse until then, not allowing people to get close enough to comfort her. Having experienced this emotional dialogue with her son, Pam began to forgive herself and to allow herself to accept the comfort from others that she needed so desperately.

Pam was now a very good candidate for relaxation training. In our next session, we discussed her grief and decided to pair tragic reminders with relaxation training. First, I asked Pam to list a sequence of sad images involving her son, from the least grief-producing to the most grief-producing. The least potent was her final argument, with Dave and his storming out of the house. Her strongest grief-producing image was of him at the funeral home.

When we began her relaxation training, Pam quickly reached a very deep level of relaxation, saying that she felt as though nothing could bother her. In her most profound states of relaxation, Pam's muscle tonus became extremely relaxed, her heartbeat and breathing slow and regular, her facial expression placid, and her hands and feet warm. The next step was to give Pam the idea that the more distressing the thought of her son's loss, the more deeply relaxed her body would become. Pam observed that it would be a loving monument to her son to pair warm loving feelings with the reminders that once triggered acute pangs of grief.

The procedure produced results quickly. Within a period of two to three weeks, Pam reported that when she drove by the park where her son once played, she experienced a warm, loving feeling. When she walked past his room, she felt love and fulfillment. The songs on the radio, that she once avoided, became reminders of her love for her son, and their good times together.

A Surgical Error

A piercing sizzle of blue-white light illuminated the sterile operating room. A confident surgeon meticulously removed nodules from the throat of an apparently anesthetized young woman. However, beyond the world of the technically precise laser surgery, in the woman's mind, something very different was happening. The powerful anesthetic that had rapidly led her into unconscious oblivion had worn off. Trapped in the prison of her still-paralyzed body, she was forced to bear the excruciating pain of the burning laser on her sensitive throat. She was unable to move or scream.

With one final surgery required to complete the procedure, her surgeon and the anesthesiologist assured her that the previous event was a one-in-a-million fluke that could not happen again. Nonetheless, Kim was willing to completely lose her voice rather than risk the horror of enduring such trauma again.

When Kim first entered my office, she spoke in hoarse, barely audible tones. She seemed tied up in knots emotionally. There was a tightness about her facial expressions, and she constantly spoke with a furrowed brow.

After a few sessions, Kim agreed to tell me about what she experienced during the surgery:

My doctor told me that I was going to have some nodules removed from my vocal cords and that the laser surgery was very routine and had a good chance for success. He said things hardly ever went wrong, and that the success rate was very high. My anesthesiologist told me that I would be given a mild muscle relaxant, and then an intravenous anesthetic which would make me unconscious for the whole procedure. He told me I would have no memory of the operation.

I remember feeling so relaxed after taking the Valium, and when the I.V. hit my veins, I was only conscious for a few more moments. I rapidly lapsed into unconsciousness, completely unaware that anything could go wrong.

The next thing I remember is hearing voices. People were talking to each other casually. Then I began to notice a tingling sensation in my throat. The tingling gradually turned into a sizzling burning sensation, and I tried to raise my hand and open my eyes only to find that I could not move. My throat hurt so bad, I knew I couldn't talk even if I could speak. The most horrifying part was to hear the sizzling of the laser, and smell my burning flesh. It felt like a hole was being burned in my throat, and that I was drowning in my own blood.

I encouraged Kim to continue to fully express and ventilate all the details of her surgical ordeal. She focused on all five sense modalities and went into as much terrifying detail as possible. During the process, Kim often became anxious and frightened, but tried to block these feelings. I pushed her forward, allowing her to fully express what had occurred. After three sessions of recounting the details of the trauma and her feelings, Kim was ready for relaxation training.

Kim was clearly aware that her fear was self-protective. At the same time, she realized she must have follow-up surgery, in order to speak normally. At this point she made a conscious decision to go ahead with the surgery and to allow me to teach her how to relax into her distress and fear. If we had simply tried to relax Kim into the distressing images, without this awareness and conscious decision making, the procedure probably would not have worked.

Kim was a difficult subject for relaxation training. It took two supervised sessions, over a two-week period, before she learned how to relax on her own, even though she practiced twice daily at home with a relaxation tape. After finally learning bodily relaxation, Kim and I constructed her distress hierarchy. She rank-ordered her various memories and fantasies about her surgical experience. Kim's distress hierarchy included memories and fantasies of being paralyzed, drowning in her own blood, choking, and being unable to speak again.

We then began pairing profound physiological relaxation with the memories and fantasies on her list. It was easy for Kim to relax into her least distressing memory: being given Valium. She experienced difficulty relaxing into the image of receiving an intravenous anesthetic, since this would render her incapable of responding if something went wrong. Nonetheless, within two weeks, Kim learned to relax into this image. After we overcame that hurdle, Kim's progress was rapid.

Another technique that helped Kim was *hypnotic anesthesia*. Here Kim learned to recall and reexperience a sensory numbness in her hand, and then to generalize it to her throat. With this tool, Kim had an ace up her sleeve. Even if there were a problem with the I.V. anesthetic, Kim would be able to reduce her pain through the sensory recall of numbness.

Kim's second surgery went like clockwork. There were no complications. The anesthetic worked as predicted, and she did not need to use sensory recall of numbness until she was in recovery. I did not hear from Kim for several days after her surgery because she was unable to talk. When she did call, she told me that things had gone well, and she felt she had learned an important lesson about relaxing into distress.

Nightmares From A Distant Past

Late one night in 1968 in the dense jungles of North Vietnam, a twenty-year-old private and his crack army commando team sought out the Vietcong. Suddenly, his unit was besieged. Bob was on point when the attack occurred, and the first thing he saw was his right flank man's face blown away. Although injured in the firefight, Bob and four others were able to escape. Bob continued to fight in Vietnam for another year and a half before returning home.

Twenty years later, Bob is still plagued by nightmares about his experiences in Vietnam. He finds that war movies, guns, hunting trips, and documentaries on Vietnam elicit acute anxiety attacks. To use Bob's own words:

It seems so weird. I've even had to give up duck hunting. I'll be out there in the blinds waiting for the ducks to come in, and I start getting this feeling that something is going to get me. The same thing happened about five years ago deer hunting, so I just quit going altogether. I really hate to give up hunting because it's something me, my boy, and my dad like to do together. I also notice when I see war movies, I start having this vague feeling about dying. I feel like I'm going to die, or something is going to happen to me, although I know it really won't.

I keep having this nightmare of one afternoon in a fight when I killed this young V.C. When we were going through his things, I saw that he had a wife and a kid just like I did. I knew that could have been me, but it wasn't.

I know I'm safe now, and I don't have anything to worry about, but I still keep getting these overwhelming feelings of anxiety. Sometimes they just come on out of the blue for no apparent reason. The dreams sometimes get really bad.

When I met Bob he was a forty-year-old truck driver suffering from what psychologists call a *posttraumatic stress disorder*. This occurs when people who have been exposed to severely traumatic situations have trouble letting go of or getting over the trauma. Raised as a devout Christian, Bob had trouble in Vietnam reconciling his religious values with having to kill during the war. Face-to-face with the young dead Vietcong, who just like him had a wife and child, that reconciliation became even harder.

Bob's case was more difficult than the others described so far. Because he had the posttraumatic stress disorder for so long, it had deeply permeated his life. Although Bob acknowledged that he had had problems in Vietnam, he could not understand why he had anxiety attacks when he was no longer exposed to reminders of Vietnam, or even thinking about it.

In therapy, Bob returned to his experiences in Vietnam and expressed and reexperienced them in vivid detail. Closing his eyes, Bob described all the sights, sounds, smells, and feelings of his patrols and combat in Vietnam. Often during these sessions, Bob perspired, his voice became shaky, and his breathing rapid and shallow. He continued expressing and ventilating his feelings for about six months. It seemed whenever Bob began expressing his anxiety, he would shut off his feelings, thus perpetuating the problem.

Bob was allowed to fully ventilate and express his feelings of regret over killing another human being. Bob had an open-chair conversation with the Vietcong he had killed. During this imaginary conversation, Bob finally realized that the Vietcong youth would have killed him if the tables were turned, and this appeared to alleviate most of Bob's guilt.

Eventually, Bob could begin relaxation training to overcome the distressing memories. Bob realized that the function of his posttraumatic stress disorder was to prevent him from being killed in a combat situation. He understood that his feelings of anxiety were appropriate in Vietnam, where they had strong survival value, but that worrying about survival while on a duck hunting trip or watching a movie was inappropriate and debilitating. Bob realized that his anxiety no longer served a useful purpose, and instead, crippled his enjoyment of life.

Bob learned the relaxation training sequence to let go of tension and relax the nervous system, with supplemental multisensory imagery journeys to the beach and other pleasant locations. After practicing these procedures for two weeks, Bob was ready to begin desensitization.

He was taken to a deep level of relaxation, and encouraged to reexperience the horrifying events of his combat tour in Vietnam. Clearly aware that he was no longer in the combat situation, Bob was urged to relax more deeply, the more distressing or upsetting the memory. I described to him some of the scenes based on his reports to me, and Bob added details himself.

After our first desensitization session, Bob came out of deep relaxation saying, "Boy I really feel weird. I was thinking about Jeff getting killed next to me, and killing that V.C., and it didn't really affect my emotions." When I asked Bob how he felt now he said, "Fine." He told me that he felt a little bit dazed, but not upset. Most importantly, he reported feeling no anxiety or fear.

Bob's subsequent monthly visits were for "boosters" of relaxation training and imagery. He was encouraged to listen to his feelings closely and learn what they were telling him and then, and only then, to relax into them. Bob also found large muscle aerobic activity highly effective in eliminating any remaining bouts of anxiety.

The Cost of Comforting

Janet, a forty-five-year-old insurance agent on leave from her job, came to my office with an impossible problem. As Janet talked to me, her husband lay in bed, struggling for his breath in the last days of a battle against lung cancer. Janet was a nervous wreck. She was unable to sleep more than an hour at a time, and the tranquilizers her physician gave her were not helping. Janet felt an overwhelming dread that her husband was about to die. Her life had come to a standstill.

During visits with her husband, she was crippled by feelings of helplessness and couldn't wait to leave. She confided, "I just can't handle sitting there helplessly watching the man I love so much dying a slow and torturous death."

The first phase of helping Janet cope with this "impossible problem" was to allow her to fully express and ventilate her feelings. Instead of talking to her husband and expressing her distressing feelings, which might have made him feel worse, she used the open-chair technique during our therapy sessions.

A strong factor in Janet's favor was that she was an intensely emotional person who tended to wear her feelings on her sleeves. When I gave her permission, encouragement and a safe environment in which to express and ventilate how she felt about her husband's tragic illness, the open-chair sessions became impassioned.

Lance, honey, I love you so much . . . but I just can't stand to sit in that hospital and watch you suffer. I've seen you lose eighty pounds and turn from a strong healthy man into a frail dying person. It's hard to listen to you wheezing and gasping for breath, even with your oxygen. I love you so much I just wish it would be over for you. When I make that wish, I feel guilty because I know I shouldn't want you to die. I feel so helpless . . . I want to do something. I just can't stand it anymore. I don't know what to do. I'm losing my mind!

Janet was amazed that after her first session of freely expressing her feelings about her husband's illness, she became calmer and her outlook brightened. The session had temporarily relieved her of the psychological burden of feelings she kept hidden to protect her husband and family. Janet had spontaneously let go of a tremendous amount of bottled-up distress.

What purpose was Janet's despair and distress serving? This was a question that had to be answered if Janet was ever to be completely free of these feelings. When we explored what her feelings were telling her, Janet realized that she felt obliged to give her husband comfort and love during his last days. The question was how to do this—how much to give—without damaging herself further. She knew she could not tolerate being around her husband for very long without suffering acutely herself. What she needed was a compromise that would allow her to express her love, comfort her husband, but not drag her down into utter despair. Janet finally decided that by making three thirty-minute hospital visits each day, she could give her husband the support and affection she knew he needed without endangering her own well-being.

The first stage of her therapy was successful and Janet began to follow the visitation schedule we developed. She had a better understanding of her feelings, and so they were not as intense as before. Her visits with her husband were still not free of distressing feelings, however. Her therapy then entered the phase of learning to relax into distress. Janet learned to pair up a relaxation response with images of her husband's desperate illness and eventual death. During the last few weeks of her husband's life, Janet came to my office twice weekly, and we rehearsed having her relax into her husband's eventual death.

When Janet's husband finally died, she handled it well. She told me:

> I don't really have much left to cry about because I feel like I've already cried myself out. I know my husband's in a better place now. It's a relief that he's no longer suffering. He knows, and I know, that I did my job by comforting and loving him as

much as I could during those last days and weeks. Although it has only been a few days, I feel like I'm already ready to get going with the rest of my life.

Janet was most grateful for learning how to relax into the actual perceptions of her husband's desperate illness. In one of her last sessions she confided, "I don't know how I could have sat there and watched him struggle to catch his breath without the relaxation and desensitization. You've got to tell other people about how effective this is and how it works."

Research on grief has taught us that it typically dominates a six-week period for healthy, well-adjusted people. In Janet's case, it occurred over a two- to three-day period. Once you become aware of your feelings, fully express and ventilate them, learn what they are telling you——and let them go——they will disappear.

A Wall of Flames

Another example of the power of neutralizing distress comes from the case of Nancy, a twenty-eight-year-old alcoholic referred to my office by a personal injury lawyer. This is what happened on the night of September 13, 1987, in Nancy's own words:

Pedro, our dog, started barking. I woke up, and noticed the smell of smoke.

I looked out of our bedroom, and could see an orange glow coming from downstairs. I immediately felt a rush or tingling in my body, jumped up, and shook my husband and told him to get the kids and get out. As I headed for Danny's (one-year-old son) bedroom, I heard my husband getting out of bed behind me. I grabbed Danny and threw a blanket over him. We ran down the stairs, and jumped between the flames. I knew I could hear Bob getting Brad (three-year-old son) just behind me. I remember the heat was really intense, and all I could think of was getting out the door.

The second we were out the door, I got my son away, and looked back for my husband and other son. I thought I could make them out in the flames, but couldn't really tell for sure. By then, neighbors had gathered around, and I could hear the fire trucks coming.

Then I heard screaming. I immediately ran for the door as fast as I could. A wall of flames burst up and knocked me back but I kept going forward. I was tackled by our neighbor, and he dragged me away. . . . Next, I broke free, and ran around and started ripping at the shutters. I pulled about four or five of the slats off before the explosion knocked me away and down to the ground.

About an hour later, when the flames were doused, the fire-fighters found Nancy's husband and other son curled up together by a door, dead from smoke inhalation.

Nancy's loss had occurred approximately nine months before her visit to my office. She had sought to escape the overwhelming pain of this loss by drowning her sorrows in alcohol. Alcohol is a sedative and a painkiller, yet the Nancy's pain could not be numbed. She was plagued by recurrent thoughts: "Why didn't I grab my other son?" "Why didn't I wait for my husband?" "We should have just all died together."

When I began working with Nancy in therapy, I introduced her to the open-chair technique, hoping that she would be able to express her feelings to an imaginary husband and son. This proved too difficult for Nancy, and she walked out of the session when we first tried it. In our next session, I tried allowing Nancy to gradually go over the details of the night of the fire. As she described everything that had happened, and what she herself had done, she realized that if she had stayed behind to save her husband or her other son, all four of them would have been killed. Only after this realization could Nancy could go through with the gestalt open-chair technique with her dead husband and son.

Nancy's ventilation of feelings was one of the most awesome displays of emotions I have ever seen. I encouraged her to continually ventilate and express her feelings, using details and reminders. After three more sessions Nancy felt she had "cried almost all I could cry." And with an analysis of her feelings, Nancy realized that her guilt and despair no longer served a purpose. Having realized that there was nothing she could have done to save her loved ones that night, her recollections became less ominous and dreadful. Her memories became more like a movie whose outcome she knew she could not control.

As in other cases of psychological trauma, it was important for Nancy to learn to maintain a profound level of relaxation while recalling the anguish of that night. Nancy could begin relaxing into those memories once she had emotionally come to terms with both the events of that tragic night and her behavior under duress. In deep relaxation, as she recalled the horrifying sequence of events, her facial expression remained smooth and serene, her breathing deep and regular, and her muscle tone completely relaxed. She eventually could relax even more deeply into the most distressing details of the tragedy, such as hearing the screams from inside the burning house.

Neutralizing Job Stress

A less dramatic but equally useful application of the principle of ventilation and desensitization/neutralization is in combating job stress. Most of us have jobs where our financial and emotional security is strongly influenced by supervisors. In the past eleven years I have had many patients who suffered from job stress due to conflict with a supervisor. There are also other causes of job stress——corporate mergers, layoffs, takeovers, and recessions——but coping with an impossible boss heads the list of stress producers. No matter how well you perform, and how diligent and conscientious you are, your life can be made miserable by a supervisor who dislikes you.

John was a fifty-five-year-old employee of a large company in northern California. During his thirty-five years at this company, John had two nervous breakdowns. Both incidents, according to John, were caused by intense conflict with his supervisor. John reported that his supervisor continually dumped dirty jobs on him, allowing another man in a similar position to sit back and read the paper.

John and I discussed the possibility of his leaving his job, but this was a tough pill to swallow since John had only five more years until retirement. Although John began to work on commercializing a passion that he had for a long time, forming and selling ceramics, it generated only a modest income. John felt he had to remain at his job to make enough money to maintain his lifestyle. But John just could not stand his supervisor.

John recognized that his frustration and anger was serving the purpose of prompting him to change a very unfair situation. Unfortunately for John, despite repeated attempts at assertively changing the situation, his efforts had met with only further frustration. John was left with three options: (1) stay on the job and have another nervous breakdown; (2) quit and lose his retirement benefits; or (3) relax and tolerate the unfair situation until retirement.

After about six weeks of counseling, John decided to try option three: relax, tolerate, and retire. He learned the relaxation techniques quickly and found he could enter a deeply relaxed state almost at will. John also learned a few techniques of assertiveness and began refusing to do jobs that were not within his job description. Although this eased the pressure somewhat, Jonh still brooded over the unfairness of his position.

Then, John was instructed to pair up typical unfair occurrences at work with a profound level of physiological relaxation. John had trouble doing this, but with practice, he learned to relax more deeply the more unfair the situation became. Whenever his assertiveness met rejection, it was very important for him to have the relaxation training to fall back on. To supplement desensitization and to relax into the unfair situation, John used the technique of thinking that he was "only working for the money."

As of this writing, five more months have passed with John still working in the same job. He is that much closer to retirement and continues pursuing the option he chose. He knows that if his job stress becomes intolerable, he can always take a medical leave or quit. He probably will not have to do this because his relaxation training has given him a less expensive and less disruptive means of relieving his stress.

IN SUMMARY . . .

Yes, you can survive and overcome the most horrifying events life can throw at you. I know this because I have seen it happen often with patients, and in my own life.

Your feelings serve a purpose——often as a call for action——to solve some problem or change your circumstances. Not only must you listen to your feelings, but you must also assertively try to solve the problem your emotions have underlined. Then, and only then, is it possible to let go and relax into the distress.

The four steps to overcoming distressing emotions are:

1. Fully express and ventilate the feelings.
2. Understand what function or purpose the distressing emotions are serving.
3. Discover your sphere of influence and take action to solve the problem if you can.
4. Learn how to relax deeply into those things you cannot change. Accept and neutralize them.

The more distressing the thought or situation, the more deeply relaxed your body needs to become. This will in effect neutralize the overwhelming distress. It is impossible for you to be emotionally upset when your body is profoundly relaxed. As many of my patients have told me, "The same thoughts and memories are going through my mind, but they're not doing anything to me emotionally."

11 | Your Inner Voice

The Power of Beliefs, Expectations and Self-Talk

Have you ever listened closely to what you say to yourself? We all have a little voice inside that talks to us constantly. Psychologists call this the *self-talk phenomenon*. Psychologists assign self-talk different degrees of importance in influencing our behavior and feelings, but all agree that what we say to ourselves influences what we do and how we feel.

THE WORDS WE USE

In the middle of this century, linguist Benjamin Whorf postulated that the language we use to explain and understand our world determines how we experience it. It is language that produces and maintains the extreme cultural differences observed throughout the world. For example, Eskimos have seven different words for snow, making their experience of it more precise and detailed than an Indiana farmer's. This degree of precision in describing snow would be useful in adapting to the Eskimo's environment, but not much help to an Indiana farmer. Hopi Indians, on the other hand, have just one word for all flying objects. When Hopi Indians see a jetliner soaring across the sky at 36,000 feet, they use the same word they would use for a sparrow flying from tree to tree. This conceptualization would not have promoted the development of air travel.

From an awareness of the importance of words as structural elements of our experience, psychologist George Kelly developed an understanding of personality called *constructive alternativism*. His idea was that people understand their world by labeling events. Kelly suggested people form their ideas about the world and its events, and form their conclusions, by using markedly contrasting words—opposites—which he called *dichotomous constructs*. People think of reality in terms of good or bad, black or white, hot or cold, love or hate. These are but a few of the labels we use daily. Kelly maintained that people with more accurate labels for interpreting reality could better predict and control events. People with few and inaccurate labels have poor representations of what is occurring, are unable to predict events, and feel little control over their lives.

For example, John, a twenty-seven-year-old single man, was experiencing considerable distress because he felt sexually excited by a woman who was the opposite of everything he thought he wanted. A talk with John revealed that the main construct (label) he relied upon to explain relationships was: love versus hate. With some exploration, John recognized that he could be sexually attracted to someone without loving her. John therefore developed a new dichotomous construct: love versus lust.

Often patients express a strong hatred for someone, but feel guilty about harboring the thought. I have found it to be effective, with people who experience strong feelings of hatred, to suggest a new construct. Instead of thinking of the hated person in love or hate terms, substitute the construct: love versus indifference. When a patient thinks of someone who is hated, they label the feeling as total indifference. As a result, they no longer experience guilt.

Although people differ considerably in how they think about the world, in 1964 psychologist Charles Osgood discovered that there were three primary constructs that people used, regardless of their cultural background: strong versus weak, active versus passive, and good versus bad. Osgood's work showed that we have a common underlying system of primary constructs. We also employ secondary constructs to experience and understand the world—such as happy-sad, black-white, fast-slow, love-hate. These vary greatly from person to person and from culture to culture according to their different values. However, the more diverse and accurate the labels or constructs you use to interpret your world, the more sensible and predictable it will become.

The Self-Fulfilling Prophecy

An even more powerful way your thoughts and words can influence your feelings and behaviors is what psychologists call the self fulfilling prophecy. *Self-fulfilling prophecy* implies that when you expect something to occur, you tend to make it happen. In 1969, psychologist Robert D. Rosenthal found that when teachers were told that certain members of their class were "intellectual bloomers," they tended to treat them differently. There were no "intellectual bloomers," but the teachers' expectations that these students were budding geniuses led to completely different treatment of them and vastly improved their grades.

The self-fulfilling prophecy can be one of the most powerful determinants of a person's behavior. Consider for a moment the example of the "bad child" in a classroom. Often in education, a difficult child is labeled a "behavioral problem." There are usually parent/teacher conferences, trips to the principal, time-outs during class, and detentions after school. Once a child is labeled a behavior problem, the other children and the teachers tend to treat that child differently. They begin to expect negative behavior. When you consistently look for something to support your preexisting idea about a person, you will usually find it. We call this the *inductive fallacy*. It means that you can search for, and find, examples to support your conclusions, no matter how obscure and atypical these examples.

Darrell, a twelve-year-old with a mild behavioral problem, was a victim of a self-fulfilling prophecy by a teacher. Early in the year Darrell was labeled a "behavior problem." His teacher was very sensitive to any mistake Darrell might make. It did not matter how many other children were making the same mistakes; Darrell became a target. Darrell was most recently suspended for throwing paper in the classroom. Upon closer questioning, the teacher admitted that two other children started the paper-throwing and that at least seven other children were involved. Yet, due to the self-fulfilling prophecy, Darrell was the one sent to the principal's office. His teacher needed an acceptable explanation for the disruptive behavior and had one: the "behaviorally disturbed" Darrell.

The self-fulfilling prophecy can be extremely important in shaping your response to others and to yourself. If, for instance, you look forward to your retirement as a golden age to enjoy countless recreational activities, unlimited travel, and the best time of your life, you will tend to have an exceptionally enjoyable retirement. On the other hand, if your concept of retirement includes being put out to pasture, and becoming slow, grey, old and useless, you will create a very miserable time for yourself.

If, however, you set your expectations far too high, you are likely to be chronically frustrated over never getting the things you really want. So make your self-fulfilling prophecies positive yet realistic. Realize that the things you look for are the things that you will tend to find. When you expect the best from others, you will find that they tend to meet your expectations. If you have a bright and positive outlook, you will to be delighted at how often you find evidence to support this self-fulfilling prophecy.

Placebo: The Power of Positive Expectant Faith

A *placebo* is a substance with no medicinal properties that causes a patient to improve because of the patient's belief in its efficacy. Usually, to test the efficacy of a new drug, researchers will give half the test patients the actual drug and half, a sugar pill or placebo. If the drug's effects are greater than those of the inert sugar pill or placebo, the drug is determined to be effective.

While a placebo is often associated with an inert pill, it also refers to an underlying belief or expectation about healing. Psychologist Jeanne Achterberg points out that the word placebo comes from a Latin word meaning "I will please." Achterberg reviews substantial evidence showing that the placebo effect accounts for healing in from thirty-to-seventy percent of all drug and surgical interventions. She goes on to note that even repair of injured tissues has been encouraged with the use of placebo.

For instance, Achterberg cites Volgyesi's 1954 report that patients hospitalized with bleeding ulcers responded in a very interesting way to treatment. They were divided into two groups, each of which received simple water injections. Group 1 was told that the injections would cure them, and Group 2 was told that they were given experimental injections of undetermined effectiveness. Seventy percent of the group who were told that the injections would cure them showed excellent improvement and maintained that improvement for a follow-up year. Only twenty-five percent of the second group showed such improvement.

My colleague, Dr. Martin Rossman, presented an extreme example of the power of *positive expectant faith*, an underlying belief or expectation that a serious condition would be healed. To use Dr. Rossman's own words:

When I was in my second year of practice, working in the county medical clinic, a middle-aged woman named Edna came in for a checkup. She was a likeable, talkative person who said she was there because "the doctors worry me so and tell me I better keep an eye on my blood pressure." Her chart revealed she had been diagnosed with a precancerous condition of the uterine cervix two years before. The gynecologists she saw wanted to take biopsies and remove the affected areas. Edna had turned this recommendation down four times, and each successive note by her gynecologic consultant was more frustrated and concerned in tone. There was mention of possible psychopathology and "irrational beliefs about healing."

When I asked Edna why she was unnecessarily risking her life, she smiled broadly and told me that "Jesus will heal me, so I don't need surgery." She said she prayed and talked to Jesus every day, and he promised he would heal her if she put her trust in him. I asked her how she communicated with

Jesus, and she told me, "I see him when I pray, and he talks to me just like we're talking now."

I explained the medical concerns the other doctors and I had about her. Then I told her I had no doubt that Jesus could heal her if he wanted to, but wondered how long it would take. She was surprised when I asked her if she would get in touch with him and ask him if he would agree to heal her in the next six weeks.

She closed her eyes, and after a few minutes smiled and nodded her head. "Yes, he says he can and will heal me in six weeks." She agreed to have another pelvic exam and pap smear then and to have a biopsy if the pap smear was still abnormal. "But it won't be," she said. "I know that now . . ." and she left, smiling more widely than ever.

I felt good to have gotten a commitment from her to have a biopsy if her prayer proved ineffective. Six weeks later she returned. Her cervix looked normal on examination. Three days later her pap smear report came back: perfectly normal. Edna's story . . . points to the potent healing effects of faith and belief.

The power of placebo or positive expectant faith affects you as an individual and can also affect people around you. In the 1960s psychologist Jerome Frank decided to conduct a study to learn which psychotherapy method was most effective. Frank had specialists in the fields of psychanalytic, behavioral, and humanistic psychology treat patients with different psychological disorders. Frank measured different expectations, beliefs, characteristics, traits, and other factors to find what worked best in counseling. To everyone's surprise, Frank found that humanistic, psychoanalytic, and behavioristic treatments were all equally effective. The single best predictor of any therapeutic success was the therapist's own belief in the technique being used.

According to Frank, a placebo gains its potency through being a tangible symbol of the physician's healing power. Various types of patients throughout the world have been administered placebos of one kind or another. The common feature of placebos, be they medical, surgical, a sugar pill, voodoo curses, or visits to religious or medical shrines, is that they all serve to alter patients' expectations about their health. In more than fifty percent of the cases patients administered placebos show a decrease in nausea, pain, anxiety, depression, and even in such clear-cut physiological problems as tumor cells. Apparently expectations cause a profound physiological change at a biochemical level. It is not only the patients' attitude that changes. Just as we have already learned that your behavior clearly affects your neurochemistry, we now have a compelling implication that your beliefs, expectations, and thoughts also influence your neurochemistry and physiology.

The power of positive expectant faith, or placebo, is most effective when combined with the most technologically and scientifically valid medical interventions. There is nothing inconsistent about combining all the tools of science with the power of your expectations and beliefs.

WARNING: Just because positive expectant faith has been shown to affect healing, it does not mean that medical or surgical intervention is ineffective or undesirable. Often, it is lifesaving.

COGNITIVE THERAPY TECHNIQUES

Cognitive psychologists have developed techniques involving thinking, planning and problem solving to help improve our moods and behaviors. Because much of our thinking occurs through self-talk, cognitive psychologists have developed the tools to help you change yours.

Rational Self-Talk

Psychologist Albert Ellis developed a treatment program for emotional disorders that he calls *Rational Emotive Therapy*. Central to Dr. Ellis's therapy is the idea that negative self-talk and irrational beliefs must be replaced by positive self-talk and rational beliefs. To use Ellis's own words, "Irrational thoughts and sentences create emotional distress."

Dr. Maxie Maultsby describes rational thinking as having the following characteristics:

- It is based primarily on objective fact as opposed to subjective opinion.
- If acted upon, it usually results in the preservation of life and limb instead of premature death or injury.
- If acted upon, it produces your personally defined goals more quickly.
- If acted upon, rational thought prevents undesirable personal and/or environmental conflict.
- Rational thought minimizes your inner conflicts and turmoil.

Ellis believes that many typical self-talk sentences are irrational and unrealistic. When we notice one of these in our thinking, we must dispute the statement and replace it with a rational one. Ellis has identified what he claims are the ten most common irrational ideas that interfere with fulfillment in life and has provided ten rational alternatives:

1. Irrational Idea: You must, yes must, have love or approval from all of the people you find significant.
   Rational Idea: Sure it would be nice to have the love and approval of everyone you find significant, but you certainly don't have to have it to survive.

2. Irrational Idea: You must prove thoroughly competent, adequate, and achieving.
   Rational Idea: Being competent, adequate, and achieving are values which you strive for and more times than not achieve. But no one is perfect!

3. Irrational Idea: When people act obnoxiously and unfairly, you should blame and damn them, and see them as bad, wicked, or rotten individuals.

Rational Idea: When people act unfairly it's okay to be angry with their behavior without damning or condemning them. Change is always possible.

4. Irrational Idea: You have to view things as awful, terrible, horrible, and catastrophic when you get seriously frustrated, treated unfairly, or rejected.
Rational Idea: Frustration and rejection, just like achievement and acceptance, are part of life——so learn to experience and appreciate them.

5. Irrational Idea: Your emotional misery comes from external pressures and you have little ability to control or change your feelings.
Rational Idea: Most of your emotional misery comes not from external pressures, but from your interpretation of them.

6. Irrational Idea: If something seems dangerous or fearsome, you must preoccupy yourself with, and make yourself anxious about, it.
Rational Idea: If something is dangerous or fearsome, remove yourself from the danger, then forget about it.

7. Irrational Idea: You can more easily avoid facing many life difficulties and self-responsibilities than undertake more rewarding forms of self-discipline.
Rational Idea: It's much easier to take responsibility for your actions through self-discipline.

8. Irrational Idea: Your past remains all important and because something once strongly influenced your life, it has to keep determining your feelings and behavior today.
Rational Idea: Once you've learned your lessons from the past, it is easy to let it go.

9. Irrational Idea: People and things should turn out better than they do and you must view it as awful and horrible if you do not find good solutions to life's grim realities.
    Rational Idea: Sometimes there aren't good solutions to life's grim realities. Life isn't always fair or fun.

10. Irrational Idea: You can achieve maximum human happiness by inertia and inaction, or by passively and noncommittedly enjoying yourself.
    Rational Idea: One of the best ways to enjoy your life is to overcome inertia and get active.

If you find yourself thinking these irrational thoughts, you are setting yourself up for some major disappointments and frustrations. You must challenge them, dispute them, and find realistic, positive substitutes.

Reframing

Reframing is a cognitive psychology technique in which you learn to refocus your thinking on a positive outcome rather than trying to avoid or eliminate negative ones. It is easy to understand reframing by looking at some simple examples of how it can be applied to typical life problems:

1. Negative: I'd better not blow that presentation today.
    Positive: My presentation will be clear, compelling, and convincing.

2. Negative: Don't hit the ball into the net.
    Positive: I'm going to hit the ball within one foot of the base line.

3. Negative: I'd better not say something to upset him.
    Positive: I'm going to make him feel warm, comfortable, and loved.

4. Negative: I cannot act like I'm bored.
   Positive: I am bubbling with excitement and enthusiasm.

5. Negative: Don't blow all of your money.
   Positive: I'm going to wisely invest my money and multiply it tenfold.

6. Negative: Gosh, I hope we don't have another fight tonight.
   Positive: I'm looking forward to a peaceful and enjoyable evening.

Thought Stopping

An effective cognitive psychology technique for removing unhappy or maladaptive thoughts is a twofold process called *thought stopping*. First, you construct a list of pleasurable or enjoyable scenes that do not involve the person, event, or situation you want to forget. The scenes or images can be adventurous, funny, interesting, or pleasant in any other way. Second, when you have your list of positive thoughts and images ready, think about the person, event, or situation you wish to forget. The moment the thought you want to forget enters your mind you need to shout (out loud or to yourself silently) STOP! Then immediately begin thinking about some pleasant event or situation from your list. As you continue to practice thought stopping, you will find that you are banishing negative or unhealthy thoughts from your mind and substituting positive rewarding ones.

Silent Ridicule

Silent ridicule is a technique that changes a distressful or pain-producing thought into a humorous one. Laughter is often a good replacement for the distress or pain that some memories can cause. Silent ridicule is often very effective when you must interact with the person or situation that has hurt or disappointed you in the past. For instance, you may imagine your large, intimidating, scary supervisor as a giant baby wearing diapers, with a cigar in his mouth. This image is inconsistent with your being intimidated or bullied.

Stress Inoculation

Stress inoculation training is a technique developed by psychologist Donald Meichenbaum in 1975. Patients imagine themselves in a stressful situation while maintaining a positive image of themselves and continually reinforcing their behavior with positive self-statements such as, "I'm doing great."

A good example of stress inoculation training was a patient named Marie, who had a terrible fear of speaking in public. After teaching Marie relaxation training and positive imagery, she was taught to rehearse a speaking engagement while saying self-statements that built her self-esteem, such as:

- I know my material inside and out.
- I am competent and effective.
- I am a dynamic entertainer.
- The crowd loves me.

Cognitive Restructuring

Cognitive restructuring refers to altering destructive thoughts to enable a person to think more productively and effectively. An example of cognitive restructuring goes back to George Kelly's constructive alternativism. Think of the constructs or labels you use to interpret and categorize reality. Most people use constructs such as good/bad, active/passive, or strong/weak. Kelly has found that people with broader ranges of constructs have a much easier time interpreting, understanding, and predicting reality.

If, for instance, you are a person who sees things as distinctly black or white, you are likely to categorize people as good or bad. While this works for certain issues, it becomes useless when you are dealing with someone who is multifaceted and complex. Would you categorize your company's C.E.O. as generous or stingy when he refuses to give employees a raise, but donates a million dollars to a charity?

What about love versus hate? Do you find yourself flip-flopping between loving and hating your spouse or significant other when he or she pleases you or lets you down? It is usually more effective to develop a wide range of constructs to handle different events. If, for instance, your C.E.O. donates a million dollars to charity yet denies employees a raise, you might categorize him on a dimension of *insensitivity versus generosity*. A husband who ignores his wife might be thought of along the dimension of *love versus neglect*. A workaholic mother might be thought of by her husband and her children along a dimension of *loving versus overextending*.

You see, constructs are just as broad and creative as you want them to be. They do not have to be semantic or linguistic opposites to be useful.

Restructuring Pain. A completely different use of cognitive restructuring comes from the work of Ronald Melzack in the treatment of chronic pain patients. Melzack found that patients who describe their pain with emotionally loaded adjectives such as unbearable, miserable, and intolerable have more difficulty handling pain than patients who use more sensory-oriented words such as stinging, cutting, or pulling.

William was a forty-two-year-old unemployed electrical engineer who had been suffering from chronic spinal stenosis and a mildly herniated disk in the lumbar region of his back. Doctors agreed that William would not be a candidate for surgery, and he had to tolerate a considerable amount of pain. William described his pain as unbearable, intolerable, and excruciating during his initial visits.

In therapy, William became aware that these labels only served to make him more miserable. After relaxation training, directing William into alternative activities, and cognitive restructuring, he began to think of his pain as discomforting and annoying. As

William put it, "There's a big difference between thinking of my pain as unbearable versus annoying. I used to think of it as something I couldn't tolerate and would consider suicide. I now think of it as an annoying, noisy neighbor that I can easily put up with."

Another excellent example of cognitive restructuring is the treatment of Patrick. He was suffering from a severe cervical strain with edema and reactive depression, due to having lost his job. I learned, in talking with Patrick, that he thought of his neck as a brittle bone that was about to snap in half if he moved the wrong way. With some education from Patrick's physician and me, he became aware that this self-statement about his neck problem was inaccurate. He learned that what he was feeling was soreness in the soft tissues and muscles around his neck and spinal cord. When he relabeled his pain "muscle soreness" instead of "a bone that was about to snap in half, with nerves flying out all over the place," Patrick became more active and cooperative in his recovery.

Research in social psychology has shown that labels also strongly influence our expectations and perceptions of people. Psychologists have constructed experiments in which they told two groups of subjects that they would be hearing a lecturer whom they described with a series of adjectives. These adjectives included such words as competent, intelligent, brilliant, creative, and either warm or cold. The adjectives "warm" or "cold" were the only differences between the instructions for the two groups of subjects. The exact same presentation was given to both groups.

Researchers found the simple construct warm versus cold had a profound influence on how the experimental subjects rated the presentation. Describing the speaker as "warm" or "cold" influenced the audience's expectations of the speaker and their subsequent reactions and evaluations.

Donna was a forty-two-year-old married school teacher, the mother of an eighteen-year-old son who had recently started college. Donna was frustrated because her son was failing his courses, not trying, and partying too much. She saw her son as irresponsible and had difficulty expressing her love and support to him. Interviews revealed the main constructs Donna used to describe her son: good versus bad, responsible versus irresponsible, and love versus hate.

With some work, Donna realized that she still loved her son, although she abhorred his irresponsibility and lack of accomplishment in school. We decided to try some alternative constructs to help Donna better represent her feelings toward her son. After two sessions, she came to these constructs: appreciation versus disappointment, maturity versus immaturity, and cautiousness versus impulsiveness.

Although Donna continued to retain her constructs of good versus bad, love versus hate, and responsible versus irresponsible, she felt happier when she used the new ones to describe her son's behavior. Through these statements she was able to see that she could still love her son, but would have to be patient and realize that he was immature, impulsive, and somewhat irresponsible.

The fewer constructs you have, to understand and interpret reality, the more likely it is that you will irrationally distort events. Increase your vocabulary of constructs and realize that the more accurately and precisely you describe the people and events of your life, the more you will understand, predict, and, yes, even control your feelings and behaviors.

Self-Talk For Jump Starting a Good Day

If you are like most of us, when the alarm goes off, you hit the snooze button and try to drift back to sleep. You say things to yourself like, "I'm really tired," "I don't want to go to work," or "I need more rest." Once the alarm goes off again, you are confronted with the reality that you must get up and face another day.

The little voice inside your head begins to bombard you with statements like: "I've got to get up now," "I can't rest anymore," "I didn't get enough sleep," and "I'm feeling really stiff and tired." Then you get up and make your way toward the bathroom with the little voice continuing its barrage: "Boy do I feel stiff this morning," "I wish I could get some more sleep," and "I hope I can make it to the shower." As you go through the motions of taking a hot shower, your little voice continues: "You'd better hurry up or you're going to miss that 9:00 a.m. appointment," "Hurry up and get some breakfast and a cup of coffee down," or "You'd better not blow that big deal today."

Think for a moment about how your day might go if you substituted some positive self-talk by the little voice inside your head. Start out by trying the following self-talk sentences to jump start your day:

- Wow, I just got the perfect amount of sleep last night!
- My body feels rested and refreshed and I'm ready for a new day.
- I have powers I haven't begun to use.
- My mind is perfectly calm, crystal clear, and totally aware.
- My body feels light and limber.
- The more I move around, the better I will feel.
- I feel a surge of energy developing deep within my spirit.
- I am going to see how much enthusiasm and excitement I can generate on my job today.
- I'm going to spread positive energy and goodwill to everyone I meet.
- I'm going to keep my mind open and aware of opportunities and surprises.

Pick one or more of these sentences and let them replace the negative self-talk in the morning. You will find that if you do this, your perception of your day and the way you feel will change dramatically.

If you are riding to work on a subway or a bus, notice the one happy passenger, not the eight miserable ones. If you are driving your car and hit gridlock, realize that you cannot control the pace of the traffic and focus on something like the color of the sky, the design of a building, the flashy red Porsche off to your left, or a song on your cassette or compact disc.

IN SUMMARY . . .

Your thoughts, beliefs, expectations, and self-talk can exert an irresistible influence on your feelings and behaviors. The self-fulfilling prophecy teaches that in life you tend to find what you are looking for, fulfilling your own predictions through your behaviors. So why not prophesy positive things for yourself? Use the cognitive psychology techniques of thought stopping, silent ridicule, cognitive restructuring, reframing, and self-talk for jump starting a good day. You will quickly see that your positive thoughts can make you feel and perform better.

12 Positive Relationships

The Healing Power of Love

A brilliant psychiatrist, Harry Stack Sullivan, developed *interpersonal psychiatry* in the early part of the twentieth century. One of Sullivan's ideas was that there were developmental epochs, or periods, that offered relationships of distinctly different qualities to the developing person. These stages were: infancy, childhood, juvenile, preadolescent, early adolescent, late adolescent, and adulthood. Sullivan thought that during each of these phases, there were particular people who played crucial roles in the developing child's life. Parents, while crucially important during infancy and childhood, played a less prominent role during the juvenile and adolescent eras. The best friend, or chum, played an important role during preadolescence, while later adolescence focused more on a relationship with a member of the opposite sex.

Sullivan noticed in working with his patients that many who suffered horrendous infancy, childhood, and juvenile emotional and physical abuses would experience dramatic turnarounds during the adolescent era, provided they had a good relationship. In fact, Sullivan even found that people who had bad adolescent periods could heal these wounds through a positive relationship in adulthood.

The power of positive relationships was revealed dramatically when I was a consultant to an adolescent residential treatment facility. I had been assigned to work with a deeply troubled adolescent girl whose prognosis for restoration of normal functioning was poor.

Penny was a victim of severe parental abuse and neglect. After being abused, neglected, and finally abandoned by her natural parents, Penny was placed in an adolescent residential treatment center and diagnosed as having a "schizophrenic disorder, paranoid type."

During my first meeting with Penny, she exhibited the common signs of schizophrenia, including a flat, blunted affect, a distant gaze, and a sense that she was encased in a wall of ice. He eyes showed a look beyond hopelessness, a vacancy. Penny looked soul dead.

Penny had been medicated with a major tranquilizer called Haldol, and although this helped her organize her thoughts, it made her emotional state even more flat and lifeless. Without the Haldol, Penny complained of common signs of schizophrenia including hearing voices without knowing where they came from, seeing shadows around her that other people couldn't see, and feeling as if everyone was talking about her. Most modern practitioners of psychology and psychiatry consider schizophrenia an incurable disorder best managed through medication.

After six months of futility in our one-on-one weekly sessions, I heard Penny mention that there was a boy in school who was interested in her. Shane, a sixteen-year-old juvenile delinquent with a history of antisocial behavior, had taken a definite interest in Penny. Shane had been labeled a "behavior problem," but was not considered schizophrenic or severely emotionally disturbed. Shane had trouble controlling his impulses and did not respond deferentially to authority figures. Shane would not, however, have a girlfriend who was crazy or who had been diagnosed as having a schizophrenic disorder.

Penny told me, in one of our next sessions, that she had sneaked out of the treatment facility in the morning and spent three hours getting to know Shane. She told me that Shane was "a guy who wouldn't hang out with people who had serious emotional problems," and that she had spent most of her time just listening to him talk. As Penny listened, she formed an idea of what Shane liked and what he would not tolerate. In short, Penny realized that if she wanted Shane, she could no longer act like a paranoid schizophrenic.

Thus began the turning point in Penny's emotional healing. Penny learned to laugh, cry, become angry, express her feelings, and behave as a normal fifteen-year-old girl would. To Penny, Shane was her knight in shining armor and her emotional savior. Shane, despite his insensitivity, rebelliousness, and impulsiveness, let Penny know in no uncertain terms that she was "his girl."

A month into the relationship, Penny began to insist that she no longer wanted to take her medication. Finally, her psychiatrist granted a tranquilizer-free trial period. During this trial period, Penny continued to improve, appearing more and more normal. Penny even began getting into trouble for such behaviors as sneaking out at night, talking in class, and smoking. In her case, these were improvements because before, Penny had been completely withdrawn. Before Shane came along, Penny valued nothing.

In essence, a sixteen-year-old juvenile delinquent helped Penny more than all the psychiatrists, psychologists, and treatment facilities she had been involved with for the past eight years. The simple power of her relationship with Shane taught Penny how to laugh, cry, shout, play, live, and love.

ATTENTION

What Shane gave Penny was crucial in her turn around. Shane noticed her, accepted her, made her feel valuable. The attention we receive from others is one of the most powerful determinants of our behavior and experience. I first became aware of the power of attention while working at an inner-city hospital.

Nineteen-year-old Louanna was admitted to the inpatient psychiatric unit following a suicide attempt. While on the unit, Louanna unsettled the staff every day by telling them she had swallowed open safety pins. The tricky part was that sometimes

Louanna actually swallowed open safety pins. One never knew for sure until X-rays were taken.

I offered the staff a behavior management plan for Louanna in which she received five minutes of undivided staff attention for every thirty minutes she would not complain to the nurses that she had swallowed a safety pin. After a full day of not reporting that she had swallowed safety pins, Louanna would get a half hour of undivided attention from the staff and a trip to the coffee shop to have a snack.

The behavior management plan worked like magic, and Louanna never complained of, or swallowed, another safety pin. After talking with Louanna, she let me know that the reason she was swallowing safety pins, or telling staff she did so, was to get them to notice her. She told me that she was never noticed by her mother and did not know who her father was. She had never had a boyfriend or a close friend. Her bizarre behavior was a desperate cry for attention.

Most of us will not face such bizarre behavior, but the need for attention is pervasive, and shows up in other ways for almost everyone. How often, for instance, have you noticed children underachieve in school, act out, break things, argue with you, or do other worrisome things just to get attention?

Matthew was a twelve-year-old boy, brought in by his parents for what psychologists call an obsessive compulsive disorder. Matthew became so upset choosing the clothes he would wear to school that he would often end up in a crumpled heap on the floor, sobbing uncontrollably. Matthew's condition had gotten so bad that my colleague, a psychiatrist, suggested that if I could not get him to show improvement within a month, he should be admitted to an inpatient psychiatric hospital.

There are many theories about obsessive compulsive behavior, but I knew that the most powerful determinant of children's behavior is the attention they receive from their parental figures.

It became apparent to me, after talking with Matthew, that he was getting very little attention from his father.

I called Matthew and his dad in together, and we made a pact: for every day that Matthew did not show bizarre behavior selecting clothes and dressing himself, he would receive a half hour of undivided attention from his father between the hours of 5:30 and 6:00 p.m.

This behavior management contract was very specific. All Matthew had to do to get his dad's attention was not have an emotional breakdown when selecting and putting on his clothes. It did not matter what else Matthew did or did not do. The only behavior we were concerned with was his not disintegrating when selecting and putting on his clothes. The crucial component of the program was Matthew's father's willingness to participate and his unfailing consistency in following through with the deal.

The first day Matthew continued to show disorganized behavior, and did not receive his special time with his dad. The second day, however, Matthew did not show any severe problems, and received a half hour of quality time with his dad, doing whatever Matthew wanted. Matthew continued to test our pact, but before long he was looking forward to his half hour of undivided attention from his dad every day. The obsessive-compulsive behavior had disappeared within two weeks simply as a result of one-half hour a day of undivided daily attention from his dad.

Many of us become caught up in the rat race of our work and life and we put our children on a back burner. We justify this by thinking "I am working to support my family, pay for the children's college," and so on. We know they need our attention and, at some level, feel guilty over our neglect. We often try to buy our children's respect and affection with material gifts. But, the most important thing to children is the quality time and attention they

244 | | LIFE GUIDE

get from their parenting figures. However, the power of attention in influencing the behavior of others is not limited to children.

HOW TO SHAPE YOUR PARTNER'S BEHAVIOR

I cannot count the number of times I have had husbands, wives, boyfriends, or girlfriends come in complaining about something their partner does that they would like to change or eliminate: "If only I could get Jane or John to stop doing _____, everything would be fine." Well, there is a powerful way of going about influencing your partner's behavior. The principle is called *differential reinforcement/extinction*. When you use this, you subtly teach your partner the things you like and dislike. The rule of differential reinforcement extinction is as follows: *When your partner is doing something you dislike, ignore him or her; and when your partner is doing something that you like, provide much attention and affection.*

Often people pick a fight with their spouse just to be noticed. The key to overcoming such problems is to notice your spouse when he or she is being nice. Do not wait until your partner picks a fight with you or does something irritating to get attention. A good example of structured attention came from Joe, a graduate student.

Joe and his wife got together every night from 10:30 to 11:00 p.m. and spent that half hour giving each other undivided attention. It did not matter what test Joe had the next day, what papers were due, what deadlines Janet had to meet at work, or anything else that was going on. From 10:30 to 11:00 p.m. was Joe and Janet's special time. Joe completed his intense graduate training without sacrificing the quality of his marital relationship.

Although attention is probably the single most important determinant for the power of relationships, there are many other important points that can either make or break a relationship.

GOOD COMMUNICATION IS NEEDED

We hear a lot about the need for good communication in a relationship, but what does it mean? Communication is a process through which you let somebody know exactly what you think and how you feel. Two important components of communication are the content and the style. Style refers to how you communicate the message. If you present your message in an accusatory or hostile way, people will often not perceive correctly what you are trying to say.

An example of this is expressing your feelings when you are hurt or upset. Many of us tend to respond to our hurt feelings by lashing out in anger or resentment. This alienates the people who have hurt our feelings, and makes it unlikely that they will change. A better way of expressing hurt feelings and anger is to tell people assertively that they have hurt your feelings.

Characteristics of Good Communication

Immediacy. For communication to be effective, it needs to be timely and immediate. By this, I mean that your communication must occur soon after the event that prompted it. If I do something to hurt your feelings, and you fail to let me know about it for over a year, the odds are that your message will not have as strong an effect on my behavior as it would have if you had told me within one minute of the incident.

Specificity. For communication to be effective, it must be specific. Avoid generalizing what you are trying to say. You should go into precise and exact details about exactly what occurred, how it occurred, and how you feel about it. Consider the following examples of specific and general communication:

General: I felt uncomfortable with your behavior at Christmas.
Specific: I was disappointed when you came to my house drunk on Christmas day and called my mother a slut.

Genuineness. Effective communication is genuine. By genuine I mean don't say something insincere. Don't say, "It's wonderful to see you" if its only "nice to see you." If you have no strong feeling or opinion about someone's problem or an event, say nothing. If you try to make up something phony to impress someone, or say what you think they want to hear, your insincerity will shine through in your nonverbal behavior. Even if you manage to trick them into believing you are sincere, this will mislead them and encourage misunderstandings down the road.

Congruence. Congruence refers to the consistency between what you say and how you say it. If someone has hurt or disappointed you terribly, and you are smiling while talking about it, this is an obvious inconsistency. On the other hand, if you smile joyfully while giving someone a hug and letting her know how much you appreciate and love her, this is congruent with your spoken message.

The Sandwich Effect

The sandwich effect (mentioned earlier in Chapter 3 on Assertiveness) is a powerful communication tool used to present constructive feedback. Constructive feedback is a polite way of saying someone has done something you do not like and you need to let him or her know it. The sandwich effect works by sandwiching the critical message between positive statements. For example:

> Bobby, I value our friendship and appreciate all the fun we've had together. But I was disappointed when you didn't take the time to see me or talk to me on the phone during my last visit. I hope we can create some time in the future so we can continue to develop our friendship.

THE POLITICS OF RELATIONSHIPS

There is more to a relationship than communication. The simple reality is that politics is very powerful in determining the quality of any relationship. Politics concerns power and control. Whenever I work with a couple and ask who is in control of their relationship, they invariably tell me that it is fifty-fifty. They usually go on to elaborate that each person has a fifty percent say-so in how every issue is decided.

If you think about this for a moment, you will realize just how unlikely this is. Imagine what it would be like if all household responsibilities were divided fifty-fifty. In essence, I would mow half of the lawn and my wife the other half. She would do half the dishes and I would do the other half. A much more effective way of looking at the politics of relationships is to look at who is the boss in what areas. This is especially important when examining areas of competence and control.

Despite eleven years of effort on my part, my wife has convinced me that I will never know how to load a dishwasher. This is one of her areas of influence, and she is the boss. On the other hand, I think she has been, and still is, dangerous with the lawn mower. Therefore, mowing the lawn is my area of competence and control.

One of the best things you can do to determine the politics of your own relationship is to sort out the important areas of your life and decide who has more say-so in which area. The extent to which somebody has control over a particular area of your life should reflect that person's ability to handle the area and his or her motivation to do so.

In your relationship there will be some areas in which you do need to divide responsibility equally. However, you should know that the more equal the power distribution in any area of your life, the more likely it is that there will be serious conflict.

Here is a group of areas in which I feel my wife is the boss:

- All aspects of my business involving billing, posting, and accounting.
- Most, if not all, aspects of interior home decoration and design.
- Meal selection and preparation, except on the weekends.
- All handling of personal and business bills and accounts.

On the other hand, my wife has designated me the boss in the following areas:

- Disciplining the children.
- Handling major financial investments.
- Recreation director for family vacations and scheduling of fun events.
- Development of my private practice, teaching, writing, and career.

The following areas are ones in which my wife and I feel we have about fifty-fifty say-so:

- Where we live.
- Where our children attend school.
- Basic rules for the family.
- Who our mutual friends are.

My wife and I agree that the more things we can agree to let the other handle, the better off we are. The more that power and control are clearly and precisely allocated, the less likely there will be a major conflict.

Remember, politics is at least as important as communication. The essential rule of the politics of your relationships is to decide who is the boss of what and to allow you and your partner to mutually develop a fair and equitable sharing of power and responsibility.

PAST RESENTMENTS: THE DEAL BREAKER

If you and your partner (1) know who holds the power in the important areas of your life, (2) are communicating clearly, and (3) are providing each other enough positive attention, things are likely to be going well in your relationship. Unfortunately there is still a very powerful phenomenon that can wreck a relationship: *past resentments.*

Past resentments refer to things your partner has done or failed to do that hurt your feelings. If unresolved, these hurt feelings grow into continuing resentments over what happened. We often save our past resentments if are not assertive in our communications at the time the troubling incident occurred. People with the most past resentments are usually the peace-makers, who will do anything to prevent a conflict or a fight. Their resentments build up because they have suppressed or blocked an appropriate and timely expression of their feelings for fear of creating conflict or an argument.

Relationships are killed when one partner begins to try to change and the other partner is so angry and upset over previous hurts and injustices that he or she continues to be angry even when the partner is showing the desired behavior. The partner who is trying to change learns that efforts to reform are not being recognized, and quickly lapses back into the old pattern that created the problem in the first place. I have found too often that when a negligent husband finally changes, after twenty years of ignoring his wife, the wife has so much past resentment that she cannot acknowledge and accept her husband's new behavior and eventually leaves him anyway.

To eliminate your past resentments, reconsider what you have already learned in Chapter 4 about forgiving.

1. You must first acknowledge that you have been hurt or disappointed.
2. You must learn to acknowledge that you have had strong feelings about this hurt or disappointment.
3. You must fully express and ventilate these feelings.
4. You must determine how you will protect yourself from similar hurts or disappointments in the future.
5. You must try to understand how the person who hurt or disappointed you became able to hurt you in the first place.

If you find you are seething over with past resentments and hostilities, spend a half hour in the evening writing out your exact feelings, holding back nothing. There is no need to tell your partner how you feel at this time. Just be sure to ventilate on paper all the feelings. And develop an idea of how you will protect yourself from similar hurts in the future.

Past resentments can be carried from one relationship to another. For instance, if you have been badly emotionally hurt by someone in a previous relationship, you can carry a very guarded and defensive attitude into subsequent relationships. You want to give your new partner a fair chance. At the same time you don't want to set yourself up for the same kind of hurt or rejection. The easiest way to avoid this is to become aware of your emotional investments and never put all of your emotional eggs in another person's basket. In other words, put your relationship with yourself on an equal par with your most important relationship with anyone else.

HOW TO CREATE MUTUAL RESPECT

If you look to your partner to meet all your emotional needs, you are applying pressure unfairly. You are also setting up the relationship for a disastrous ending. You must realize that you and your partner share common ground, but each has needs that can only be fulfilled individually.

Mutual respect comes by acknowledging that your partner has these needs and desires that you are unable or unwilling to fulfill and vice versa. For example, I hate to shop, but my wife loves to browse through malls. She and her mother spend countless hours enjoying this activity, but I find it boring. Realizing this makes her happy, I encourage her. On the other hand, I love sailboarding. I find it an exciting and exhilarating sport. And I spend as much time as I realistically can out on the bay. My wife has never gotten the hang of this sport, but respects my love for it and enjoys seeing me having fun. Some shared activities we both enjoy are downhill skiing, watching movies with our children, and going for casual bike rides.

If you try to spend every waking moment doing everything you can to make your partner happy, you will not only burn yourself out, but make your partner feel overwhelmed and smothered. To develop a mutual and lasting friendship, develop as many shared activities and interests as you can with your partner, but always save some special activities just for you.

RELATIONSHIP RULES

In relationships, as in civilizations, you must have mutually agreed-upon rules. The people who make and implement these rules are you and your partner. It is necessary, when making your relationship rules, to make rules that are fair and that you and your partner can live with. Relationship rules are essentially expectations that you and your partner have for each other. Typical relationship rules cover such things as monogamy, listening to your partner whenever he or she needs you to, sharing enjoyable activities, and expressing differences of opinion.

Most partners enter a relationship with unspoken rules, expectations that they think their partners should meet. But often the other partner is unaware of these expectations, a paradox that inevitably leads to disappointments and conflict. The antidote is to make very clear to your partner what types of rules and expectations you have about the relationship. Hash things out. Do some collective bargaining. Explore what you really need, not just what you want. Find out what you can tolerate, even if it is something you do not like. Be explicit and clear in letting each other know what you expect and need from each other.

An interesting aspect of relationship rules is what I call the "major-minor rule." In abiding by the major-minor rule, partners agree to never do anything to seriously jeopardize a relationship. An example of the application of the major-minor rule occurred when my wife wanted to visit her father in Los Angeles. Before her departure I suffered a serious back injury. Given my insecurity regarding my injury, I let her know that her leaving would be a serious blow to our relationship. She realized this and postponed her trip. On the flip side, I had once scheduled a week-long ski trip with some friends and canceled out at the last minute because my wife developed pleurisy. Briefly, you are free to have minor disagreements about who does what, when. If the behavior of one member of the couple threatens the relationship (major), however, the other partner should have veto power.

The Honeymoon Myth

Anyone who has been married or in love knows the honeymoon phase. This is when partners are obsessed with each other. You do not need to be doing anything in particular to feel high during this stage of a relationship. You are happy just being around the other person, and life takes on a special quality. You want to spend every waking moment with your partner. You even lose sleep over him or her.

Unfortunately, the honeymoon high eventually cools down. For most people it cools gradually and, unfortunately, it can cool faster for one partner than the other. This decline of the honeymoon phase does not mean that you are no longer in love with your partner. It means only that the obsessive infatuation is no longer present.

At a marital workshop, the speaker told the newlyweds to place a penny in a jar every time they made love during their first year of marriage. They were instructed to place a penny in separate jars each time they made love during each of the three succeeding three years. The results are usually consistent among couples. There are more pennies in the first jar than in the next three jars combined. This does not mean a decline in the love couples experience. It means that the quality of love changes for couples who remain together. The honeymoon phase is gradually replaced, in successful marriages and relationships, by a kind of "conjugal affection," a term used by Erich Fromm to refer to an emerging mutual respect and intimate friendship.

Not being as sexually excited by your partner as you were the first year of your relationship does not mean that your relationship cannot work. One of the most frustrating things I hear in my practice is men or women telling me that they still love their partner but they are not "in love." I believe what these people mean is that they still care for their partner but are no longer as sexually excited as they think they should be. In successful couples

I have found that the honeymoon phase, although not omnipresent, remains accessible. It can easily be rekindled at special times, like when they are on a romantic vacation or when the children are visiting friends.

Some people continue to chase the honeymoon high through multiple relationships. They are chasing a high they will never be able to maintain. These relationships last anywhere from three months to two years and fracture because one partner is no longer turned on. You cannot treat relationships like cars——trading them in every few years for new models. If you do this, your life will be a long string of superficial and meaningless encounters.

In short, realize that the honeymoon phase of your relationship will not last forever, but can easily be rekindled under the right circumstances. Allow your mutual respect, love, and friendship with your partner to develop and replace the initial honeymoon high.

The Magic Bullet For Relationships

Good communication, power, past resentments, establishing the rules of a relationship, developing mutual respect, and attention are all very important in making your relationship work. But often, for one reason or another, they just do not seem to get the job done. Couples on the brink of divorce ask, "Is there any magical thing we can do to fix our relationship?"

I believe there is a magic bullet. It is the principle that *it is extremely difficult not to like, and eventually love, someone you are having a lot of fun with.*

I know this sounds superficial, but it is powerful and effective. No matter what has happened in the past or how little attention you received, no matter how many power conflicts or how poor your communication, if you frequently do things you love to do with a partner, you will associate your partner with these activities and feelings. Your partner becomes a conditioned part of the fun times. You tend to associate fun and enjoyable things with the people with whom you share them. If your partner is one of these people, you have gone a long way toward making your relationship work.

If you feel your marriage or relationship is on the verge of breaking, give yourself a month or two of seeing how many truly enjoyable things you and your partner can experience together. Do not try to solve any problems. Just be in the right places together, doing the things you really love. If you follow this principle, it often will act as a magic bullet that will turn your relationship around.

IN SUMMARY . . .

Your relationships with other people have a powerful influence on your behavior and your emotions. Remember the eight ingredients of a good relationship:

1. Practice clear, immediate, specific, genuine communication.
2. Know the politics of your relationship; who is the boss of what?
3. Learn how to let go of past resentments, but protect yourself.
4. Establish and follow reasonable and fair rules for your relationship.
5. Demonstrate mutual respect.
6. Give your partner the quality time and attention that your partner needs and that you feel comfortable with.
7. Notice what your partner does that you like and ignore what your partner does that you don't like.
8. Use the magic bullet of liking and eventually even loving the person you have fun with regularly.

13 Time to Start Living

Are you just existing from crisis to crisis, or are you really living? I disagree with William Hazlitt's idea that the art of living is knowing how to enjoy a little and endure a lot. Life is a wondrous journey, full of highs and lows, despair and joy, frustration and fulfillment, and everything between. To suffer, at least some, is a necessary part of our human condition. Yet most of our misery we bring on ourselves, or could easily overcome with desire, knowledge, and conscious effort.

"Instructions," "directions," or "keys to emotional strength;" it really doesn't matter how you think of it. The point is that the tools are available to cope with life's crises, to go beyond existing and to start living fully. These are the keys to emotional strength and they are worth looking at once more.

SITUATIONAL ENGINEERING

Your problems are not all inside your head. Legendary psychologist, B.F. Skinner, reportedly said that before you change yourself you should try to change your environment. No matter how much self-exploration and in-depth analysis you do, to a large extent your problems are reactive to the situation in which you are living. How stable and happy can you be if you are living with a physically abusive alcoholic husband, a faithless wife, or a spouse who continues to write checks and drain your savings account to pay for a drug habit? Can you maintain a normal and balanced life when the company you have worked for for twenty-five years is about to be involved in a hostile takeover, and your experience and dedication amount to absolutely no job security? How likely are you to keep from developing a serious alcohol or drug problem if all of your friends abuse alcohol and drugs and encourage you to join them? What you do depends on your interaction with your environment—everything from where you live, to your work. Before you take the journey of self-discovery, you must take a clear and focused look at your environment and discover both its opportunities and barriers.

Gateway situations represent critical decision points in your life. These include who you will marry, how much formal education you will receive, how many children you will have, and what type of jobs or career you plan to develop. The decisions you make with respect to gateway situations have an enormous impact on the quality of your life, so consider your options carefully.

Many of us already have made decisions regarding gateway situations, but have never carefully assessed what exists for us or against us in different aspects of our situation. Using the simple rating technique I have described, you can discover where potential problems or opportunities lie. Many of us have stayed in disastrous situations or relationships due to the familiarity of the misery. That is, we would prefer to endure the misery of something that is predictable than to risk the unknown.

Once you are fully aware of the constraints and opportunities in your situation you can decide what to do. Your options include:

- Accepting the situation as it is.
- Trying to change or correct the situation into one that is more favorable to meeting your needs and values.
- Leaving the situation and finding a better one.

The order of these options is critical. Sometimes people exaggerate the problem they have in a good situation. Others give up quickly and find themselves running from their problems, moving from place to place and never resolving typical stressors they will face anywhere. More often, people stay in miserable, dead end situations with virtually no hope of improvement, feeling this is normal. They feel that they deserve and must tolerate this misery. This is a myth that has created tremendous undue suffering.

YOUR FEELINGS ARE YOUR FRIENDS

There is truth in the insights of psychologist Fritz Perls, who believed that whenever an emotion is fully expressed, it disappears. Your emotions, both pleasant and unpleasant, are your friends. Your feelings are there to help you, and the sooner you learn to recognize, experience, and express them, the sooner you will be on your way to living a happy life.

As a human being you are entitled to a wide range of emotions. Feelings we all experience include anger, sadness, fear, guilt, envy, jealousy, disappointment, frustration, and despair. Often, we try to avoid experiencing these unpleasant emotions by distorting them through psychological defense mechanisms such as suppression, denial, acting out, displacement, rationalization, intellectualization, reaction formation, identification, minimization, and projection. When we use these psychological defense mechanisms to distort or block out unpleasant feelings, the feelings do not disappear, but build up and create new problems.

A good way to express and ventilate blocked-out feelings is through therapeutic letter writing. When you write letters, focus on details and specifics, and write down all your feelings regarding the distressing event. As long as you may have trouble experiencing unpleasant emotions, you will also have trouble feeling joy, acceptance, ecstasy, jubilation, delight, surprise, and enthusiasm. All your emotions, both pleasant and unpleasant, are telling you something important about what is valuable to you or your present state of affairs. So recognize you feelings, express them, and experience them.

HOW TO STAND UP FOR YOURSELF

To be happy and effective in life, you must know how to stand up for yourself. Being assertive is closely related to expressing your feelings, but goes further. You not only know what you feel, but you express these feelings clearly and appropriately to others.

Contrary to what some people may think, being assertive does not mean being aggressive. It means, as Wayne Dyer put it, that you will not allow yourself to be victimized. It means being able to express your feelings, both positive and negative, and clearly getting your point across to people with whom you need to communicate.

How often have you found yourself biting your tongue when somebody hurt your feelings and saying to yourself, "I better not say anything to him or he might get mad." The key idea is that if you are not assertive and fail to tell people where you stand, they probably will continue to take advantage of you. What's more, they may not know that they are hurting your feelings as they continue to contribute to the resentment you are building. Then, something occurs that is the last straw and you either end the relationship or lash out in anger.

To avoid this explosion:

- Tell people your emotions when you feel them.
- Communicate your feelings clearly. Explain to people how their behavior affects you.
- Be genuine in expressing your feelings.
- Use the sandwich effect. When being assertive, first say something positive, followed by something critical, and end with something positive. This will make it much more likely that you will get what you want.

LETTING GO OF THE PAST

Before you can let go of problems from your past you must learn from them. You already know what your basic emotions are and how to experience and express them. You have learned how to be assertive and to keep your feelings from building up. However, there still may be skeletons of resentment, anger, fear, and distress rattling around in your psychological closet. What can you do about them? Four ghosts from the past often wreak devastating consequences on life. These are anger, guilt, fear, and grief.

Each emotion serves a purpose. Anger and fear both protect you or someone you love. To let go of suppressed anger and fear you must develop a plan for protecting yourself and the people you care about. If you don't, anger and fear are likely to turn into chronic frustration, irritability, and anxiety.

Guilt, on the other hand, lets you know that you either did something wrong, or failed to do something you should have done. The purpose of guilt is to teach you a lesson, so that you will not make the same mistake again. Once you realize the purpose of guilt, you can promise yourself that you will never make the same mistake again. When you firmly commit to not making the mistake again, you are free of guilt.

The fourth ghost, grief, serves the purpose of letting others know that you have suffered a loss and gives them a chance to comfort you. When you experience grief, you must be open to the emotion of acceptance so as to receive the comfort and support of others.

Often, problems from the past lay buried beneath layers of psychological defense and other emotions. Through the technique of clustering (picking an emotion and writing every thought that comes into your mind about it) or clustering to people in your life—e.g. mother, father, sibling, spouse—you are likely to become aware of buried emotional problems. After uncovering any problems from the past, therapeutic letter writing is effective in ventilating, expressing, and releasing them.

YOUR BASIC NEEDS AND HOW TO MEET THEM

Once you have engineered your situation, learned to recognize and express your feelings, become assertive, and let go of unnecessary psychological baggage from the past, your basic and higher order needs will come quickly into focus. Basic needs, such as food and shelter, are obvious and not too difficult to meet. Higher-order needs, such as stimulation and self-actualization, are more of a challenge, but easily attainable by following a simple six-step problem-solving strategy:

1. Clearly specify, in goal-directed terms, which need is unmet.
2. Assess your situation with respect to barriers and opportunities to meet your particular need.
3. Assess your psychological resources; your strengths and weaknesses.
4. Brainstorm and develop several alternate plans to meet your needs. Then assess your plans and choose the best one.
5. Implement your plan and watch how it works.
6. Evaluate the outcome compared to your original goal. If the outcome is unsatisfactory, select and implement your alternate plans in order of preference.

When you fall into the trap of not having some of your basic or higher-order needs met, don't stay stuck, feeling frustrated and hopeless. Try to change things. Get busy and carry out the problem-solving strategy. You will be surprised how quickly you get back in control and change things.

YOUR EMOTIONAL INVESTMENTS

Your emotions, just like your money, can be invested. It is not enough just to know what is important to you. You must show your values in your daily behavior. To discover what is truly important to you, divide your day into a twenty-four-hour time pie and notice how much of your time is spent doing various activities. Since most of us spend around eight hours working and eight hours sleeping, that leaves about eight hours of free time to invest according to our values. You are what you do, so do what is important to you.

There is a distinction between process and end-state values. End-state values represent states of existence that are often temporary. When you achieve a goal or finish a project, the splendid ambience soon disappears. Process values are more important and permanent. They represent how you go about achieving your goals. Make sure that your process values are acceptable behaviors with which you can live comfortably.

To understand human motivation and values, you must recognize the role of the opponent process model of motivation. Extreme emotional states are often followed by equally strong but opposite emotions.

BEHAVIOR DYNAMICS

There is truth in Thomas Huxley's statement that the great end in life is not knowledge but action. To be happy, you must engage in behaviors and activities that are healthy and good for you. The psychological discipline of behavioral medicine has taught us that there are certain behaviors and experiences that are beneficial to you. Often, when you are feeling most down or depressed, you will not feel like doing the things that will make you feel better. The motivational fallacy—believing that you should only do things you feel like doing when you feel like doing them—is an unreasonable principle for running your life. It actually does not matter whether you feel like it or not. You can dramatically improve your mood and raise your self-esteem by going on behavioral autopilot and doing the right behaviors regularly, such as: large muscle activity, aerobic exercise, pleasant event scheduling, and adrenalin highs.

These behaviors act at a neurochemical level in your brain. Research from laboratories throughout the world shows that sixty-to-ninety minutes of sustained aerobic activity is correlated with clear, neurochemical changes associated with optimal moods.

GETTING BACK IN CONTROL

Your mind and body were designed to be calm and relaxed, so quit fighting it and learn how to let go. The stressors we face in life often put our body in an alarm mode. We often become stuck in this reaction. To break out of a stress/alarm mode you should practice relaxation training regularly. The techniques described in Chapter 8, such as letting go of tension, autogenic training, self-hypnosis, and multisensory imagery are proven and effective techniques that have reduced stress, anxiety, and tension for millions of people. It is often effective to record relaxation scripts and practice them where you will not be disturbed. Eventually, you can memorize the scripts, and use them without the tapes. Regular relaxation training is a necessary part of coping with a stressful and unpredictable world.

While the relaxation scripts described in Chapter 8 are excellent ways of getting back in control, in a pinch, it's often effective to use the following simple, brief relaxation exercise: Take ten slow, deep breaths. With each breath in, suggest to yourself *calm*, and with each breath out suggest *relaxed*. As you do this, imagine yourself vividly in a relaxing, safe, secure situation.

YOUR SPHERE OF INFLUENCE

To stop existing and start living, you must discover your personal sphere of influence. Serenity depends on understanding control. It means learning how to control the things you need to control, accepting the things you cannot control, and developing the understanding or wisdom to realize your personal boundaries of influence. Do not spend useless hours worrying or spinning your wheels over things you have little or no influence over. Do not fall into the control traps of learning to be helpless or overcontrolling, or being an emotional ostrich, a chronic worrier, or a self-deceiver. Concentrate on the important things you can control and influence, such as your feelings, your thoughts, your behaviors, your physical health, and the quality of life for you and those you love.

Your responsibilities represent a special aspect of your sphere of influence. If you perceive a situation that needs correcting and you have the ability and knowledge to correct it, it is your obligation to do so. But life is more than just meeting responsibilities and obligations. To meet your responsibilities, you must first take good care of yourself and engage in behaviors and activities that recharge your emotional batteries.

You will someday undoubtedly face difficult problems requiring your sustained and diligent efforts. An effective way to cope with chronic or difficult problems is to use the technique of time-structured problem solving, in which you set aside a specified amount of time to work on the problem, and then let it go and focus on something else. Remember, you can psychologically let go of a problem by feeling complete about it even if it is unfinished. Also, remember the phenomena of temporal windows of influence, when your actions can have dramatic results.

YOUR INNER VOICE

There is a tremendous power in your beliefs, expectations, and self-talk. The apostle Matthew witnessed this power when he saw Jesus heal the blind men by touching their eyes and saying, "Go be it done for you as you have believed."

You must get the little voice inside your head, your self-talk, on your side. An important feature of self-talk is the self-fulfilling prophecy. This means that you tend to find the things in life you look for. If you look for problems, you will find them. If you look for enjoyment and fulfillment in life, you will be surprised how often life meets these expectations.

The labels you use for the events that occur in your world also have an important influence on how you feel and what you do. Adopt useful constructs, or labels, that help you accurately organize and predict events in your world. Avoid dysfunctional or distressing labels such as "overwhelming," "disastrous," "insurmountable," or "horrible." Think instead in positive goal-directed terms. Think in terms of desired outcomes, not in terms of avoiding the undesirable. When you do, you will more likely achieve what you want out of life.

The placebo effect, the power of positive expectant faith, is probably the single most powerful healing agent in the history of medicine. Your belief that something good will happen to you accounts for from thirty to seventy percent of all medical cures.

Often our emotions become twisted and manipulated by irrational thought or ideas. When you find yourself becoming victimized by emotions that seem to have no constructive purpose, examine your underlying assumptions. Irrational ideas such as "you must have the love and approval of all," or "you must prove yourself thoroughly competent and adequate in achieving," are likely to have set you up for frustration and disappointment. Try to make your underlying beliefs and assumptions realistic, positive, and rational.

Reframing is a cognitive psychology technique in which you concentrate on positive, as opposed to negative, outcomes. If you continue to focus on what you do not want, it will draw much of your mental energy, and pull you in the direction of failure. Focus instead on the desirable goal or positive outcome.

For distressing thoughts that continually run through your mind, try the technique of thought stopping. When you recognize a distressing, negative, or dysfunctional thought, think or shout to yourself, "Stop!" and immediately focus on a pleasant image or memory.

Use self-talk to bolster your self-esteem and confidence. When you are in the pinch of a stressful situation, say things to yourself like: "I'm doing great" or "I'll be fine." Use self-affirmations to jump start a good day. Affirmations such as: "Wow, I just got the perfect amount of sleep last night!" and "My mind is perfectly calm, crystal clear, and fully aware" are excellent ways to start your day with optimal energy and vitality.

POSITIVE RELATIONSHIPS

The power of a loving, trusting, warm, honest relationship is perhaps the most powerful key to emotional strength. Often, love has proven to be all that people really need. Your relationships with other people have a powerful influence on your behavior and feelings. The ingredients of a good relationship are:

- Clear, immediate, specific, genuine communication.
- Knowing the politics of your relationship: who is the boss of what.
- Learning how to let go of past resentments, while still protecting yourself.
- Establishing and following reasonable and fair rules for your relationship.
- Demonstrating and accepting mutual respect.
- Giving the people you love all the quality time and attention they need and that you can offer.
- Giving the people you love the attention they deserve when they do the things you support, and ignoring distressing, negative, or dysfunctional behaviors.
- Using the magic bullet of learning to like and eventually love someone you are having fun with often.

THE BIG QUESTION

At a psychological level, many answers are in already. This does not eliminate the clear necessity of wrestling with life's most compelling political, social, and global issues. The welfare of humanity, including basic needs and the expression of human values, is a direct function of the political, economic, social, and global ecosphere in which we live. There is no contradiction between the need to resolve these larger human issues and taking good care of yourself and living life to its fullest. When you feel your best, you mind is alive, creative and open to developing the solutions that humanity desperately needs. You are likely to be more socially, politically, and globally responsive to the issues facing our generation and subsequent generations when you take care of yourself.

There is an urgency. Your biological clock is ticking and your time is not forever. The big question is: What will you do with the time you have? Are you going to exist? Or, will you live?

Notes on Sources

INTRODUCTION

viii **FORTUNATELY THESE ANSWERS EXIST** William James, *The Principles of Psychology*, 2 vols. (New York: Henry Holt and Co., 1890). Many consider the publication of James's *The Principles of Psychology* to be the starting point for the field. Although not specifically offering answers, *The Principles of Psychology* sets forth the basic questions psychology has since explored.

SITUATIONAL ENGINEERING

2 **IN THE LATE 1960s** Stanley Milgram, *Obedience to Authority: An Experimental View* (New York: Harper Colophon Books, 1974). Milgram's studies were to assess the extent to which an experimental subject would obey a perceived authority figure.

2 **IN ONE EXPERIMENT** Ibid. Milgram actually designed a series of experiments to assess obedience to authority. Variables manipulated included: closeness to the victim, other individuals who confront authority, and perceived health of the victim.

4 **IN THE LATE 1950s** Irving Goffman, *The Presentation of Self in Everyday Life* (Garden City, New York: Doubleday, 1959). Goffman used anecdotal material and observations of day-to-day life to point out the compelling power of perceived expectations.

YOUR FEELINGS

31 **PSYCHOLOGISTS DEFINE EMOTIONS** Karen Huffman, Mark Vernoy, Barbara Williams, *Psychology in Action* (New York: John Wiley and Sons, 1987). Various authors have given different definitions of emotions, but the one presented by Huffman, Vernoy, and Williams focuses on the critical physiological, cognitive, behavioral, and evaluative aspects.

32 **SCHACTER AND SINGER DIVIDED** Stanley Schacter and Jerome E. Singer, "Cognitive, social, and physiological determinants of an emotional state," *Psychological Review* 69 (1962): 379-399. Schacter's and Singer's experiments were basically designed to assess the extent to which the same physiological reactions could be experienced qualitatively differently based on cognitive and social (situational) variables).

33 OTHER PSYCHOLOGISTS   Peter Lewinsohn, et.al. *Control Your Depression* (Englewood Cliffs, New Jersey: Printice Hall, 1978). One of Lewinsohn's key contributions to the treatment of depression was his demonstration that a person's mood (depression) can be improved simply by engaging in enjoyable behaviors and activities.

37 IN 1972 PSYCHOLOGIST PAUL EKMAN   Paul Ekman, "Universals and Cultural Differences in Facial Expressions of Emotion." in N. J. Cole (Ed.) *Nebraska Symposium on Motivation: Volume 19*, ed. N.J. Cole (Lincoln, NE: University of Nebraska Press, 1972). Ekman's research confirms the universal similarities of facial expressions as genuine indicators of affective states.

42 THERAPIST FRITZ PERLS DEVELOPED   Fritz Perls, *Gestalt Therapy Verbatim* (Lafayette, CA: Real People Press, 1969). The open-chair technique was one of several powerful techniques Perls developed to ventilate and express emotions. Other famous techniques include the "hot seat," and "dream work." *Gestalt Therapy Verbatim* provides numerous examples of these techniques.

YOUR PERSONAL RIGHTS

51 ASSERTIVENESS INVOLVES EXPRESSING   Wayne Dyer, *Pulling Your Own Strings* (New York: Harper Row, 1978). Dr. Dyer's classic work on assertiveness training offers a one hundred item questionnaire at the end of the book to help determine if you are assertive, aggressive, or submissive.

LETTING GO OF THE PAST

73 GUILT, ACCORDING TO MY   Benjamin B. Wolman, *Dictionary of Behavioral Science* (New York: Van Nostrand Reinhold Co., 1973). Wolman's *Dictionary of Behavioral Science* provides an excellent and concise survey of most of the key terms in the science of psychology.

79 ABOUT A CENTURY AGO   William James, *The Principles of Psychology* (New York: Dover Publications, Inc., 1890 by Henry Holt and Co. and 1918 by Allice James. First Dover edition published in 1950). James's classic example of encountering a bear in the woods was his theoretical starting point for proposing that the recognition of physiological changes serves as the foundation for subsequent emotional experiences.

89 ELIZABETH KUBLER-ROSS IDENTIFIED   Elizabeth Kubler-Ross, *On Death and Dying* (New York: McMillan, 1969). Kubler-Ross is considered to be the first to discover the developmental sequence of how human beings handle losses. Her pioneering work gave psychologist and psychiatrists criteria by which they could assist grieving patients.

WHAT YOU NEED AND HOW TO GET IT

100 PSYCHOLOGIST ABRAHAM MASLOW   Frank G. Goble, *The Third Force: The Psychology of Abraham Maslow* (New York: Pocket Books, 1971). Frank Goble presents what is considered by most to be the best popular overview of Dr. Abraham Maslow's psychology of self-actualization.

102 CARL ROGERS, A MAJOR FORCE   Carl Rogers, *On Becoming a Person* (Boston: Houghton-Mifflin, 1961). Carl Rogers is one of the founders of humanistic psychology. His philosophy is based on the idea of acceptance, stressing that if patients feel that their emotions are accepted, a natural healing process will unfold.

102 EARLY IN THE TWENTIETH CENTURY   Goble, *The Third Force*. "Ashley Montague also refers to several surveys early in the 20th century that produce some shocking statistics. A typical one: Dr. Henry Chapin reported on ten infant asylums located in the United States in which, with one exception, every infant under 2 years of age died." Dr. Montague attributes this disaster to the fact that these babies were not loved.

102 RESEARCH BY HARRY HARLOW   Harry Harlow and M.K. Harlow, "Social Deprivation in Monkeys," *Scientific American* 207(1962):136-46. Harlow conducted a series of experiments in which he found, among other things, that infant monkeys who were allowed to have physical contact with a terrycloth surrogate developed into socially appropriate adults.

104 MASLOW FOUND THAT PEOPLE   Abraham Maslow, *Motivation and Personality* (New York: Harper and Row, 1954). Maslow's basic theory of need fulfillment stated that once basic needs were met, higher order needs became manifested. The highest needs that humans came to know were those of self-actualization. This, according to Maslow, meant fulfilling your unique potential as a human being.

YOUR EMOTIONAL INVESTMENTS

117 EARLY IN THE TWENTIETH CENTURY   Sigmond Freud, *New Introductory Lectures on Psychoanalysis* (New York: W.W. Norton and Co. Paperback Edition, 1965). [Translated from the German and edited by James Strachey] Freud's idea of object cathexis basically represents Freud's position on the quantitative aspect of motivation.

BEHAVIOR DYNAMICS

136 SOME RESEARCHERS   Edward E. Jones, et. al. *Attribution: Perceiving the Causes of Behavior* (New Jersey: General Learning Press, 1971).

136 THE FACT THAT IT   Peter Lewinsohn, et. al. *Control Your Depression*. Lewinsohn believes that not only does a depressed mood lower activity, but a lowered level of enjoyable activities is likely to create and exacerbate depression. Lewinsohn feels that it is a mutual cause and effect relationship.

He goes on to state "the more we do, the less depressed we feel; and the less depressed we feel, the more we will like doing things."

137 I REMEMBERED READING Ibid. Lewinsohn notes a subset of pleasant activities exist which is especially important in regards to depression. He refers to these as mood related activities and they fall into three basic groups: (1)social interactions in which a person feels wanted, liked, and respected, (2) activities associated with feelings of competence and independence, and (3) activities that are intrinsically pleasant (for example, laughing, or being relaxed). In addition to the aerobic lift I received through large muscle activity, my mood may have been altered through a sense of competency over accomplishing my goal.

145 SCIENTISTS HAVE JUST BEGUN P. Thoren, J.S. Flores, P. Hoffman, D.R. Seals, "Endorphins and Exercise: Physiological Mechanisms and Clinical Implications," *Medical Science Sports Exercise* (United States) 22(August 1990): 417-28. The above researches discussed recent experimental and clinical findings suggesting that prolonged rhythmic exercise can activate the central nervous system by triggering increased discharge from musculo-skelative-sensitive afferent nerve fibers arising from contracting skeletal muscle. They review evidence supporting the concept that many of the cardiovascular, analgesic, and behavioral effects of exercise are mediated by this mechanism and that the same or similar mechanisms are responsible for the central and peripheral effects of acupuncture. Based on this hypothesis and supporting evidence from human and animal studies, they suggest a mechanism and a potential therapeutic role for exercise in the treatment of selected patients with disorders as diverse as hypertension, addiction, depression, and anorexia nervosa; P.M.; Radosevich, J.A. Nash, D.B. Lacy, C. O'Dovan, P.E. Williams, and N.N. Abumrad. "Effects of Low and High Intensity Exercise on Plasma and Cerebrospinal Fluid Levels of Ir-beta-endorphin, ACTH, Cortisol, Norepinephrine, and Glucose in the Conscious Dog" (Nashville, Tennessee: Vanderbilt University School of Medicine, Dept. of Surgery, 1989). 498(1):89-98. The above researchers found that exercise increased the circulating levels of beta-endorphins in dogs.; G. A. Sforzo, "Opioids and Exercise: An Update," *Sports Medicine* (New York: School of Health Sciences and Human Performance, Ithaca College, 1989) 7(2):109-24. Sforzo's research showed that moderately high and high intensity exercise stimulate the release of opioid peptide beta-endorphin into circulation. This event may be subject to considerable intra and interindividual variation. Sforzo speculated that endorphin levels probably remained elevated for fifteen to sixty minutes following exercise. Although Sforzo felt that the duration of exercise did not seem to be critical, he noted low or moderate (less than 75% VOR max) intensity efforts do not stimulate this response.

145 SEVERAL STUDIES HAVE SHOWN Scott J. Hinkle, "Psychological Benefits of Aerobic Running: Implications for Mental Health Counselors," *U.S. Journal of Mental Health Counseling* 10(October 1988): 245-53. Hinkle reviewed studies indicating that aerobic running has antidepressant and antianxiety effects and is beneficial to self-esteem and creative thinking.

GETTING BACK IN CONTROL

158 THE FOLLOWING SCRIPT Edmund Jacobson, *Progressive Relaxation* (Chicago: Univ. of Chicago Press, 1938). The details of the original progressive relaxation exercise are described in this classic.

158 THE MULTISENSORY IMAGERY William Fezler, *Creative Imagery: How to Visualize in All Five Senses* (New York: Simon and Schuster, 1989). Dr. Fezler has developed and enhanced an earlier self-hypnotic script that he wrote with Dr. William Kroger.

165 I HAVE ADDED TWO AUTOSUGGESTIONS Paul Eckman, "Universals and Cultural Differences in Facial Expressions of emotion," in N. J. Cole (Ed.) *Nebraska Symposium on Motivation.* It is apparent from Eckman's pictures that there is excessive facial in people expressing distressing emotions, throughout all cultures. My personal observation on biofeedback measures of chronic pain patients indicate excessive muscle tension in the sternomastoid and trapezius muscles.

171 THE FOLLOWING SELF-HYPNOSIS SCRIPT William S. Kroger and William D. Fezler, *Hypnosis and Behavior Modification: Imagery Conditioning* (Philadelphia: J.P. Lippincott Co., 1976). In addition to presenting an excellent script for self hypnosis, Kroger and Fezler's classic addresses the application of hypnosis and imagery conditioning to a wide range of psychological and physical disorders.

YOUR SPHERE OF INFLUENCE

183 IN 1975, PSYCHOLOGIST Martin E.P. Seligman, *Helplessness: On Depression, Development, and Death* (San Francisco, California: W.H. Freeman and Co., 1975.) Seligman's classic work pointed out how important the issue of perceived lack of control is in influencing depression. His more recent book, *Learned Resourcefulness*, is more oriented towards treating and overcoming depression.

195 IN 1938, A BRILLIANT Wolfgang Kohler, *The Place of Value in a World of Fact* (New York: Liveright, 1938). Kohler equates value with what he calls requiredness of an object or activity. He believed that, if perceived, certain situations represented a call for action on the perceivers part. This, Kohler believed, could serve as the foundation of a scientific study of value.

NEUTRALIZING DISTRESS

204 PHYSICIAN JOSEPH WOLPE Joseph Wolpe, *Psychotherapy by Reciprocal Inhibition* (Stanford, California: Stanford University Press, 1958). In this classic paper Wolpe proved that certain emotional states are incompatible with each other: eg. it is impossible to be anxious when you are profoundly relaxed.

YOUR INNER VOICE

221 IN THE MIDDLE OF THIS CENTURY Benjamin L. Whorf, *Language, Thought, and Reality* (Cambridge, Mass.: MIT Press, 1956). Whorf emphasized that the language we use to describe events and experiences can actually influence the experiences themselves. Although complete linguistic determination has been virtually disproved, there is strong evidence indicating that the labels we use to understand reality influence our experience of reality.

222 FROM AN AWARENESS George Kelley, *A Theory of Personality: The Psychology of Personal Construct* (New York: W.W. Norton and Co., 1963). Kelley's theory of constructive alternativism is based on the assumption that human beings have a deep-seated motivation to understand and predict their world. Kelley deals extensively with the psychotherapeutic implications of constructive alternativism and offers therapists a repertory construct grid in which they can map all the constructs they use.

222 ALTHOUGH PEOPLE DIFFER CONSIDERABLY Carl Osgood, "The Nature and Measurement of Meaning" *Psychological Bulletin* 49(1952): 197-237. Osgood worked with various constructs and developed what he called the semantic differential.

223 IN 1969, PSYCHOLOGIST ROBERT D. ROSENTHAL Robert D. Rosenthal, "Interpersonal Self Fulfilling Prophesy" *Proceedings of 1977 APA Convention* 4(1969): 371-372. Rosenthal found that not only teachers' expectations altered students' performances, but that the expectations of other people could strongly influence the behavior of those with whom they interacted.

224 PSYCHOLOGIST JEANNE ACHTERBERG Jean Achterburg, *Imagery and Healing* (Boston: New Science Library, 1985). Achterburg's work is a scholarly review of the applications of imagery to various psychological and physiological disorders. Volgysi's report is cited in Achterburg's work.

225 MY COLLEAGUE, DR. MARTIN ROSSMAN Martin Rossman, *Healing Yourself.* (New York: Walker and Co., 1987). Dr. Rossman's book is intended to help the reader overcome specific physiological problems. Much of Dr. Rossman's work is based on earlier work by Dr. Irving Oyle.

22 IN THE 1960S PSYCHOLOGIST JEROME FRANK Jerome Frank, "The Influence of Patients' and Therapists' Expectations on the Outcome of Psychotherapy" *British Journal of Medical Psychology*, 41(1968):349-356. It is interesting to note that the efficacy of therapy was not a function of the patient's belief in the method, but of the therapist's belief in the method used.

227 PSYCHOLOGIST ALBERT ELLIS A. Ellis and R. Harper, *A Guide to Rational Living* (Englewood Cliffs, New Jersey: Printice Hall Press, 1961). Dr. Ellis has created an extensive cognitive therapy modality based on understanding and challenging irrational thoughts and replacing them with rational beliefs.

228 DR. MAXIE MAULTSBY DESCRIBES Ibid. Dr. Maxie Maultsby's work is described by Ellis in the *New Guide to Rational Living*.

232 STRESS INOCULATION TRAINING   Donald Meichenbaum, *Stress Inoculation Training* (New York: Pergamon Press, 1985). Dr. Meichenbaum's work represents a concise and clear exposition of how stress inoculation training works.

232 AN EXAMPLE OF COGNITIVE RESTRUCTURING   George Kelley, *A Theory of Personality: The Psychology of Personal Constructs* (New York: W. W. Norton and Co., 1963). Since Kelley believed that the basic motivation of human beings in to predict and understand reality, it necessarily follows that people with broader and more effective constructs have an easier time interpreting, understanding, and predicting reality.

233 A COMPLETELY DIFFERENT USE   Ronald Melzak, "The McGill Pain Questionnaire: Major Properties and Scoring Methods" *Pain* 1: 277-299, 1975. Melzak's McGill Pain Questionnaire has patients rate their pain on sensory, affective, and evaluative dimensions. It is an instrument commonly used by clinicians in the management and evaluation of chronic pain patients.

POSITIVE RELATIONSHIPS

239 A BRILLIANT PSYCHIATRIST   Harry Stack Sullivan, *The Interpersonal Theory of Psychiatry* (New York: William Allenson White Foundation, 1953). Sullivan was perhaps the most notable of the post-Freudians. His focus on interpersonal versus intrapsychic processes served as a springboard for the subsequent development of dyadic and family systems therapy.

252 THE HONEYMOON PHASE   Erich Fromm, *The Art of Loving* (New York: Harper Row, 1956). In this timeless classic, Fromm distinguishes and discusses the different types of love.

TIME TO START LIVING

255 I DISAGREE WITH WILLIAM HAZLITT'S IDEA   William Safire and Leonard Safir, *Words of Wisdom* (New York: Simon and Schuster, 1989).p. 219. Hazlet's quote is sighted in Safire and Safir's section on quotes about life.

258 IT MEANS, AS WAYNE DYER PUT IT   Wayne Dyer, *Pulling Your Own Strings* (New York: Avon Books, 1978). Dyer's classic introduced the general public to the concept of assertiveness training.

26 THERE IS TRUTH IN   Thomas Huxley, *On Elemental Instruction in Physiology* (1877). From John Bartlett's *Familiar Quotations* Emily Morison Beck, Ed. (Boston: Little Brown & Co., 1980): 823.

263 THE APOSTLE MATTHEW   Matthew 9:29 NRSV. Another translation interprets Jesus as having said, "According to your faith let it be to you."

Index

abuse, 26,27,96
acceptance, 35
acting out, 39,58
addiction, 6
adrenaline highs, 150
  benefits of, 151
  sources of, 151
aerobics, 33,144
  activities, 144
  benefits of, 146
  calculating training level, 146-47
  capacity, 145
  in treating depression, 149
  list of, 148
  table regarding age, 147-48
aggressive(tion), 3,36,51,52
alcohol(ic), 4,5,27
anger, 12,34,48,58,73
  cause of, 92
  close relatives, 92
  displacement of, 93
  options, 97
  release techniques, 94
  substitutes for, 97
anticipation, 35
anxiety, 5,49,204
  hierarchy, 204
assertive, 23,51-55,258
  bill of rights, 57
  talk, 64
  techniques, 65-69
attention, 28,241
  negative, 11
  positive, 11
  power of, 241-43
attribution theorist, 136
autogenic training, 165
autosuggestions, 165
awe, 36

basic needs, 100-105
  barriers to, 108-10
  how to satisfy your, 106-108

behavior dynamics, 261
behavioral autopilot, 136-38
behavioral inertia, 136
behaviors, 1-4,7,10,16,19,20
believe/beliefs, 4,56
brainstorming, 107
brief relation exercise, 179
broken record, 65

calming your mind techniques, 163
catharsis, 41
chemical dependency, 26
chronic lethargy, 143
clustering, 75
codependency, 122
cognitive processes, 31
cognitive restructuring, 232
  and pain, 233
communication, 20, 245
  characteristics of good, 245-46
congruence, 246
conjugal affection, 252
conscious, 2
constructive alternativism, 222
constructs, 222
  dichotomous, 222
contempt, 36
criticism, 69
  giving/taking, 69-70

denial, 39
depression, 33,49
desensitization, 84
differential extinction, 244
differential reinforcement, 244
dignity, 57
disappointment, 36
disgust, 34
displacement, 39,58
distress, 24
diversifier-emotional, 126
divorce, 11-13,25
drugs, 4-6

addict, 125

education, 8,22-23
emotional constipation, 41,46
emotional health, 21
emotional investment, 117,120,126, 260
  octopus, 117
  unwise, 120
  wise, 126
emotional jail time, 73
  definition of, 73-74
emotional ostrich, 186
  example of, 187
emotional reinvestment, 128
  example of, 129
emotional zombie, 41
emotions, 1,14-15,31
  table of, 34-37
empty nest, 14-15
endorphins, 145
enkephelons, 145
environment, 1-4,16
envy, 37,58
equifinality, 110
expectation, 33,110
experiment, 2-3

fear, 24,27,34,73,78-88
  blocked, 85
  cluster to, 83
  components of, 79
  realistic vs. unrealistic, 86
  stress as chronic, 80
  unrealistic, 82
  versus anxiety, 84
feeling talk, 64
feelings, 4,7,10,16,19
financial insecurity, 25-26
finishing vs. completing, 193
flight or fight response, 78
fogging, 68
forgiving, 95-96
  5th step process, 95-96
  6th step process, 95-96
  process of, 95-96
  therapeutic letter and, 95-96

free information, 67
functional fixedness, 109

goldenboy effect, 184
greeting talk, 64
grief, 45,73,88
  stages of, 89-90
  why, 88
guilt, 12,51-52,73-78
  techniques for exposing, 74-75

happy, 10,17,19
hatred, 56
heart rate, 147
  maximum, 147
  minimum, 147
  never exceed, 147
high blood pressure, 27
honeymoon myth, 252
hostile, 3
hypnotic desensitization, 204

"I am" strength bombardment exercise, 103
identification, 40
inductive fallacy, 223
in-law problems, 20
inner voice, 263
intellectualize, 31,40
interpersonal psychiatry, 239
irrational idea, 228
  most common, 228-30

jealousy, 37
job rating, 18
job stress, 114
joy, 35

leaky onion, 41,48
learned helplessness, 183-84
  example of, 184-85
leisure activities, 21-23
loneliness, 44
loss, 45,90
  example of, 90-91
  techniques for coping with, 90
love/loving, 4,6-10,12,13,21,35,102

magic bullet for relationship, 253
marriage, 6,9-11,18,19
mental health, 10
migraine headaches, 93
minimization, 40
mistakes, 74
  commission, 74
  omission, 74,77
molestation, 85
mood altering activities, 139-40
motivational fallacy, 135,261
multi-sensory imagery scripts, 157
  beach, 163-65
  mountain cabin, 168-69
  orchard, 174-75
  rainbow, 178-79
mutual respect, 250
  how to create, 250-51

needs, 10,11,15,16,20,26,99
  basic, 100,259
  esteem, 102-03
   example of, 113-14
  love/belonging, 102
   example of, 112
  pyramid, 100
  reality of dollar, 104-06
  safety, 101
   example of, 111
  satisfaction of, 106
  self actualization, 104
  sex, 100
  sleep, 100
  stimulation, 104
  survival, 100
negative assertion, 68
negative inquiry, 68
nervous, 25
no, 60
  how to say, 60,61
nonverbal behavior, 62
norepinephrine, 32
not goals, 109-10

obedience, 2
  to authority, 2

object cathexis, 118
obligations and preferences, 197
  techniques for balancing, 197-98
occupation, 8,9,13,18
open chair, 31,42,43,49,96
opponent process theory, 130-32
optimism, 36
overcontroller, 185-86

paranoia, 7
parenting, 10,11
passive activities, 144
  list of, 144
passive worrier, 186
past, 248
  resentment, 248
pattern of control, 183
peer pressure, 4,6,19
PEST, 74
personal tractor beam, 182
placebo, 224
politics, 246
  of relationships, 246
positive expectant faith, 224
posttraumatic stress, 24
  examples of, 24
power/powerful, 1,2,4,6,7,16,18,19
problem solving, 23,106
  barriers to, 108-10
  six steps of, 106-08,260
problem solving set, 108
process values, 130
progressive relaxation, 158
psychological defense mechanism,
  39,41,58
punishment, 2

rage, 47
rational thinking, 228
  characteristics of, 228
rationalization, 39
reaction formation, 40
reflective listening, 67
reframing, 230
rehearsing, 71
relationship rating, 19,20
relationships, 19,20,23,27,253

politics of, 246
  rules, 251
relaxation training, 24,27,158,167
relaxing your body, 158
  script, 158-63
relaxing your nervous system, 165
  script, 165-67
role playing, 71
remorse, 35
resentment, 248
  past, 248
respect, 57
responsibility, 28,195
  ingredients of, 196-97
retirement, 13,14

sadness, 34
sandwich technique, 71, 246
second guessing fate, 78
secondary gain, 45
self-deceiver, 187
  example of, 187-88
self-disclosure, 68
self-esteem, 13,14
self-fulfilling prophecy, 223
self-help, 4,10
self-hypnosis, 169-70
  deepening, 173-74
  principles of, 175-76
  script, 171-73
self-talk, 222
  for jumpstarting the day, 235-36
  rational, 227
sensation seekers, 150
silent ridicule, 231
situation, 1-4,6-8,10-16,19,25,28
  gateway, 7,10
  living, 19,21-23,26
situational engineering, 255
  change, 27
  constraints, 17,23
  opportunities, 17,23
  rating scale, 16,18,20,21,26
situational requiredness, 195
special space meditation, 176
  script, 176-79
sphere of influence, 262

children, 190
control vs. peripheral, 182
example of, 199-201
feelings, 188
job, 191
recognizing, 182
spouse, 190
your personal and health, 189
strategy, 191-93
  for taking charge, 191-93
stress, 1
  inoculation training, 232
  management principles, 80-81
submission, 37
submissive, 51-55
suppression, 39
surprise, 34

talk, 4,69,222
terminal values, 130
therapeutic letter writing, 45
  exam of, 46-49,76
time structured problem solving, 82
trauma, 24

ulcers, 12,27
unrealistic expectations, 110
unwise emotional investors, 120
  chronic worrier, 124
  codependent, 122
  drug addict, 125
  workaholic, 120

vacation, 27
values, 16,20,130
  process, 130
  terminal, 130
victimized, 51
violence, 26

wise emotional investors, 126
  diversifier, 126
  example of, 126
workable compromise, 66
workaholic, 120
worry, 24,124
worst case scenario, 72